FUTURE
BOSTON

Tor books by David Alexander Smith

Future Boston
In the Cube

FUTURE BOSTON

THE HISTORY
OF A CITY
1990–2100

EDITED BY
DAVID ALEXANDER SMITH

A TOM DOHERTY ASSOCIATES BOOK
NEW YORK

Contents

FUTURE
BOSTON

BOSTON IN 1772

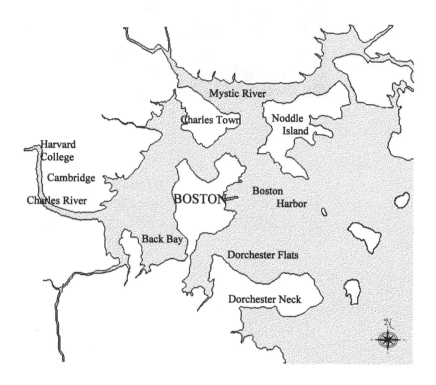

Just before the American Revolution, Boston is a peninsula between the tide-flooded Dorchester Flats and the wide, estuarial Charles River.

All around Boston, numerous rivers and streams flow across often-flooded farmland.

Boston itself is already crowded and heavily built up. The eastern edge of the city is dockland and wharves; its commercial life depends on the sea.

BOSTON WILL SINK
DAVID ALEXANDER SMITH

BOSTON WILL SINK, CLAIMS MIT PROF

TIME MAGAZINE, OCTOBER 29, 1923

GEOLOGY PROFESSOR W. O. Crosby of the Massachusetts Institute of Technology is not what George F. Babbitt of Zenith, Ohio would call a troublemaker on the scale of John L. Lewis or Adolf Hitler. Yet he stirs a controversy in Beantown fully as loud as Mayor James M. Curley's banning of the opera *Salome* as "a danger to public morals."

Professor Crosby sifts river mud to develop his conclusions. A huge volcano blew up in Boston, he says, 500,000,000 years ago, long before Prohibition or even before Uncle Joe Cannon became Speaker. The volcano's caldera—its throat—gradually filled with silt. Then the glaciers scooped out a channel that is now the Charles River and Boston Harbor, leaving the debris farther south to create Cape Cod, and left the soft round drumlin hills that Bostonians later cut down to make land from the Back Bay and Dorchester Flats.

To people who laugh at his theory, Professor Crosby points to the 1885 excavations for the Boston subway. Under Boylston Street, twenty feet below present sea level, the diggers found an Indian fish weir that could only have worked on the tides. So Boston must have sunk, he claims.

Submerged petrified tree stumps have been found up and down the Massachusetts coast. More proof, says the prof.

How can the Hub of the Universe (as Boston calls itself) sink? According to Professor Crosby, rock can move. Continents, he thinks, slide around on the Earth's mantle like bread on top of French onion soup. If the subterranean magma cools, Boston could sink like tomato paste oozing from a can whose bottom has been cut out.

If Boston goes down the drain, warns the professor, everyone should move to Quincy or Marblehead, towns built on granite outside the caldera.

Does anyone take him seriously? Treasury Secretary Andrew Mellon sees the news as more reason to invest in the stock market. "After all," says the Secretary, "it can't collapse like that." President Calvin Coolidge, former governor of the Bay State, when asked about Boston's sinking, replies, "I hadn't noticed."

BOSTON IN 1990

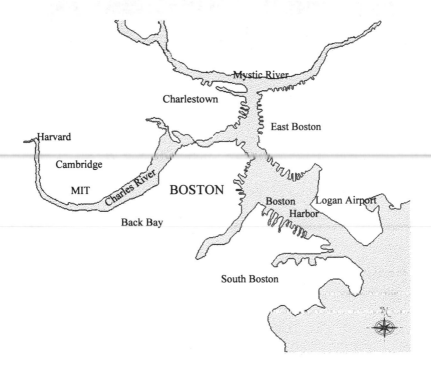

By 1990, the city has expanded. Much of Boston, including the Back Bay and South Boston, is built on filled land. Noddle Island has been enlarged and is now joined to the mainland, creating East Boston and Logan Airport. Boston's financial district, the city's two tallest buildings, and most of its residential district are all built on land borrowed from the ocean.

The water is still there, but underground. An intricate series of sluice gates, runoff drains, reservoirs, and canals channels water through the city.

Across the rivers and under Boston Harbor, bridges and tunnels connect Boston with its suburbs.

Boston stands an average of only four feet above sea level.

The city has begun to sink, but almost no one knows it.

SEEING THE EDGE
SARAH SMITH

EIREEN DIDN'T COME home.

Saturday, a week before Christmas, Jerry woke up to the sound track of "Rudolph the Red-Nosed Reindeer." Eireen's kid Travis was sitting on the edge of Jerry's lumpy sofabed, shivering in his thin pajamas and watching the Saturday morning cartoons. Travis wiped his nose on his sleeve and turned his flat black eyes Jerry's way. "Mama not here, Je'y."

Jerry tunneled into his sleeping bag; he didn't want to hear this. "She looks after you on weekends," Jerry said. "Because I work Saturdays."

"She not here." Travis stared over at Jerry, daring him not to do something about it. Weird-looking little kid, slant eyes under a wiry Afro, and mean like his mother. Already at four his conversation was mostly things Jerry didn't want to hear.

After a moment Jerry groaned, twisted himself out of his sleeping bag, groped into the kitchen for something for the two of them to eat. There wasn't much.

All you need in life is the right programming language. Jerry had believed that from eleven on, when he started programming LISP; he had Common Lisp, Prolog, C++; by high school he knew more about computers than the teachers did. He was going to MIT, he knew it. But he'd been failing French and English and Social Studies because they were boring and gym because it was gym, and his school counselor had had a little talk with him about technical schools, and so Jerry said a personal farewell to eleventh grade and hitched to Boston.

The first thing he'd learned in Boston was the meaning of "recession." He'd slicked down his hair so he looked old enough to hire, said he was taking a leave of absence from MIT, and knocked on every office door around Kendall Square. He had got some part-time work programming for a little company, Intelligent Analysis. When they paid him, he'd find a real place to live.

"Can't you stay here by yourself until she gets home?" Travis didn't say anything, just blinked. He was only four but he knew who was responsible for him when Eireen wasn't here. Jerry sighed.

"You can go to work with me if you don't screw up."

Eight A.M., freakin' cold, the wind coming right through Jerry's jacket. In Kendall Square Dollar-a-Pound was opening. During the week it was a rag-rendering factory, but on Saturday morning the owner, Bruce, broke open a bale of old clothes, and if you found something you wanted you could buy it for a dollar a pound. Inside it was warm and a lot of people were already shopping. Jerry looked for a winter jacket while Travis played solemnly, jumping onto the piles of old rags and clothes. A spike-haired punk guy was trying on women's '60s stuff in front of the mirror; mamas on welfare pawed through kids' clothes and Cambodians stuffed bags with clothes to sell. Travis looked up at every Southeast Asian voice, but you wouldn't catch Eireen in a place like this.

Sometimes you could find great jackets here, wool coats, down vests, gloves even. But today Jerry didn't find even a dirty ripped coat. Upstairs Bruce owned a classier place called the Garment District. The clothes were on hangers and Bruce sold bomber jackets, perfect, for fifteen bucks sometimes. A bomber jacket would suit Jerry fine. He looked up the stairs longingly. But Intelligent Analysis wouldn't pay him anything until New Year's, and he had thirty-eight bucks cash.

At IntAl the office smelled like coffee and Cheez-Its, a sure sign that Pete Walters was here. Pete stuck his head around the edge of his cubicle and slid up his glasses to see who'd come in. He was dressed like usual—big sloppy Afro, brass rat ring from MIT, plaid flannel shirt, suspenders that held up his jeans—pretty casual, but no telling whether he'd let Travis stay.

"Morning, Hacker."

"Morning."

"Who's the boy?" Pete said absently, but didn't listen for the answer. Okay. Jerry didn't want to get in trouble with Pete, who was a wizard programmer. Pete's first company had made him rich, Jerry'd heard, and now he was just marking time until he got his next big idea.

"Hey, dude, you can draw with these markers," Jerry told Travis quietly and pointed him at the only blank whiteboard. Travis stared at it, the markers loose in his hand. Jerry powered up his machine and got to work. IntAl was programming a NOAA catalog call-up system, storing and retrieving weather pictures; pretty boring code, vanilla-flavored, but the hours fit in with taking care of Travis and Pete didn't ask questions, which was good because back in Schenectady someone was probably wondering where Jerry was.

"Want to come here, Hacker, take a look at something for me?"

Pete was peering at his screen, clicking on parts of pictures with the mouse to zoom them in and out. "That's Boston," Jerry said. "Boston, the Cape."

"Uh-huh. Friend of mine lives down in Hingham says there's something wrong with the edge of the caldera. His cellar's got water in it or something." Pete chuckled. "You see anything?"

"Edge of the what?"

"'A deep cauldron-like cavity at the summit of a volcano.'"

"Volcano?" Jerry pulled up a chair. Pete zoomed the picture out to full size. Boston met its harbor in a jagged C; the north horn was Revere Beach, the south one Hull. Rivers and wetlands made bright white marks on the photograph.

"Boston is the caldera of an extinct volcano," Pete said, putting on his assistant-professor voice. Moving the mouse, he drew a ring around the city and the inner suburbs close to Route 128—the highway that circled the city. "You look at the composition of the rock, you can see it." Pete clicked and a yellow overlay drew itself over the NOAA picture, a ragged yellow circle from Revere south to Hull and Nantasket Beach and extending out into the ocean. "Outside this circular area," Pete said, "all the rock is granite. Every time you're driving out of town and you have to drop down a gear, like that mother of a hill on Route 2, you're driving up the edge of the volcano onto that granite."

Pete pushed up the contrast on the picture.

"In here's Boston Basin, completely different kind of rock. Conglomerate, tuff, melaphyre." Pete tapped his pencil around the circle of the Boston Basin. "You have here a plug, fourteen miles wide, the lava plug of your volcano, which fills your caldera and is geologically completely different from the area surrounding it."

"Yow, well, volcano. Is it going to erupt or something?" MIT had better last until he went there.

"No, man, it's dead." Pete shook his head and reached for a Cheez-It from the box on his desk. He stared at the picture for a couple of minutes and snapped his suspenders while he chewed.

"But the edge does look just that little bit different," he said finally.

At the whiteboard, Travis was methodically erasing a flowchart. Pete spit out his Cheez-It and started yelling at him. Travis began to cry. Jerry went over and took the eraser out of his hand. The kid smelled funky, like a mouse.

"You scare me!" Travis accused Pete, still sobbing.

"He's just my landlady's kid," Jerry said, embarrassed. "She didn't show up this morning."

"He can't come here if he erases work." Travis left snot trails on Jerry's sleeve. Pete went out to the front desk, grabbed the jar of candy canes, held the jar out to Travis without speaking. Travis sniffed.

Pete zeroed in on the shoreline just below Boston. "Now look at that edge, right there." Between 1979 and '80, no difference around Boston itself.

"The waterline's higher at Revere and Hull," Jerry guessed.

"Uh-huh. Look at '80 and '81."

'81 was higher than '80. '82 higher than '81. Hard to tell, because the winter storms changed the shore a little every year. Jerry studied the pictures one by one, watching the slow creep of the water up Nantasket Beach.

"Is that like the greenhouse effect?"

"Uh-uh. You don't see this out around Quabbin. But look at the Charles, up in the estuary."

Jerry looked past the shadow of the Museum of Science and the Charles River Dam, up toward the wide Charles River between the Back Bay and MIT, up farther still. On the shore, in the later photographs, white dots began to bloom like mildew.

"That's standing water," Pete said. "And it shouldn't ought to be there at all."

* * *

Saturday, four P.M. When Jerry opened the basement door to Eireen's apartment he was greeted with smells: something moldy, a cheap sugary perfume, fish sauce.

And silence.

He turned on the lights. Everything was exactly the way he had left it, his sleeping bag sprawled like a corpse on the couch, TV off. Eireen still wasn't home. Travis turned on the TV very low and sat in front of it, watching silently, not taking up space.

Jerry looked quickly in the bedroom. Eireen's dirty red silk dress was still thrown over the bed. Jerry had met Eireen through an ad in the *Herald*. "Free room and board in exchange for child care after school and evenings." Sounds like a room, right? And a bed? The whole apartment was the size of Jerry's parents' kitchen. Travis's foam rubber mattress was crumpled on the floor by the sofa bed where Jerry slept. Eireen had her own room and her king-size bed, which completely filled it. The bathroom smelled and water was always backing up through the drain.

It was getting dark. Jerry asked Travis if he wanted to go to the park. Travis shook his head. He wanted to wait for his mother.

Eireen had a VCR and for a while they watched an old PeeWee Herman tape. Jerry rinsed out his underwear in the kitchen sink. Travis asked if they could rent another tape from the store down the street. Jerry said no. Travis was a leech; every day when Jerry picked him up from the town day-care center, Travis begged to stop at Woolworth's, said he was hungry, managed to find a candy bar or a Teenage Mutant Ninja Turtle he just couldn't live without. Jerry had been taking care of Eireen's kid four weeks now and the kid had whined him out of at least ten bucks.

Eireen was a bad mother. She fed Travis on hot dogs, Coke, potato chips, and double-cheese pizza flavored with fish sauce. Most of the time Jerry despised her.

Right now he wished she'd come home.

* * *

Sunday Eireen didn't even phone to say where she was. Sunday evening Jerry and Travis went to McDonald's and Travis ordered $2.67 worth of Happy Meal to get a plastic monster in a plastic car, worth about five cents.

Monday morning Jerry dropped Travis off at day care, glad to be rid of him, and went to work. At lunch Pete asked Jerry to eat with him at the Department of Transportation cafeteria, the DOT Cafe. Jerry bought a big hot sandwich, hoping Pete would pay, but he didn't. $2.55. Food cost a lot.

Pete drew on a paper napkin. "I'm still thinking about that water. About a decade ago, NOAA thought the Boston caldera was sinking about four inches a century," Pete said. "But that water, man, it's coming in faster than that."

My landlady hasn't come home, Jerry thought. *She went out Friday and left her kid with me.* Travis was running out of underwear. At home in Schenectady, Jerry's mother had a washer and dryer. Why didn't Eireen have like one of those little washer-dryers you could put in an apartment? She was irresponsible.

Jerry shifted his shoulders. His underwear was scratchy.

"This lady I live with," Jerry said. "I mean I don't live with her. I live in her house, I take care of her kid. I haven't seen her for three days now."

Pete didn't even look up. He didn't hear. He was still looking at that picture on the napkin, that geological O.

"Don't talk about this to anyone yet, Hacker, you understand?" Pete said.

For a moment Jerry didn't know what he was talking about.

Tuesday afternoon. Jerry took Travis for a walk to the Dummer Park playground. Travis played silently, by himself, in among the swings and the slides, dropping a ragged mitten, then finding it again.

Jerry wondered where Eireen came from. He didn't

know whether she was Vietnamese or Cambodian. When he had asked her, she said "I Amer'can" and gave him a look that cut glass. "Travis' father Amer'can so'dier." She showed him a picture of a black man with his arm around a much younger Eireen. Jerry didn't know whether her name was Eileen or Irene. She didn't have her name on the mailbox. She didn't get mail. He'd asked her where she had lived before Boston. "Buffaro New York." Another time she said Texas.

Squatting down, Travis pushed his plastic monster around in the sandbox. Jerry shivered in his fall jacket. The mist was turning into rain. "Let's go back."

On North Harvard Street Travis pointed out the Christmas lights and the Christmas-tree seller. They stood by the lot full of trees and sniffed the smell of Christmas. Travis, who begged for toys all the time, didn't say anything about Christmas this afternoon. In the puddles on the street, the lights wavered.

Man, it was cold.

Wednesday afternoon Travis's day care ended until after New Year's. Wednesday evening they finished the last of the food in the refrigerator, a frozen package of lima beans. Travis wanted cookies. There weren't any cookies. Travis went into a temper fit. "Where my *mama*? I want sweet. You bad man." Jerry heard Eireen in his voice. Where was Eireen?

What was he supposed to do, take Travis to work every day?

He was down to twenty-six dollars and eighty-three cents. He took Travis out to a convenience store. They bought Wonder Bread, milk, peanut butter, Ritz Crackers. Travis wanted cookies. Jerry said he could have Ritz Crackers. Travis picked up a big bag of Chips Ahoy. The tears ran down his cheeks and the snot ran out of his nose into his mouth. "Cookies! You no' get cookies I stay here!"

Already Jerry'd spent nine dollars. It made him angry. "All right, you creepy little kid! *Stay* here."

He slammed out of the door. From outside he looked back in. There was the kid in his worn-out sneakers, standing in the middle of the store, still clutching the big bag of cookies like it was some kind of toy. The tears were running down his face. He looked frightened. In the pit of his stomach Jerry realized something but didn't want to know what it was. "Oh, shit," Jerry muttered. "Oh, shit, man." He went back inside the store, bought the Chips Ahoy too, $3.09, and he held Travis by the hand while the two of them walked back to the apartment.

Travis fell asleep on his foam rubber mattress. Jerry stayed awake watching the late night news, trying not to think about Travis or anything. The TV showed a fat police officer pointing at some bushes. In New Bedford the police had found another body. Whores had been disappearing from Weld Square and showing up later, dead in the bushes at the side of the highway.

So what? Eireen didn't live in New Bedford.

"I should call the police," he told the phone, trying out the idea.

Finally he rolled out the sleeping bag on the sofa and closed his eyes.

In the middle of the night Travis climbed silently into his sleeping bag. There wasn't enough room for the two of them. Jerry didn't say so, didn't send him back; it was cold. The kid smelled like the inside of a bum's shoes. Jerry lay awake until morning.

Thursday Jerry took Travis in to work. Pete's big workstation was on but in screen-save mode; he didn't come in all morning. Jerry set Travis up playing Spacewar on the demo machine. Travis shot evil spacecraft, crashed into planets, went into orbit around the sun. The kid had talent. Jerry debugged and tested, muttering to his code.

They had a real lunch, leftover pizza from the refrigerator, some cranberry juice from a machine. For dessert, candy canes from the front desk. It was a feast compared to what they'd been eating. Travis fell asleep under the desk on Jerry's coat, snoring a little.

Then, while the code was compiling, Jerry heard Pete come in. Instead of going to his machine, Pete just stood at the door of the office.

"Hey, Hacker?" Pete was just grinning and standing there, swaying a little. He carried a big paper bag that clanked like glass.

Everything Jerry wanted to say came to the edge of his lips and stayed there. *Help.* I've only got $13.60 left. I want to go to MIT. Give me a loan. Tell me where I can leave this kid.

Except Pete didn't care. He put down his bag and leaned against the top of his big monitor, then he sat down as though somebody had cut the strings that worked his legs. He fished in the bag and brought out a bottle of Jack Daniel's, opened it and threw the top in the trash. Left-handed, he clicked around with his mouse, started calling up the same pictures: Boston Harbor 1979. 1980. 1981. Pete took a big swig of the liquor and wiped his mouth with his sleeve.

"Hacker," he said to the air more than to Jerry. "Big news, man. I'm gonna be famous."

He fumbled with the mouse and the picture swooped around the screen. "Gonna have my name in the papers. Get interviewed on the evening news. Ted Koppel. All that shit." He laughed. "It's been happening since the sixties, man. Right here in Boston." The laugh trailed off. "Right here," he said to himself. "Right here where I live."

"I need to talk to you—Pete, listen—"

"What you want, Hacker? You still got landlady trouble? Hacker, you have got *no* problems. You can have your very own condo." Pete's voice rose a little. "Just walk into anything in Boston, it is yours. Just make sure you get your-self the second floor, you understand? Maybe the third?"

Pete put his right hand over the center of the picture like it had some texture, like he was feeling the land with his palm. The picture drifted from Cambridge across the Charles to Dorchester and Roxbury, the mouse moving. "Codman Square's going to drown, man, Codman Square where I grew up. You ever go to Revere Beach when you were a kid? No more Revere Beach, man. Nobody's going to finish those condos they tore down the roller coaster for." Pete's breath was ragged. "Back Bay, Faneuil Hall, Fenway Park. Where're the Red Sox going to play? No more Kendall Square. What are all those white profs at MIT going to do? No more AI Lab. What are you going to do about this shit, MIT?" He banged his bottle down. "Fuck it!" he yelled. "Right here where I live! In my fucking city!"

He stood up, a big, swaying bear of a man, terrifying Jerry because Pete's eyes were lost and staring and tears ran down his face.

"Pete—"

"Hacker, Boston is going down like an elevator. Boston is over. You go back where you came from."

Pete punched his machine off, not bothering to get out of his program or park the drive heads. Jerry heard him stumble out the door.

Jerry stared at the code scrolling past on his screen.

Travis hadn't even woken up. Jerry put out his hand to-ward the telephone. I'm going to call the police. They'll take care of Travis. They'll fly me back to Schenectady, I'll go back to school. The kids at school will say "What happened to you?" and I'll tell them I went to Boston, I got a job hack-ing LISP. I'll apply to MIT, they'll take me, no problem. Meanwhile I'll just be another kid at school.

The code kept scrolling blurrily down the screen, and Jerry didn't dial the police. He put his head down on his knees. He was still hungry. But when he went back to the refrigerator for another slice of pizza, he remembered they'd eaten it all.

Friday, two days before Christmas. Jerry woke up late, cramped and hungry. This was one of his days off. Usually he went in to work anyway; not today.

"Go Aquarium," Travis announced.

Jerry thought about the $13.60 in his pocket. "No. Not today." Travis burst into tears.

"Want to go Aquarium—with—my—*mama!*" Suddenly Travis was up in his lap, burrowing against his shirt. Jerry hugged him, feeling stupid, not knowing what else to do.

"She's going to come back today," Jerry said. "It's Christmas in two days, right? She just went away to get some money for Christmas so she could buy you presents."

Travis blinked, unsure. It could happen, Jerry thought. Eireen was the kind of person who did things at the last minute, bought food only after almost everything was out. She was a Christmas Eve shopper, all right. She must have left a message, but it had to have got lost. She was that kind of person. She'd be home. Today.

They spread peanut butter on Chips Ahoy for breakfast. Jerry asked what Travis wanted his mother to bring him. Sniffling, Travis explained all about the presents he wanted: Nintendo, and a bike, and a real dog, and Teenage Mutant Ninja Turtles. "But I no get." The apartment was cold. They sat on the sofa, breathing the moldy air, both of them wrapped in the sleeping bag.

"Je'y," Travis said. "Where my mama?"

"Your mama just isn't here today, kid. I told you she'll be back. We'll go to the Aquarium together, you and me, dude, how's about that?"

Tears rolled down Travis's face as if Jerry had told him bad news.

He sniffled all the way on the subway to the Aquarium, needing to be told again and again that they'd see the penguins, they'd see the dolphins. The two of them sat at the front of the subway car to look at the tunnel. The driver let Travis stand next to him. Just before the car went up the rise to one of the stations, Jerry saw a puddle on the tracks. The lights dimmed as the train clacked mushily through it.

"Funny," the driver said. "I never seen that one before."

It cost seventy-five cents and ten cents for the subway, three dollars for Travis at the Aquarium, a horrifying six dollars for Jerry.

They watched the dolphin show. Travis sat in front stoically while the dolphins splashed him. They went into the Aquarium building itself. It was dark. At the bottom of the building the penguins flew silently through phosphorescent water. The big tank at the center of the building glowed green, filled with circling fish and sharks. It was dark and silent, almost nobody here this afternoon. Travis put his hand into Jerry's.

They found a tour and followed it, filling their minds with facts about water. The tour leader told them that land is always sinking under water.

They stared up at the big tank. Travis didn't say anything, just held Jerry's hand.

In the tank, fish flickered through shadows.

Friday afternoon, five P.M. Jerry found Pete's name in the phone book. He let the phone ring. An answering machine slurred in Pete's drunken voice. "Dr. Peter Walters is spending some time in the desert . . ."

After dinner Friday night they were out of milk and bread. They ate the last of the Chips Ahoy in front of the television. The kid smelled worse than ever.

Jerry said to Travis, "I'm going to give you a bath."

The bathroom smelled like dirty clothes and some of Eireen's stockings were still hanging over the sink. Jerry worked out how long it had been since he'd seen her; he was frightened to realize it had been a week. In the soap-dish, the sliver of soap still had one of her black hairs stuck to it. Jerry peeled the hair off before he gave the soap to Travis. The water foamed out of the old faucet into the pit-ted bathtub. Travis, naked, danced on one thin leg before he splashed into the water. Jerry put a little green dish deter-gent in the bath and it foamed up; Travis splashed and slapped at the bubbles, and Jerry took an old washcloth and scrubbed at him. Travis floated his plastic monster from McDonald's like a boat. They washed his hair with Eireen's shampoo. Jerry took a shower and the hot water lasted until he was done.

They settled down on the couch for the night. Clean, Travis smelled different. He smelled okay.

Early Saturday morning, when he went into the bathroom to pee, Jerry found Eireen's purse.

It was stuffed down behind the door beneath a couple of towels, the same big red plastic purse she always carried. He looked at it stupidly and then dropped the towels back down over it. In the living room Travis was still sleeping, sprawled out on the couch, the covers kicked off him and his mouth open a little. Jerry went back in the bathroom and lifted the towels off the purse like you'd lift a blanket off a dead person to see their face.

In the purse, with her lipsticks and Tampax and con-doms, with a half-full box of Tic Tacs with a roach in it and some Chinese haw flake candy, with a nail file and some balled-up Kleenex and a Danielle Steel novel with the cover cut off, Jerry found some white powder in a plastic enve-lope and, wadded up like the Kleenex, in small bills, nearly eighteen hundred dollars.

He opened her wallet. There was her driver's license with her picture on it. Eileen Nyo. He hadn't known she could drive.

He talked to her picture. "Boston is sinking," he said.

"And it's Christmas Eve and you owe me, Eireen, you owe us both."

He flushed the white powder down the toilet and counted the money with methodical adult fingers. Then he went to wake up Travis.

First they went to Dollar-a-Pound. Jerry filled a trash bag high with kids' clothes. Three pairs of jeans all together in the kids' pile, all the right size for Travis. A pair of canary yellow corduroys. A lot of T-shirts, some sweatshirts, one with a picture of the Turtles. "You want some socks?" Bruce asked. "I got a truckload of socks last week." Travis went rummaging in the piles of clothes and came up with a really bad Travis-size jacket, fake orange-and-black fur with a furry orange hood that stuck out in a ruff. He looked like a lion. As they were waiting in line to weigh out, the kid in front of them discarded a black leather bomber jacket because it weighed too much, four pounds.

Yow.

Next, Purity Supreme on North Harvard Street. They bought frozen TV dinners, Ring Dings, ice cream on a stick, Spaghetti-Os. They bought All-Temperature Cheer and Air Wick. At Video Unlimited they rented two tapes, and they ate lunch in front of the TV watching *The Black Cauldron*.

"I'm gonna clean up. Okay?" Jerry asked Travis. He folded Eireen's red dress and stuck it in the back of her closet. He filled a trashbag with their dirty laundry, the sheets, the towels from the bathroom, and while Travis wasn't looking, Jerry smuggled Eireen's purse in the trashbag out of the bathroom and hid it high on her closet shelf. They spent the afternoon at the laundromat watching their clothes spin. On the way home, Jerry bought Travis a pair of red high-top sneakers from the discount shoe store and they grabbed a couple of free pine boughs out of the Christmas-tree lot on North Harvard Street.

That night they slept in the sleeping bag on Eireen's

lumpy king-size mattress. Travis wore his new red sneakers to bed.

All night the pine boughs smelled really good.

Sunday. Christmas Day. After their frozen turkey dinners for breakfast they opened up a can of jellied cranberry sauce, and, eating it with spoons, they finished it all.

What do you do after you eat on Christmas? "We're going into Boston."

Suddenly the weather was like some kind of crazy miracle. A freak front had come through, it had to be sixty, seventy maybe, like spring. They both wore their jackets open, Orange Fur Monster and Black Leather Bomber Hacker, while they rode the trolley down Commonwealth Avenue into Kenmore Square, and Jerry showed Travis the big red triangular Citgo sign. Before the trolley went underground they got off and began to stroll through the streets like a couple of king dudes. Suddenly they were in tourist-calendar Boston, walking through the Back Bay by brownstone house fronts, Orange Fur Monster and Bomber Hacker sauntering down the street, picking where they would live.

"We're going to live on the top floor," Jerry told Travis. "Because the water's going to rise."

They raised their feet high—one pair of dirty black Reeboks, one pair of little red high-topped sneakers—and played wading through the water. They imagined swanboats in the Frog Pond, and stealthily they sawed through the boats' huge locks with the edge of Travis's monster toy and stole a boat each. "We're gonna need boats, dude, 'cause all this is going to be underwater." The water rose just like in a bathtub and the Frog Pond overflowed, and the pirate kings raced each other with the swanboats, paddling madly, and then they turned their swanboats into spaceships and flew all around the sky. But Travis said they needed ice cream from Friendly's, so they let the swanboats and the water and the spaceships go away for now.

They walked through the Financial District licking their ice-cream cones, tilting their heads back to look at the tops of the buildings. They got lost and Travis began to lag a little, when they unexpectedly found the waterfront between two streets and saw the Fort Point Channel. Travis looked at the channel and his eyes widened.

"Je'y, what that ship?"

"Yow," said Jerry.

He had never seen anything like it before. It bobbed on the water, silly and indestructible like a cork toy, a real live three-masted eighteenth-century ship. Boston Tea Party Museum, he read on the sign by its wharf. Orange Fur Monster ducked under the railing that was supposed to keep people off the wharf; Bomber Hacker swung his legs over it and followed. On Christmas Day there was no watchman; they jumped down and stood on the deck, two dudes who could do anything.

"We no live in house. We live *here*," Travis said.

"Yow." Travis ran around yelling and waving an invisible scimitar.

There, across the water, down the channel, by the harbor, there was Boston. The ship shifted and the rigging creaked and swayed like a pirate ship. The winter afternoon was closing in. In the sunset light the buildings glowed.

The deck moved under Jerry's feet, and something passed under him like a wave. Jerry talked to the city. *You're sinking.*

Boston creaked and swayed around him, shimmering, changing. Yachts sailed through the half-submerged arch of Rowe's Wharf. The Customs House tower dissolved into a lighthouse, gondolas slid over the park grass and bumped the windows of the brownstones. Gulls screamed and waves boomed against the drowning buildings in Kendall Square, and MIT was gone. With every one of his heartbeats Jerry could feel the caldera sinking, jarring, in tiny waves, right here, right now. Here was his future Boston and it wasn't going to be programming, no, not MIT, no, but what he knew right now, mold-smell, a whore's purse filled with small bills, the good way it feels not to be hungry. He wasn't going to be hungry again. Things were going to work for him. He felt himself crossing some edge between what he had thought he wanted to be and what he was.

Travis tugged at his hand. The kid looked up, very solemn, holding out his plastic monster in its car. "Je'y? I give you fo' Christmas." Jerry knelt down by him so they were equal height and Travis said solemnly into his ear, "This *my* *favorite*," and pushed it into his hand.

"You my favorite too, Trav." He was stuck with the kid. It was okay.

"We live here?"

The drowning, frightening future city glittered across the water like an eternal Christmas. Jerry grinned.

"This is ours," he said to Travis. "We live here."

NOMADS
ALEXANDER JABLOKOV

CAIUS FITZPATRICK, TOPCOAT over his arm, swung around a corner in the casual slouch he termed "worker's walk." It was the gait of the man in to fix the pipes, replaster the wall, rehang the doors; deliberately incurious about anything but the task at hand, and not too energetic about that either. Caius had supervised countless workmen, and knew the walk well. It made one's presence seem reasonable anywhere.

The building was the former lodge of some extinct fraternal organization, and these upper floors were a warren of studios, converted from their one-time ceremonial uses. Caius imagined war-paint-spattered initiations, ritual antler storage, ceremonial washings. He peeked through doorways, finding men and women in various stages of undress sprawled exhausted on the floor. Intent on their own business, they made no notice of him as he wandered from door to door, looking for Linda.

Somewhere below, down the wide oak stairs he had just climbed, the dance concert continued, not noticing his absence from the audience. He could hear occasional strains of the recorded music above the casual chatter of the relaxing dancers.

In one small room two ballerinas in white tutus faced each other, each with one leg up on the bar, their hair in severe buns. As they leaned toward each other, each with a leg above her head, whispering some secret, they might almost have been one ballerina stretching in front of a mirror. A larger room beyond was filled with people in brightly colored leotards, faces made-up to look like birds. They earnestly discussed their just-finished performance. At the end of this studio stood an elaborate baldachino, now bedraggled, its canopy hanging down in strips. Caius wondered what Grand Dragon or Imperial Sultan had once sat enthroned beneath it.

When Caius had been in high school his class had gone on a field trip to the Boston Aquarium, to see how it worked behind the public areas. Caius remembered the dark tanks in the back corridors, one containing oddly pigmented indigo and pale-blue lobsters, one a hideous, gape-jawed goosefish, one an electric eel. Sick seals had gazed wanly at the passing children from their wet infirmary. An eight-foot monitor lizard beaded like a handbag had ignored them, more interested in a cockroach that had incautiously wandered into its cage. An inhabitant of Indonesia, the monitor had been found by a perplexed householder in the industrial suburb of Revere, who had stalked into his garage to prove that his children had certainly *not* seen a dragon, as they claimed. Caius felt now as he had then, that he had strayed into a place of initiates, the secret creators of the public scene. He was one of them, he reassured himself. He belonged here, as he did everywhere.

He ascended a creaky set of stairs and paused at a doorway. Two women sat, knees together, each holding a red carnation. One of them, hair shading from black at her scalp to red-blond around her shoulders, was Linda.

"Is he PC?" the other dancer asked Linda, then took a luxurious bite of a chocolate bar.

Linda frowned. "I wouldn't call him that. He's cute, though."

"Ha. So political correctness isn't everything, huh?"

"Well . . ." Linda thought. "Of course not."

The other woman finished her chocolate. "I'm sure glad we stopped boycotting Nestlé's. Why were we doing that?"

"Baby formula. Third World."

"Yeah, that's right." She looked up, smiled at Caius, and nudged Linda. "Heads up."

Linda raised her high-arched eyebrows, then uncurled, somehow arriving on her feet. Her movements seemed unconsidered, but always got her where she wanted to go.

"Did you enjoy it?" she asked. She still wore her leotard but had pulled on sweatpants, and leg warmers over those, all in clashing colors.

"Yes," he answered. "You danced well." And she had, her usual distracted manner completely transformed into focused intent. He wished she could be that way with him. With a long-eyelashed wink, Linda's friend dodged past them and out the door. Caius took a step forward.

She fended him off. "Please, Caius. I've been working. I stink like a horse."

"Hey," he grinned. "I grew up in South Boston, remember? I've never smelled a horse in my life. It'll be an experience." He grabbed her. She was still sweaty, warm and damp under his hands. He kissed her neck. Salty. She did have the sour smell of too much life. Was that really what horses smelled like? It was thick and sharp. And it was hers.

She let him kiss her a moment longer, then twisted out of his arms with a dancer's liquid strength. Even his construction worker's muscles couldn't hold her. Not without a struggle.

"I do smell foul." She laughed and ran over to the window. It looked out over the low roofs of East Cambridge row houses. Cylindrical water towers stood like sentinels on the flat rooftops of industrial buildings. They had obviously fallen asleep on their watch, for beyond the sturdy brick warehouses with their entirely unnecessary brick cornices rose the anonymous towers of the Kendall Square redevelopment which had swallowed, among other things, one of Caius's favorite diners. Beyond those were the even higher towers of Boston itself. All built by Fitzpatricks, as Caius's father would automatically have pointed out.

Linda slid the window open and leaned out, catching the breeze. Her high cheekbones and slanted eyes were a legacy from her Thai father, who had been brought back to the American Midwest as a lasting souvenir of her mother's Peace Corps work. Linda shivered melodramatically. "It's cold. I feel winter. Deep winter." She turned to him. "Let me shower. Meet me downstairs. Twenty minutes."

The street outside the studio was dark and slightly ominous. Newspapers and McDonald's wrappers blew in the gutter. The dance studio's arched windows glowed yellow above him. Chilled by a sudden breeze up the Charles, Caius paced the street.

He had met Linda one glorious late-summer day, in front of the Robert Gould Shaw Monument, a meeting arranged by a mutual friend with a love of quirky combinations. Caius liked the view of the Common from the corner on which the monument stood, with the gold dome of the State House rising high above.

The Saint-Gaudens high relief of the white officer and his black troops of the 54th Massachusetts Infantry, marching off toward death and glory in the assault on Fort Wagner, had not proved the best rendezvous point. Linda had found the sculpture vaguely racist. The white officer was mounted while his black troops marched. Racial differences in hair, lips, and noses were clearly obvious. And it was cast in the nineteenth century when *everyone* was racist. And all

Caius had ever seen was a strikingly effective sculpture, a memorial to brave men.

Refusing to be deterred, he suggested roller-skating on the Esplanade. Despite his ungainly, large-handed Irish workman's body, he turned out to be somewhat better at it than she, since he didn't worry about damaging himself by running into trees and light poles.

By the end of the day, they were tired, and friends. At Goodspeed's he bought her a beat-up copy of the memoirs of the picturesquely named George Roberts Twelve Hughes and took her to dinner at a Brazilian restaurant. It was a day he felt he would always think of.

Still waiting for her, Caius found that he had walked into a small, barren park. On the other side of it was the African Methodist Episcopal Church, where the black congregation appeared Sundays in the neatest and most precise clothing Caius had ever seen, men and boys in sharp suits, women and girls in frocks with ruffles and hats. And white gloves. Caius had never known a woman who wore gloves except to keep her hands warm. He had only seen these people here, at this church, Sunday mornings. How did they live the rest of the week? Caius pictured their small starched-and-pressed houses above ironed lawns, shades decorously drawn. Where? The moon, perhaps. Nowhere in the Boston Caius knew.

On his side of the park, ominous in the deserted night, was a low, aluminum-sided building called Biomorphics, a genetics research lab spun off from MIT, its windows a line of glass as blank as the slit in a helmet's visor. At the corner of the lab, against the brick wall of the next building, was a makeshift shelter made out of pieces of plywood, refrigerator boxes, and sheets of plastic. Caius glanced at it. It was actually put together quite well, with a slight overhang on the roof and bends in the plastic to give the wall stability. Resting in it was a long-haired, bearded man in a tattered overcoat and beat-up orange Reeboks. He sat in the shelter expectantly, as if it were a sleigh taking him to some important destination.

Caius slid his eyes quickly across the derelict, and quickened his step.

"Hey buddy, you got fifty-three cents for a bottle of Cabernet?"

Despite himself, Caius slowed.

"C'mon. The Fetzer's on sale. At $5.89. I call that a good value. You won't be wasting your money on someone who buys Thunderbird, for crissakes. Or Riunite. I'm fifty-three cents short."

"Did someone give you pennies?" Caius stopped.

The other grimaced. "What, are you kidding? They walk by with their girlfriends, they don't want to seem like assholes, so they reach deep into their pockets . . . and shit comes out. Assholes, after all. Actually, I have $5.40, but four of the pennies are wheat ears, and I save those."

"For your collection?"

The man's eyes narrowed. His skin was wrinkled, dirt rubbed into the folds. Stubble surrounded his mouth. "Don't get smart. Someone gave me a Standing Liberty dime last week too. I stashed that, believe it. Times will get bad, currency worthless. I'll need silver then."

Caius dug into his pocket and pulled out a handful of change. Under the man's watchful blue eyes, he carefully counted out fifty-three cents.

"Much obliged." The man stood up. His hair was tied back in a ponytail. "You're probably heading back to the bright lights—and the liquor stores." He fell into step beside Caius, who for one frantic instant thought about claiming he was going in the other direction. But he had to get back now. Linda would be waiting. The man was big, even taller than Caius, and moved smoothly in his long coat, hands in his pockets. "So what do you do?"

"I'm a builder," said Caius Fitzpatrick. The other

grunted, as if that meant something to him. "How about you?"

The man looked at him incredulously. "What do I look like? I'm a drunken bum who sleeps in doorways."

"And drinks Cabernet."

"Hey, I have standards. Besides, I said it was on sale, didn't I?"

Caius thought about the construction of the man's shelter. There had been a logic to it, a sense not normally found, as if it were the vernacular architecture of some unexamined culture. "What did you do before . . ." He suddenly realized the question was indelicate. "Um . . ."

The man laughed, head thrown back. Several of his back teeth were missing. "Before I was free? I forgot. Completely. It's irrelevant. Now I'm free. I go where I want, I do what I want. You don't understand us, you people who live in houses." The man's eyes were ablaze and he gestured wildly with his arms, looking, Caius suddenly realized, like a dangerous drunk. "We are the new nomads. Wanderers. Free cossacks of the streets!" He glared at Caius, his eyes uncomfortably sharp and penetrating, not the eyes of a drunk at all. "And you build."

"My whole family builds. It's an honest occupation." Caius wondered why he sounded so defensive.

"I'm sure it is. But it restricts, confines, insulates."

"You don't think insulation is important?" Caius asked, glad to score a point, even against a street person. "I've seen you nomads freezing to death on the streets." He wished Linda was with him. She had a good fund of statements of liberal concern. Though this man would have frightened her. He didn't seem like the sort to react well to liberal concern. "I've seen you crowd the shelters. Is that freedom?"

"Yes! Freedom can be cold and terrifying. Unpleasant. That's the way it is. If you don't realize you're free, it's all only meaningless suffering. The trick is understanding that you're paying a price, not enduring a punishment." They stopped in front of the liquor store. The man raised his hand in salute. "Would you care to join me? I'm sure they'll give us plastic cups if we ask."

"No," Caius said. "I'm already late."

"Ah yes, the responsibilities of the unfree. I always forget. Good-bye. My name's Rum, by the way."

"Caius."

"Well, okay, it's not really my name. More a *nom de rue.*" Rum turned and strode grandly into the liquor store. Caius hurried up the street to the dance studio.

"I've been waiting," Linda said, slightly irritated. Caius was always punctual.

"Sorry. I ran into . . . a friend."

"Ah." She looked at him, Caius realized, not with suspicion, but with interest. He decided not to explain further. He needed a little mystery.

"Where do you want to eat?" he asked.

"There's a new Thai place down here," she said. "I've been wanting to try it."

"A taste of home cooking?"

"Fat chance. My dad never cooked and Mom was straight Illinois meat and potatoes. I didn't see a chili pepper until I went to college. Let's go, it's cold."

Fred Ng slapped the rough brick wall revealed once the plasterboard was off. "You guys been around a long time, eh?"

"Yeah," Caius answered, not quite believing it himself. "The first Fitzpatrick got here in 1846. First boat from Ireland after the blight. He must have been a lousy potato farmer, went under quick. Came to Boston, dug a pit up in Somerville, and started making bricks." One of the headers in the lowest course of bricks had a maker's mark in it, a GfP in a circle: George Fitzpatrick.

Fred Ng was Caius's partner in their building-restoration business: Fitzpatrick & Ng, Resurrectionists. Caius's

Aunt Alice thought the name sacrilegious and crossed her-self whenever she passed one of their trucks. Or so she al-ways told him.

"Building restoration?" Caius's father Homer had ex-claimed when his son told him his plans. "Are you crazy? Putting in antique bathrooms with bye-dettes and lace cur-tains for rich bitches to take milk baths in? Fitzpatricks are builders, not antique dealers, Caius. You trying to move up in society?" Homer peered suspiciously from his fat flow-ered armchair, an obsolete patriarch.

"No, Pop," Caius said. "I like it, that's all. I like bricks, mortar, wooden beams." *And hate steel I-beams and glass-and-stainless towers.* But he didn't say that. No sense in starting another argument about building technology. Dinnertime discussions in the Fitzpatrick household had always been about things like structural concrete and brominated glass.

"Look." Homer stood up and walked to the living room window. The Fitzpatrick house was high up Telegraph Hill, not far from the high school, and the climbing skyline of Boston dominated the view. "Twenty, thirty years ago, none of those were there. We put them up. My father. My brothers. And you. Remember how you used to visit me when you were a kid? You loved the work site."

Caius remembered the bustle, the grinding concrete mixers, the flaring torches showering down sparks. He still had, somewhere, a bolt and nut that his father had given him on one of his visits. Caius had always screwed and un-screwed the nut, over and over, when thinking seriously. It was a talisman of his father's strength.

"I'm sorry, Pop." His father had welded him book-shelves out of stainless steel strips, tiny iridescent welds with a minimum of excess metal. His childhood bed had been riveted and stood on heavy metal casters, to his mother's dismay, since it ruined the floor. Homer had wanted his son to soak the iron into his soul, but had in-stead gotten someone who was concerned with Adam fanlights and wood rafter trusses. "Fred Ng and I already have a contract, on a house in the South End."

Homer shrugged. "It's quite a jump, Caius. There's no foundation under you. Fred's a good man." He turned back to the skyline. "But we'll keep building, Caius." He knotted his big hands in fists, as if willing the buildings into existence from his living room. "We'll keep building."

As he left his father's house, Caius had imagined the towers climbing ever higher, until the sky was iron, the sun was encased in scaffolding, and the moon broken up for gravel. And busy Fitzpatricks would have done it all.

Fred and Caius climbed back up out of the cellar. The upstairs was open and it was cold, late December. Many of the men had come from Southeast Asia, from Indonesia, Malaysia, Taiwan, Thailand, recruited through some mysterious connections of Fred's. They wore heavy coats and shivered in the Boston cold.

They were in the process of rebuilding the top two floors of a brick Queen Anne row house. The new owners had requested a 'completely authentic' restoration, which demanded a heavy braced frame with tediously hewn joints and rafter plates, using up a lot of expensive wood. Caius had tried to convince them to use a simpler balloon frame, just as strong, but they had insisted.

The joining of the roof frame was almost finished. Caius watched his men working and smiled. Completely authentic. Suggano and Murathir, carpenters from two different Malay villages, had cut elaborate Asian joints to hold the frame together without the use of nails or pegs. A future restorer, a century or so in the future, would no doubt be confused to find clearly Southeast Asian workmanship in an otherwise completely consistent nineteenth-century Yankee house.

Fred raised his eyebrows when he saw Caius putting on his coat. Caius rarely left while anyone was still working.

"She must be special." Fred smiled as Caius blushed. "It's about time. I've read that the Irish marry late, but . . ."

"I'm not getting married. I'm going to a meeting about Nicaragua. At Harvard."

"Good for you," Fred laughed. "Never marry a woman your mother can stand, else the two of them will conspire against you."

Out on the street, Caius paused and looked up at the house. The elaborate brick front, surmounted by a false gable roof, was supported by scaffolding. Several of the men, veterans of construction in Hong Kong, had asked why they didn't use bamboo scaffolding, light, strong, and flexible. Caius had explained that, in Boston, bamboo was much too expensive. They had looked at each other then, their suspicions confirmed about this cold and sad northern city, too poor to afford even bamboo.

He grabbed a bunch of flowers from a bucket in the grocery store and headed down into the subway, seeing Linda. She poured just enough cream into her coffee for it to slop over into the saucer, then drank it by delicately extending her lips, barely picking up the cup, sunlight streaming through her hair from the window behind. She wandered into the shallow water at a beach on Cape Cod, her inappropriately long skirt pulled up her lovely legs, to laugh at the horseshoe crabs as they frantically pursued each other across the bottom in their urge to mate. She tossed her hair angrily, threw an antique enamel-backed brush across the room, enraged by a Supreme Court decision, and then pursued it, checking it for cracks, running her fingers across the bristles as if scratching a dog, her face sad.

"Well, if it isn't my fellow wanderer," a voice grated.

Caius looked up. Hanging over him, beard and long hair flying, was Rum. His face was lined and red, his nose bulbous. Here in the enclosed car, Caius could smell his rankness.

"Boston's not a good place for a nomad," Rum stated, as if continuing an interrupted argument. "For one thing, it's got a damn toy subway system. Now New York—there's a subway line out to Queens that takes a solid hour. They wake you up at the end and you walk out and get on the one getting back. All night! A hotel on wheels. Half the city's in ruins. Everyone camps out there like Goths."

"Why don't you go there?" Caius asked.

"Because it will come here!" Rum roared with laughter. "Everything'll fall apart and we'll be living in the ruins soon enough. And I'll know the territory. I've been burned out for years." He frowned, suddenly irritated. "And I build myself little houses, like a middle-class nomad. Old habits die hard . . ." He shook like a sheet in the wind. His teeth ground together loudly.

"Do you cart your house around with you?" Caius asked, desperate to stop the sound.

"Nah. You can find plywood and cardboard all over. In the future, though . . ." Rum shook his head. "I'm stockpiling. The stuff people throw away is amazing. Rolls of asphalt roofing. Dented aluminum panels. Cracked plexiglass domes. Carpet remnants, all colors. Hell, I'll be a chieftain with fifty wives." He coughed into his hand, a rough, tearing sound. "A big man. In the future."

The train stopped at Charles Street. High up on Longfellow Bridge, they had a view over the Charles River. "Ah, Boston. It's back." Rum stepped out, pulling his long coat around him. "See you around. Say hi to your girlfriend for me."

Caius felt a chill that had nothing to do with the cold that had come in through the open door. What did Rum know about Linda? Had he followed them from the dance studio? Did he know where she lived? Caius looked down at the hand which clenched the bunch of flowers as if it were a weapon. He sat back and rested them on his chest. Not everything in this world was hidden and mysterious.

* * *

The meeting was in an old Greek Revival building near Harvard Square, once a home of the New England Anti-slavery Society. Pictures of prominent abolitionists still lined the hallways. Caius kept trying to think of its current inhabitants as wild-eyed immigrants from other parts of the country who didn't belong here, who were trying to destroy his city with their weird concerns: animal rights, nuclear power, toxic waste, abortion, Central America. But the sternly hysterical eyes of the ancient Boston radicals hanging on the walls held the same look. It was Caius who felt out of place.

After the meeting, Caius sat on a folding chair, finishing a cold cup of tea, while Linda and several fellow activists retired to another room for a side session with Emiliano, a real Nicaraguan who studied at the Episcopal Divinity School. They flickered past the half-open double door while Emiliano leaned on a table, dryly elegant in a ventless jacket. His black hair was combed straight back, and he spoke with an engaging Hispanic accent, like a polo player or a cabaret owner. Eventually, he straightened and, with a flick of his fingers, declared the session over.

The cold overcast outside was distant from Nicaragua. Instead of further discussing land redistribution and baby formula, Caius found himself telling Linda a story from his boyhood. After long discussion, and many careful diagrams drawn on rolls of brown butcher paper, he and Henry O'Rourke had built a raft out of oil barrels, grocery store pallets, and a broomstick, all scavenged from the windswept shore of Old Harbor.

She laughed. "Did you really think you could sail to Tahiti?"

"Well, *somewhere* with palm trees on it." He shook his head. She leaned closer to him, one arm under his, the other holding his flowers. "The oil barrels were rusted through.

We sank like a stone, maybe fifty yards from shore. Henry couldn't even swim. I had to drag him to shore. And you know what my father's only reaction was?"

"No, Caius." Her cheeks were flushed with the cold and her dark half-Asian eyes gleamed beneath her lashes.

"He said, 'Caius, you're a builder, not a boatwright. Let this be a lesson to you.' "

She laughed again. He stopped and kissed her. In modern overstimulated life nothing is more tantalizing than kissing someone in an overcoat. Her lips were soft. The rest of her was concealed in thick down, a precious object packed for shipment.

Because of the snow, traffic was snarled on Beacon Street. Linda drove an aged Volvo. She turned the radio to a station that played only rock music from the '60s and '70s, music as old as her car, some of it older than she was. They stopped near a large excavation, where a sewer was being rebuilt.

A small board by the pit displayed potsherds and clay pipes from the Colonial period, dug up by workers. Some of Boston's water pipes were still wood and clay, Caius knew, from the nineteenth century. They spilled water constantly but were only replaced when they burst. He imagined the water flowing through them, coming in all the way from Quabbin Reservoir in central Massachusetts. The creation of that reservoir had drowned four villages. Hiking there, Caius had seen their ghostly foundations down through the still, forgetful water. Boston had sunk them so that it could live. Caius wondered if their spirits longed for vengeance.

The new sewer pipes loomed massive and black, their mouths gaping anxiously like fish on a dock. A white stripe of snow marked each of their backs. Steam rose out of the ground as a backhoe dug through the street. The familiar glare of a welding torch illuminated the sides of a trench, the torch itself invisible. The crew worked with lazy purposefulness, minding their tasks, each understanding a small part of the system they were rebuilding. Caius thought of the steel bolt and nut that lay in his drawer at home, and the hard work of building in a world where nothing was truly solid. He looked over at Linda as she, frowning, fiddled with the balky clutch and put her shoulder into her shifting. Her strangely dyed dark-brown to red-blond hair, like a parfait, spilled out from under her knit wool cap.

She glanced at him. "What are you thinking about?"

"Building," he replied. "The way you build things."

"You love that, don't you? Sometimes I think you like the process more than the final result. You never want to be finished."

"Is a dance performance ever finished?"

She laughed. "No. When it's finished, it's sad."

She lived on the second floor of a triple-decker. Caius loved triple-deckers because they seemed so reasonable. No one found them reasonable anymore, of course, and no one built them.

Caius took Linda's coat, and they stood in the living room, indecisive. She turned and pulled a record off the shelf. It was by a singer named Jane Siberry. Their common taste for the Canadian songwriter, a surprise to both of them, had been one of the first things that had let them know that they did not have to remain strangers.

" 'And I'd probably be famous now if I wasn't such a good waitress,' " Linda sang along to the record. She tried to dance with Caius, but he kept losing the beat of the music. Finally, laughing, she kissed him. The record played to the end. Fortunately, the arm returned automatically.

The seat was hard, and Caius twisted in it until Linda glared at him. He sat up straight and, staring at the three busily playing musicians, tried to find something he could pay attention to. The dark lacquer gleam of the grand piano, the pianist's precisely painted nails reflected back in it? The duller wooden shine of the cello, its perspiring owner pulling sounds out of it with a saw? Was the violinist wearing a toupee? His hair had slid forward over his eyes, but perhaps that was just the style.

He glanced at Linda. She seemed fascinated, her narrow eyes half closed. She wore more eye makeup than usual, and her hair was pulled back by a black, Carmen-like comb, revealing dangly Indian earrings.

They sat in the Tapestry Room of the Isabella Stewart Gardner Museum. Heavy beams supported the large room's ceiling. High arched windows opened out on the central enclosed courtyard, its lush greenery contrasting with the winter that reigned outside. Tapestries covered the walls. The room was dominated by a huge marble fireplace and a painting of Saint Michael fighting Satan.

"Sorry," Caius said, once the performance was over. "The seat's hard."

"Mine was just as hard," she pointed out. "You didn't see me jumping around." Her eyes flicked past him. "You're very possessive, you know that?"

Caius tried desperately to remember which of his remarks had occasioned this assault. "What do you mean?"

"Oh," she gasped in annoyance. "For example, in this museum we went where you wanted to go, saw what you wanted to see."

"We've been in every single gallery," Caius said, at a loss. "What didn't we see that you wanted to?"

"Stop it. I don't want to argue with you. I'm just letting you know something." She turned away, swirling her red-and-yellow Central American dress like a signal flag. He watched her graceful form slide into the next room, her shoulder blades eloquent of departure. Precariously balanced on his stumping legs, he followed.

"What are you so upset about?" Caius asked.

"Nothing," she said. "Everything." She looked at him in appeal. "Oh, Caius. When I met you, everything seemed so simple. So choreographed. Like," she groped into his idiom, "like it had been laid out with a straightedge and plumb line."

"Why isn't it simple?" he asked. "What's different?"

"I don't know. The steps are all wrong." She dipped her body in a sinuous tango, dancing with an invisible partner. She looked sadly over her shoulder at him. "I'm getting my coat. Don't come with me. I need to think." Feet moving precisely beneath her long dress, she darted out through the stairwell, with its dark, almost invisible Japanese screens, and vanished.

When he finally left the museum, he looked for her red coat, but it was nowhere to be seen. The Back Bay Fens lay across the street, ponds frozen and hidden beneath a thick layer of snow. The snow had been coming down heavily, but now the sky was clear. Cars crept cautiously along the languorous streets, their tires grumbling in undertones.

Caius walked amid the trees, feeling fallen branches snap beneath the snow. The winter sun was setting and the park filled with shades of blue, from the indigo of oak tree shadows to the pale blue of the snow itself, the color of a baby's blanket. He crossed an arched bridge over hidden water and entered a thick stand of pampas grass, huddled under its new white overcoat.

A glow caught Caius's eye, the faintest of yellows vividly warm against the cool shadows. Curious, he approached. A bearded figure, like a forest spirit, hunched over a tiny fire in a perforated coffee can. With no surprise, Caius recognized Rum.

Rum looked up and squinted across the fire to see who was disturbing his privacy. He looked older than when Caius had last seen him, his skin splotchy and drooping. He held his hands out to the fire as hobos always did in movies.

Cold and hungry, Rum still managed a condescending smile.

"Sit down, Caius." He gestured expansively at the

snow-covered ground opposite. Caius squatted, hunching in his long overcoat. "You don't look well, friend. Didn't she like your flowers?"

Behind Rum, Caius could see his shelter, a lean-to this time, its entry blocked by a heavy sheet of plastic. It had the same reasonable look as the first shelter Caius had seen against the corner of Biomorphics, a look of sensible structure. "Flowers aren't the problem. Ah—do you need food, Rum? A place to stay?"

Rum barked a laugh. "I've never wanted a place to *stay*. Want a drink?"

"No, I—"

Rum pulled a wine bottle out of the snow and shook it. "Still some left. We better drink it before it freezes. It'll be no damn good at all then. A Sauvignon Blanc. Not a great one, but hey, it'll do." He produced a plastic cup and poured. Caius sipped. Darkness had filled the Fens, and only Rum's face was now visible in the firelight. A tired face. A beaten face. The face of a man with nowhere to go.

"Bad times are coming," Rum announced with the relish of an Old Testament prophet. "Cold days. The buildings you've built will crumble, sink into the water, vanish like burst pimples."

"And we'll join you out here?"

"Ha. Out here will join you. Dogs will run the streets tearing at babies' arms. No one will sleep anywhere two nights in a row because someone will find and kill them if they do." His voice rose. "Buildings will freeze and crack. You won't recognize that world, Caius." Something caught in his throat and he bent over in a fit of weak coughing. He took a breath and shook. "Summer's a different story around here, you know. Full of faggots running around grabbing each other. Millions of them. Everybody in the city, as far as I can tell. Don't know who's home with their wives. It's a whole other world, you know. So I don't stay out here in the summer. Too noisy, and the summer people try to climb in with me. I prefer the winter. I'd like to see winter everywhere." He shivered and pulled his coat more closely around him. With the sky clearing, the temperature had dropped drastically.

"Look, Rum," Caius said. "Why don't you come with me?"

Rum peered at him with sullen suspicion. "Are you one of those funny boys too?" he demanded. "Kind of cold for that kinda thing, isn't it?"

"Don't be ridiculous."

"You have no right to say that!" Rum shouted. "You're trespassing on the future and you're dressed for the past." He pulled his loose hair back from his face, peering intently at Caius. "So how's your girlfriend?"

Caius's knees were starting to ache. His Asian workers could squat that way for hours, but he was beginning to wonder if he would ever walk again. Linda. A man always needed something to hold on to. If he let go . . . well, he could either float, or sink. Rum was sinking. Caius stood up, joints filled with sand. "She's fine," he said. "Just fine."

Rum snorted, and his eyes wandered from Caius's face. "It'll all freeze," he muttered. "You'd better be ready for it. If you're not, you might get stuck in ice up to your knees."

Caius shivered. "Rum, there's a shelter not far from here."

Rum regarded him bleakly. "There's no shelter for any of us. Don't fool yourself."

"I'll—"

"If you have them come take me to the shelter tonight, I'll just get out again. Nomads never like being put on reservations." He turned away and stared blankly off into space, obviously prepared to ignore Caius for as long as it took for him to go away.

Caius hobbled off into the high grass. The city's glowing towers rose up above the dark trees. Busy traffic roared on the Fenway. The city went about its business. Caius stood at the park's edge for a long time, realizing that he felt more like Rum shivering in his lean-to in the Fens than like any of the people in the bustling city before him.

They met for the last time in a diner called Frank's Eatery, near the building Caius was restoring in Chelsea. It was a gesture of grace on Linda's part. She didn't like diners and had always found Caius's interest in them perverse.

This one was run by Chinese, who yelled at their customers and worked with incredible speed. One had to be a pro to get served at the take-out counter. "What you want?" the counterman shrieked. "You want beef? Beef?" A moment's hesitation and you were lost, shouldered aside by more experienced patrons.

Someone tried to combine two orders: "I want the chicken, but instead of the slaw I want—"

"We no have!" the counterman shouted in a passion. "We no have! Next!"

Outside the pink-and-green interior it was that wholly unsatisfactory weld between winter and spring called mud season. The earth was so wet and soft that it seemed everything should sink into it.

"Are you still working on that house—what did you call it—stick?" she asked. Now that he knew, her Central American bracelets and earrings seemed like flaring signals. He had only missed them because he had not cared to see.

"Yes," he replied. "We'll be on it all summer. It's a complicated style."

"But you like that sort of thing," she said. "Don't you?"

He took a sip of his coffee. It was terrible. "I suppose I do."

"Oh," she uttered. "Don't be mad at me." Her tone implied that any anger on his part would be unreasonable and impolite.

Caius had heard that if a man wanted to break up with woman, he should do it in an expensive restaurant where she would be embarrassed to cry. Linda had obviously applied the lesson in reverse. What could he say to her in this diner with its shouting countermen and construction-worker-filled Formica tables that would not seem ridiculous?

"What emotion would you suggest?" he asked, finally.

She shredded her napkin. "Why do you have to make this so hard on me? It won't change anything. I'm going. It's what I have to do. I know that you've never been committed to this, the way I have. I know your politics are a little different . . ."

"Don't you feel embarrassed," he said, "turning a complicated personal failure into a simple infidelity?"

She was calm. "Don't be so analytical, Caius. These things happen."

He was desperate to find why it happened. He didn't understand why her failure to love him enough had led her to Emiliano's bed. He didn't understand why, one day, she had incautiously played back her answering machine, so that the romantic Sandinista's purring voice could tell Caius everything he should have known long ago.

"Oh," he moaned. "This is so banal."

She smiled at him and took his hand. Her gesture was a sign of the unselfish affection she had convinced herself had replaced her love for him. Her touch was disconcerting, like false skin. "I'll write from Managua. I will."

He pictured her somewhere in Central America, sitting at a table in a flowered jungle, a cracked plaster wall behind her. She wore a wide-brimmed hat. A colored parrot waddled by, its head tilted, peering at the floor tiles for dropped food. She was not writing a letter. Caius could not compel his imagination that far.

He stood up, his food unfinished.

"I have a book of yours," she said. "That book by Twelve Hughes, remember?"

He remembered. He had bought it for her the first day

they had met, the day in front of the Civil War memorial. She had forgotten that it was hers. Looking at her, he could see that she had never read it. "Keep it," he said. "Or donate it to a hospital." He turned and walked out. At the last moment, he resisted the automatic urge to pay the check. He left her with it.

A sea breeze cleared the sky. The air was clean in his lungs. He wandered the busy, indifferent streets and felt no urge to go back to the work site. Fred could handle things for the afternoon. So he walked. He walked the high span of the Mystic River Bridge, a lonely pedestrian in a world meant for cars. The highway ran between the tourist sights in Charlestown, separating Bunker Hill from the USS *Constitution*. He walked underneath it, looking for shelters, for the abandoned figure of a proud and haughty man. He saw no one.

He crossed over into Boston on the low Charlestown Bridge, shadowed by the ugly green span of the highway. He walked, soon footsore and weary. He searched the faces of drunks and panhandlers. He even asked about Rum but, nervous at being approached rather than fled from, they sidled away with muttered, incoherent replies.

With night the cold returned. Caius stopped and looked up at the stars. Perhaps Rum was nowhere to be found. He could well be dead, of "exposure" as the newspapers always had it. Overly exposed to life. He could have left this earth far behind, and be circling one of those distant points.

Caius finally stood in an area of desolation somewhere beyond the boutique streets of the new South End. His home, South Boston, lay some miles to the east, not far, really, but he didn't feel like walking anymore. He explored the lot where he stood. It was amazing, as Rum had pointed out, what people threw away. Sofas, refrigerators, carpets. And corrugated metal sheets, vinyl fake-wood panels, plywood boards. Everything he needed.

He had wanted Rum to explain, to show him how to live

in a world where nothing remained solid. Caius felt like one of those cartoon characters who had run off the edge of a cliff, but could only fall when he looked down and realized that there was nothing under his feet. He was tumbling, air in his hair. Drowning, water in his mouth. It was a world Rum knew how to live in. Had known, at least, until it killed him.

Caius chose a spot against the foundation of an abandoned brick house which rose sturdily above the surrounding garbage. Shrubs hid him from the street. He ran his fingers between the smoothly fitted bricks. Such a wall could stand for centuries. He shook his head. Permanence was not the lesson he was trying to learn.

Caius began to build. He laid the floor down first, a fiberboard panel on the soft, wet dirt. Then, after a moment's consideration, he hoisted an A-frame of two wall panels and laid a sheet of plastic over them. It wasn't much, nothing like Rum's elegant constructions, but it was late, and he was tired. It would be a long time before Caius would be able to compete with the master nomad.

He crawled in and lay on his back, covering himself with a length of carpet. Would this make him free? No. Life would find him in the morning, the ground would be solid beneath him again, and he would have to think of what to build. For now he closed his eyes, and went to sleep.

PROJECTS
GEOFFREY A. LANDIS

BEN DANGLED HIS feet over the side of the ledge and looked out across the Charles at the sunset. The day was breezy and cool, with sailboats zipping briskly up and down the basin. Across the river, Boston skyscrapers were gold-plated by the October sun.

Fifty feet below, none of the people walking along Memorial Drive even looked up. The ledge around the top floor of Walker Memorial was plenty wide, hardly a challenge, but Ben liked it for the view. It was a good place to sit and meditate.

After a while Rat came walking down the ledge, carrying a burger and a Coke from Pritchett. He was crazy, but then Ben figured that all of his friends were crazy. Everybody worth knowing was crazy.

"Hey ya, Benjy."

"Hey yourself, Rat."

Rat walked over and sat down cross-legged next to Ben. Ben reached over and grabbed a handful of his fries. The catsup was mixed half-and-half with Tabasco—a trick Rat had taken up to discourage moochers—but Ben was so used to it he was starting to prefer them that way.

"Got the midterm projects back today." Rat—his full name was Jacob Ratjszek, which he hated—was in architecture. His midterm design had been a study for a plastic sky-scraper, made rigid like a balloon by its own internal pressure. He'd worked on it for weeks.

"Yeah?"

"Yeah. 'Good imagination, but unrealistic. B+.' And a note: 'Please do something more practical for your final project.' "

"Bummer."

"Fucking professor thinks I'm a twerp."

"You mean you're not?" Ben regretted it the moment he said it.

"Damn right I'm a twerp. I've got twerp written all over me. But just one thing, Benj. I'm one twerp that these guys are god-damn going to *remember*."

Ben, Rat, and another student, Trenton Endicott, lived together in half a house in Cambridgeport. It was old, run-down, with peeling paint and warped floors and in a less-than-nice neighborhood; but it was big, close enough to the Institute to walk, and not half as expensive as most of the apartments around Cambridge.

The landlord was a medical intern whose hobby was collecting Art Deco. His wife raised Dobermans. The kitchen was her province, fenced off from the rest of the house, and filled with Doberman puppies. On Sunday afternoons she would invite poor starving students down for samples of bread, cookies, or whatever she was baking.

Rat and Trenton had two old Jaguars, bought from a junkyard wrecked and rusted, one bashed in from the front and the other from the back. They'd cut the frames apart halfway and welded them together. Covered with a tarp, the car frame sat up on blocks back behind the house, under an abandoned grape arbor, waiting for some day to come when they'd find time to work on the body. In the living room, engine parts were spread across the floor, across every chair, couch, table. Neither one of them had worked on it in months. They'd never get around to finishing it. That was yesterday's project; today's project was always newer, more exciting.

It was a crazy house.

Ben was course eight—Physics. Trenton and Rat were both in Architecture and Urban Planning. Trent was tall, blond, handsome, and quiet; Rat was short and Jewish and quirky. Ben figured himself for somewhere in the middle. He'd roomed with Rat his freshman year, and when they decided to go together on an apartment, Trent was a natural choice for a third. Trent was in the Urban Planning concentration, working on a combined master's. He'd picked Professor Tormic for an advisor.

"Man, you have got to be out of your mind," Ben had said. "The Tor has got a reputation a mile wide. He never cuts *anybody* any slack."

"Aw, he's all right," Trent said, "if you know how to handle him."

"Yeah? How's that?"

"Well, first thing is, you gotta be ready to work your ass off."

"Right."

"No, Tormic's cool. Hell, he's the only professor in the 'tute that comes to all the grad student parties, let alone come with some woman he just picked up at a bar."

"Yeah, right. Good reason to work for the guy."

Trent shrugged. "Well, that and the fact that he's brilliant."

Trent was the only one who had a regular girlfriend, Mary, a Chemical Engineering major from Connecticut. She was rather cute, in her own way—long brown hair and a taste for dressing in blue cotton shifts. Trent often spent nights at her apartment. Ben had tried dating one of her roommates for a while. He'd thought they were hitting it off pretty well, but when he'd tried to make a move, she'd let him know where he stood real fast. "You guys are just too weird for words, you know? Like, you guys are kinda interesting to hang around with sometimes, but not on a day-by-day basis, okay? Frankly, I don't see how Mary deals with it."

If Rat ever had any interest in women, he never mentioned it.

When Ben came in the next day he found Rat lying on the floor in the living room, looking on in amusement as the King of Nigeria stalked a sheet of transparent mylar that hung suspended in the air over the heating vent. Niger was stock-still, only the tip of his tail twitching occasionally. The mylar rippled and twisted with the passing air currents. Rat was cooking something up, thought Ben; he could tell by the speculative look in his eye.

Trent was in his room, scrutinizing a long spool of chart-recorder output spread across the floor. He had chart-recorder output taped up across every wall of his room, results of geological measurements he'd taken over the last few weeks.

"What's up, Trent?" asked Ben, tossing his jacket onto the pile at the end of the hall.

Trent looked up with a grin. "Good news, that's what. Tormic says he thinks we have enough to publish. Our conclusions are pretty radical, but he says we'd better publish before somebody else makes the same jump. I'm getting it ready to submit for *Urban Studies Review*."

"Hey, good for you. Go for it!"

The walls of Rat's room were covered with drawings and photos of buildings. Half of them showed skyscrapers. The other half were domes: sports arenas, churches, inflated tennis domes, observatories; covers from science-fiction books showing the cities of the future, with segmented domes rising from the plain like half-buried crystal balls.

"A dome is a competition between materials strength and gravity," said Rat.

In the middle of their living room, clearing aside the engine parts, Rat had put up a five-foot-square scale model of Boston. Trent had made it for a wind-tunnel project long ago, but Rat took it over as his own. He had put a dome over the city, made from ultra-thin plastic. The model was in front of the bay window. When the sun struck it, the air inside heated and the dome inflated.

It was Rat's project for the design course.

"See, in all the old science fiction, they always have these cities with domes over them, right? But that's stupid, no? Living inside a thing like that would be like being indoors all the time. Dull. People need to get outside sometimes, especially in good weather, don't they?"

"Sure," said Ben, although he knew some people who wouldn't even recognize the sun if they happened to see it one day.

"You really need a dome you can put up in winter, when you need it, and take down in summer, when it's nice, right? So here's my solution: a transparent mylar dome."

"Like the tennis bubble, but transparent?"

"Forget the tennis bubble, Benjy. I'm talking *big* bubble. I'm talking kilometers here. It stays inflated on waste heat generated by the city. It keeps the heat from escaping, and so you can go outside in winter in your shirtsleeves. In the summer you just roll it up and store it away. The savings in snow removal costs alone would pay for it, not to mention the energy savings."

"Pretty clever."

"Damn right it's clever. But I know what he's going to say. 'Imaginative, but not realistic.' Pfagh."

Rat joined him on the porch roof. The skyglow was just beginning to fade, and Venus stood out like a searchlight against the luminous pastel sky. They sat in silence until the stars emerged. It was a pleasant, companionable silence.

"When I was a kid," said Ben, "I used to climb up on the

roof of our house, lie down on the shingles, and try and count the stars." Rat said nothing. "Counting stars is tough; it's easy to lose track and count the same ones twice. That happens, and you have to start over again from the beginning. And the longer you're out, the more you see." The night was an endless dark and the stars seemed so close that he could almost brush them with his outstretched fingertips. "I used to say the numbers out loud so I wouldn't lose track." Sometimes he would so lose himself in contemplation that he would hear his own voice counting . . . six hundred eighteen, six hundred nineteen, six hundred twenty . . . and for a moment fail to recognize the voice, or what it was saying. "You ever do anything like that, Rat?"

"Nah." A jet crossed the sky, for a moment rivaling Venus in brightness. When its noise had faded away, Rat continued. "Guess I was too busy trying to make rocket engines. Most of them turned out more like bombs, really. Blew out every window in the block, once."

"You know what, Rat? I never did manage to count them."

"Yeah. I know what you mean." They were silent for a while, so long that Ben started to think perhaps Rat had fallen asleep. "You really think they're out there, Benj?"

"Gotta be. A hundred billion stars in the galaxy, Rat. Some of them have just got to be homes of other civilizations. If we haven't seen them, we're just looking in the wrong places. Or listening to the wrong things."

Niger appeared at the window, meowed softly, walked carefully out to rub once against Rat's shoulder, and then bounded out into the night. "Lasers, huh?"

"You got it." There had been SETI—Search for Extraterrestrial Intelligence—attempts before. But those projects had listened for radio signals. "Aliens advanced enough to discover the laser wouldn't bother with radio. The wavelength is all wrong—radio waves aren't directional enough to communicate across interstellar distances. Intelligent aliens would use lasers. But nobody's ever tried looking for laser signals. Nobody before us, anyway."

On weekends Ben went out to Haystack Observatory, where his project team had set up scopes. They searched G-IV stars, looking for narrow-band coherent light. Finding nothing.

"You just do that, Benj. Look for your aliens. And I bet you'll find them. Someday. Me, I'm going to do what I've always wanted to do."

"Which is?"

"Make tall buildings."

Early November the weather turned cool and foggy. Ben's observatory session was postponed. He wandered over to Urban Planning to see if Trent was in his office. He was expounding on his project to a pair of mystified undergraduate assistants.

"It's like this," said Trent. "The continental plates are moving, right? The Atlantic Ocean is getting wider, and it's shoving the Eastern Seaboard up into the Allegheny mountains. The plate is being pushed on the right; it's pinned on the left; and so a whole load of compressive stress builds up. Like this." He put his hands together, palm to palm, and pushed. "Now, turns out the Boston basin is a Paleozoic caldera. The city itself is built smack-dab center on the extinct volcano's throat, a big granite plug. And the pressure is squeezing on the plug." He made a popping sound. "Just like a watermelon seed. But, in this case, it squirts down. Boston's starting to sink."

"Come on. If Boston were sinking, wouldn't other people have noticed by now?"

Trent shrugged. "Nobody's gonna find what nobody looks for."

"Then how do *you* know?" asked Ben.

"Seismic tomography. The boss managed to borrow a machine over a weekend." He grinned. "He's a slave driver, but there are advantages in having a boss who's got connections with the oil companies. The data's noisy, but when you know what to look for, it's there. Now, the way I see it, the Boston civil authorities take the ostrich approach. Obviously, that's only going to work for a limited amount of time. This is a long-term thing; the city is going to sink for the next century. Boston is traditionally a city built on land-fill, but there's got to be a limit to how much you can keep building a city up. It would be interesting, wouldn't it? Every ten years or so they'd have to raise all the streets, and the first floors of all the buildings would become basements, while the basements become submerged."

Boston sinking. It seemed unreal and far away, nothing concerned with the solid, vibrant city Ben knew. "So what do you think they should do about it?"

"Personally, you mean? Just abandon the place. Heck, move the Institute down to Florida or somewhere, and what's Boston got worth keeping, anyway? Just a bunch of old houses, and a couple of skyscrapers that are going to fall over anyway. Let it sink."

The undergraduate assistants looked appropriately shocked.

"But, of course, you can't put that into a thesis," said Trent.

Ben laughed.

"Benjy—are you in on this hack?" asked Rat. "All I can tell you is that it's big. It's real big."

"Will it take a lot of time?"

"Couple of weeks, maybe," said Rat.

"Can't, then. Next week we have Haystack scheduled for twelve-hour runs, and after that I'll be up to my ass in data."

"Okay, but you'll regret it, I guarantee you."

"Are you really hard up for people?"

"No, I got lots of volunteers. I just thought you'd want to be in on it."

"Can't be helped, Rat. Sorry." Ben looked at him for a moment. "Say, this isn't going to be another 'Synthesis of Phenylated Methyl-ethylamines,' is it? You could get in a lot of trouble."

"Hey, no way. I swore off that. Besides, this one's legal. Well, almost legal. Most of it, anyway."

"Synthesis" had been a science-fair project back in high school. He'd won the local science fair and was well on his way to winning the city-wide when three men wearing charcoal gray suits and sunglasses showed up and confiscated his display. Apparently someone had finally figured out that "Phenylated Methyl-ethylamines" was a euphemism for "amphetamines." They'd taken him to the local police station and asked him questions for three hours, but eventually let him off with a warning. Rat claimed that he'd never used the stuff he made; Ben believed him, since Rat was so wired naturally that using speed would have been like putting salt in the ocean. Ben figured that he'd probably just been amused by the prospect of playing his teachers for fools.

"Yeah, right."

Rat spread his hands and grinned. "What can I say? I've got a rep."

"Tormic is up for tenure next week," said Trenton.

Rat kept scribbling away and mumbling to himself. Ben looked up. "Trouble?"

"Nah. They'll give him a hard time, but he'll make it. The man's obnoxious, but you gotta see that he's fucking brilliant."

"Yeah?"

The summer before they found their place in Cambridgeport Ben and Rat had both stayed at the Institute. Trent had gone back to Chicago; he'd found a summer job as a junior assistant in the mayor's city planning office. Ben stayed in the dorm. Rat didn't have enough money saved to pay for a dorm room; instead he set up a tent on the roof of Building 24. The door that led to the roof was kept chained and padlocked, but Rat had sawed through one of the links of the chain, replacing it with one that looked identical but could be twisted open and shut. The tent lines he tied to vents and other protrusions; the stakes he welded into the roof itself by melting the tar with a hot-air gun. There was a bathroom on the top floor, but after it was dark he didn't bother, urinating off the side of the roof into the courtyard forty feet below.

Friday evening some enterprising hacker had crashed the network. The net mainframe responded to all commands with the same misspelled message: HEY NERD! ITS FRIDAY NIGHT. WHY ARENT YOU OUT HAAVING A GOOD TIME? User Services couldn't say how long it would take to purge the system. Ben decided that it was as good a time as any to heed the message. He looked at the posters in the lobby and found a mixer in the Sala.

The party was a dud. Soggy tasteless pretzels and waxpaper cups with punch the color of radiator antifreeze and music played so loud as to make any chance of conversation impossible. The girls mostly sat around in groups of three or four. Makes it rather hard to go up and ask one to dance, Ben thought—you keep thinking, won't all her friends think I'm insulting them? If one girl won't dance, he feels kinda silly asking the next—what do they think, that he sees them as commodities? All the same?

Ben did one dance, but the girl nodded and headed off. No interest at all. He looked around one more time and split for a friend's house.

When he got there, they were having a party of their own. Bob was strumming his guitar, Trent accompanying him on one of those little plastic recorders. Mary was with him. Ben expected her to be happy that Trent's attention, for once, was on something other than his project, but she didn't look very happy.

The fireplace was burning wood scrounged from dumpsters all around the Institute, mostly loading pallets and shipping crates. Occasionally bits of paint would sizzle up in colors, releasing a quick burst of odor.

Trenton was well on his way to oblivion. His paper had been rejected by *Urban Studies Review*. "A disappointment, but they're pretty choosy. We're sending it to *Geology Transactions*; they're sure to accept it."

The Building 10 ledge was narrow, but if you followed it around there was a wide niche where you could sit and have lunch. When Ben reached it Rat was already there. As he sat down, Rat reached over and grabbed some of his fries.

Trent never went out on ledges. Once they'd offered to show him around the Walker ledge, as wide as a sidewalk and at least as safe. He just looked out the window and smiled. "Sorry, guys. I'm not into suicide."

From where they were sitting, they looked out across rooftops: weathered green brass, flat gravel, forests of ventilation ducts separated by the occasional skylight. Rat waved his hand out at it. "Looks pretty real, doesn't it?"

"Why shouldn't it look real?"

"So how do you know that this is the real world and not a computer simulation?"

"Too high-resolution for a computer simulation."

Rat shrugged. "Yeah? So it's a really *detailed* computer simulation."

"Not damn likely. *You're* in it. No computer could ever come up with a world with something as unlikely as you in it."

"Yeah, right. So how do *I* know that it isn't a simulation?"

"It's got *me* in it."

"And how do you know that you're not a computer simulation, too?"

"Because—" Ben paused. "I don't know. How *do* I know I'm not a simulation?"

Rat shrugged. "You could try jumping."

Ben looked down. "No thanks. If I am just a simulation, I think I'd just as soon not know it."

Minnesota was too far for Ben to fly home for Thanksgiving, Trent's parents were vacationing in Europe, and Rat never went home for holidays, so the three of them and Mary rented bicycles and pedaled down to Cape Cod. The water was far too cold to swim, but Rat did anyway, stripping down, shouting "Banzai!" and diving in; then immediately running out to shiver by the bonfire Trent and Mary had made from driftwood. When the fire burned down a bit, Trent wrapped the turkey in aluminum foil to roast in the coals. Trent and Mary shared a blanket and sang Beatles songs off-key as the turkey cooked, while Rat, uncharacteristically silent, huddled close to the fire, wrapped up in three winter coats. Feeling left out, Ben walked down the beach, gathering more driftwood for the fire. It was well past sunset before Trent pronounced the bird done to satisfaction.

Trent and Mary shared one tent while Ben and Rat put up a tent of Rat's own design, a geodesic dome of graphite rods and iridescent plastic sheet which he claimed was half the bulk and a third the weight of a standard tent.

Sometime after midnight a storm whipped up. Rat's dome began to whistle and then, with a nearly ultrasonic twang, shredded. Ben grabbed his sleeping bag and dashed for the other tent, startling the heck out of Trent and Mary, who had slept through the whole thing. Rat chased down the beach after the tent poles. "Hey! That's a hundred bucks' worth of graphite rods! Help me catch them! Hey, it's not funny, you guys!"

In the morning it was cool and overcast, but had stopped

raining. Ben and Rat took a bus back to Boston with their bikes and the remains of Rat's tent, while Trent and Mary cycled on down to Provincetown.

The end of November, Ben's research project hit gold. One of the nights when Ben was supervising the optical coherence survey, an undergraduate assistant was puzzled by an anomaly in the scan spectrum. When Ben checked it out, the source showed characteristics of coherent light. It emanated from somewhere near a star known only by a number, DB-4223B, a G subgiant fifty-seven light-years from Earth.

"Likely star for life?" asked Rat.

"Who knows?" Ben shrugged. "Actually, we weren't even supposed to be looking at subgiants in the first place—we were aiming at main-sequence stars. This one got on the list by mistake. But then, who knows what type of stars are even likely to have planets? This one's as good a bet as any, I suppose."

"He's obsessed, Ben," said Mary. "You talk to him. He's impossible to live with. I just can't take it anymore, it's been that bad lately."

"Yeah, sometimes I know just what you mean. He's having a hard time, you know."

"I know, but it's just too intense for me. Does he have to be so obsessive about it? Couldn't he relax, just for a few moments every now and then? I can't deal with it. I can't, I really can't."

By the beginning of December, Rat hardly came home at all. He was always working on his project. When he came in, he was usually on the phone. "You sure that they don't guard the helicopters at night? Okay, good. Do we have backup pilots for the other four?"

Ben tried not to even wonder what he was up to.

His own project was in high gear, working twenty-hour

days. They were constantly excited. It was clear that they'd found a laser in the sky, a huge one. It was putting out, Ben's professor calculated, as much power in a day as had been generated by all the power plants on Earth since the beginning of civilization. But it didn't seem to be *doing* anything—the power wasn't modulated, it didn't even seem to be narrowly focused. It just *was.*

After a long session at Haystack trying to nail down the signal, Ben came home just before dawn. Trenton was still up, pacing back and forth around the living room. He was white. "I can't believe it. I can't believe it. They denied him tenure."

After a while Ben got Trent coherent enough to tell the story. The tenure committee hadn't actually denied tenure to Tormic; what they had done was only to push the decision off to the next year. Apparently Tormic's research had been beyond question, but they had heard bad things about his teaching. And his research focus didn't really match the department's main interests—they hinted without quite saying anything outright, that he might find himself happier if he found a spot on a geology faculty. He could try for tenure again next year, except—

Except that he'd lost his cool. He insulted the tenure committee—"a gaggle of worn-out has-beens and never-wases, with turds for brains"—and the department—"morons couldn't see breakthrough research if it raped their sister and stole their wallet." They were jealous of his brains, he'd said to Trent. Well, he didn't need that bunch of jerks anyway. If he picked up a phone he could have his choice of a dozen other offers in an hour. According to Trent, Tormic had gone on insulting the committee, in excruciating detail, for half an hour. At the end of it they didn't need to fire him—he'd quit.

The next day his office was already empty. A good-bye note was painted on the door in Wite-Out: "Starting at Amoco Monday. So long, suckers!"

× × ×

Trent was rather depressed all the next week. It was four in the morning when Ben came in, and Trent was sitting at his desk, staring at his papers. In half an hour he still hadn't moved. Ben was almost afraid to talk to him, but more afraid not to.

"How's it going?"

"Okay," said Trent, without looking up.

"Thesis going all right?"

"Maybe."

"Well?"

"Got a committee," he said. He put down his calculator, pushed back his chair, and looked up at Ben. "They want me to give an informal presentation to fill them in on what I'm working on, next week. They seem pretty sympathetic. I think it'll go all right. I'm just a little nervous, that's all."

"Well, good luck, then."

"Yeah." Trent pushed his chair back toward his desk and bent back to work.

After three weeks of observation and analysis, they finally concluded that Ben's laser signal was no more than a natural optical maser operating in a supernova gas shell, a phenomenon that had been predicted by an obscure Russian astrophysicist back in the late sixties, but never before seen. Still, that was more of a discovery than most students ever made. It was plenty for a thesis.

Rat spent all his time listening to the weather radio, plotting fronts and isobars on a plastic map of the United States. He was nervous. His final architecture project had been due a week ago. He'd gotten an extension, but that wouldn't last forever. He told Ben he had the paper written, though he didn't volunteer to show it. The class required not only a paper, but a model. "Not yet," he said, but he didn't seem to be working on anything. He just sat on the floor stroking the cat and watching the Weather Channel.

* * *

Mary didn't say where she went. Her roommates said she just packed up and left. The Institute only knew that she didn't register for classes for next term. When Trent tried to call her family they hung up on him. She left a note in purple felt-tip ink.

"I have to leave for a while. I've got to get away, get some time by myself to think things through. I'm sorry. Maybe I'll see you in September, okay? Maybe things will work out."

The night was crisp and clear, the stars brilliant in a velvet sky. Ben wished that he could be out observing, instead of having to head home to work on his thesis. When he got in, he could hear Rat on the phone: ". . . the front moved through last night. Another front is coming in tomorrow afternoon, it should drop a couple of inches of snow. As soon as we hear from the weather service, we're *go* for tonight, four A.M."

"They dumped my thesis," said Trent. "I can't fucking believe it. They called it science fiction. Told me to get back to the real world. They want me to start a new project. Jesus, a new project! I'm almost through, and they want me to start over again."

"Bummer," said Ben.

The dome went up over the Institute on a calm winter night two days into finals period. It was a military operation, zero hour four A.M. The dome itself was twelve tons of mylar, suspended under a skyhook helicopter. Compressed air canisters blew it open, and four smaller and more maneuverable Army helicopters snagged the main tension lines as it slowly settled over the Institute. Rat's ground team grabbed the anchor cables, stretched them out to inch-thick steel eye-bolts that had been emplaced in quick-set concrete the previous night, and winched them to the specified tension. Another team released a controlled volume of helium between the two sheets to hold it in position until the sun rose and the greenhouse effect took over. Ben wondered how he'd kept managed to keep an operation that big so secret.

"The key rule of life," said Rat. "Never ask first, for it is always easier to get forgiveness than permission."

It was like a warm summer day inside, while snow swirled outside.

It was huge. It was magnificent. The headline in the *Globe:* "Doming the Dome: Tech Students Do it Again". In the *Herald-American:* "Saran-wrapped Science". The instant dome was on the front pages of a hundred newspapers, the latest and most audacious student caper from a school well-known for technological pranks.

Rat wasn't there to enjoy his triumph. Ben finally found where he'd gone when he returned home late, and the phone was ringing. It was Rat, calling from jail.

It turned out that Rat had used a fake Institute purchase order to buy the materials—a rather major item, since he had used nearly a hundred thousand dollars' worth of mylar alone. He was also being held by the feds, who had been less than thrilled when it appeared that the helicopters used had been "borrowed" from the National Guard.

With his usual good fortune, Rat only stayed in jail for a night. The helicopter company turned out to be his benefactors; their publicity department wanted to feature the dome for a TV ad, and it wouldn't do to have the builder in jail. They paid his bail and convinced the others that, all in all, it would be better if the theft charges were just quietly forgotten.

Geology Transactions rejected Trent's paper. "The settling of Boston is well known, and is already adequately accounted for by gradual compression of landfill. Data is interesting, but does not support such a far-reaching conclusion."

Late at night, Trent broke into Tormic's empty office and brought in a tank of liquid nitrogen. He taped plastic over the ventilation grill and around the door and chugged down a fifth of Jack Daniel's while the nitrogen boil-off slowly displaced the air in the office. No mess, no pain.

The dome lasted about a month before it tore away in a strong wind. It was beginning to get dusty anyway. The Institute had already started making plans for a stronger one next year, bigger, financed by the money they would save on heating and snow removal.

It was a warm day in March, and the ice was finally breaking up in the river. Ben was looking across at Boston, trying to see it as Trent might have, transformed into a city of canals. After a while Rat joined him on the ledge.

"You still think you'll find your aliens?"

"Eventually. Or else they'll find us."

They sat in silence.

"I look at Boston," Ben said, "and all I see is your dome. Thin plastic, glistening in the sunlight."

"Forget that. That's history. It'll never happen in Boston, anyway—the prof was right about that all along. Too conservative. Tall buildings, that's where the action is. You know Frank Lloyd Wright's mile-high skyscraper? Forget it! Technologically obsolete. Why think small? With composite fibers and dynamic control, I figure that we could build one ten kilometers tall, easy. Imagine it, will you?" He held out his arms.

Ben shook his head and smiled.

Ben kept the only remaining copy of Trent's thesis. It must have been when he and Rat moved out of the apartment that it got lost. At any rate, he looked for it but couldn't find it the next year, when Boston began to sink.

DYING IN HULL
DAVID ALEXANDER SMITH

IN THE WEE hours of February 12, 2004, Ethel Endicott Cobb
clumped down the oak staircase to check the water level in
her dining room. She always checked her floor when the sea
was lowest, no matter whether ebb tide came during the
day or, as this time, in the dark of night.

Moonlight from the window reflected on the empty
hardwood floor, a pale milky rhombus. A thin glistening
sheen of still water lay over the wood, bright and smooth
like mirror glass.

Blinking sleepily, Ethel sat her chunky body on the next-
to-bottom step and leaned forward to press her big square
thumb down into the rectangular puddle. She felt the moisture and withdrew her now-wet hand. Water slid in to
cover the briefly-bare spot, and in seconds, the surface was
motionless and perfect, her mark gone.

She yawned and shook herself like a disgruntled dog.

Gunfire in the harbor had disturbed her rest; she had
slept fitfully until the alarm had gone off. Well, she was
awake now. Might as well start the day.

The rose-pattern wallpaper was rippled, discolored with
many horizontal lines from rising high-water marks. It was

crusty at eye level but sodden and peeling where it met the floorboards. Above the waterline, Ethel had filled her dining room with photographs of the town of Hull—houses, streets, beaches, the roller coaster at Paragon Park—and the people who had lived there. Pictures of the past, left behind in empty houses by those who had fled and forgotten.

Ethel carefully touched the floor again, licking her thumb afterward to taste the brine. "Wet," she muttered. "No doubt about it." For a moment she hung her head, shoulders sagging, then slapped her palms against the tops of her knees. "That's that." She rose slowly and marched back upstairs to dress.

Cold air drafts whiffled through the loose window frames as she quickly donned her checked shirt, denim overalls, and wool socks. The sky outside was dark gray with just a hint of dawn. Her bedroom walls were adorned with more photographs like those downstairs. As the water rose with the passing months and years, she periodically had to rearrange things, bringing pictures up from below and finding space in the bathroom, on the stairway, or in her makeshift second-floor kitchen.

Crossing to the white wooden mantelpiece, she hefted the letter. Ethel read what she had written, scowling at her spiky penmanship, then folded the paper twice, scoring the creases with her fingernail. She sealed it in an envelope, licked the stamp and affixed it with a thump. Returning to the bed, Ethel stuck the letter in her shirt pocket and pulled on her knee-high Wellingtons.

By the time she descended again to the first floor, the tide had risen to cover the bottom step. Ethel waded over to her front door and put on her yellow slicker and her father's oilskin sou'wester, turning up the hat's front brim.

The door stuck, expanded by the moisture. She wrenched it open and stepped out, resolving to plane it again when she returned. Closing the door behind her, she snapped its cheap padlock shut.

Queequeg floated high and dry, tethered to the porch by lines from his bow and stern. Ethel unwrapped the olive green tarpaulin from his motor and captain's console. When she boarded her boat, the white Boston whaler rocked briefly, settling deeper into the water filling K Street. After checking the outboard's propeller to verify that no debris had fouled the blades, Ethel pushed *Queequeg*'s motor back to vertical, untied his painters, and poled away from her house.

She turned the ignition and the big ninety-horse Evinrude roared to life, churning water and smoke. Blowing on her hands to warm them, she eased *Queequeg*'s throttle forward and burbled east down K to the ruins of Beach Avenue.

Dawn burnished the horizon, illuminating the pewter gray scattered clouds. Submerged K Street was a silver arrow that sparkled with a thousand moving diamonds. The air was bright with cold, tangy with the scents of kelp and mussels, the normally rough winter ocean calm now that last night's nor'easter had passed.

She stood at the tiller sniffing the breeze, her broad feet planted wide against the possibility of *Queequeg* rolling with an ocean swell, her hands relaxed on the wheel. They headed north past a line of houses on their left, Ethel's eyes darting like a general inspecting the wounded after battle.

As the town of Hull sank, its houses had fallen to the Atlantic, singly or in whole streets. These windward oceanfronts, unshielded from the open sea, were the first to go. Black asphalt shingles had been torn from their roofs and walls by many storms. Porches sagged or collapsed entirely. Broken windows and doors were covered with Cambodian territorial chop signs of the Ngor, Pran and Kim waterkid gangs. Some homes had been burned out, the soot rising from their empty windowframes like the petals of black flowers.

A girl's rusted blue motor scooter leaned against the

front stairs of 172 Beach. Barnacles grew on its handlebars. Mary Donovan and her parents had lived here, Ethel remembered, before she moved to downtown Boston and became an accountant. A good student who had earned one of Ethel's few A-pluses, Mary had ridden that scooter to high school every day, even in the snow, until the water had made riding impossible.

Beach Avenue had been vacant from end to end for years. Still, Ethel always began her day here. It was a reminder and a warning. Her tough brown eyes squinted grimly as the whaler chugged in the quiet, chill day.

"I could have told you folks," Ethel addressed the ghosts of the departed owners. "You don't stop the sea."

Sniffling—cold air made her nose run—she turned down P Street. For three hundred years her ancestors had skippered their small open boats into Hull's rocky coastal inlets, its soft marshy shallows, to harvest the sea. In the skeleton of a town, Ethel Cobb, the last in her family, lived on the ocean's bounty—even if it meant scavenging deserted homes.

Like 16 P just ahead. She throttled back and approached cautiously.

16 P's front door was open, all its lights out. The Cruzes have left, Ethel thought with regret. The last family on P Street. Gone.

Cautiously, she circled the building once to verify that no other combers were inside.

Decades of salt winds had silvered its cedar shingles. Foundation cracks rose like ivy vines up the sides of its cement half-basement. Sprung gutters hung loose like dangled fishing rods. She killed the steel blue Evinrude and drifted silently toward the two-story frame house.

Luisa Cruz had been born in 16 P, Ethel remembered, in the middle of the Blizzard of '78, when Hull had been cut off from the mainland. A daydreamer, Luisa had sat in the fourth row and drawn deft caricatures of rock stars all over her essay questions.

So the Cruz family had moved, Ethel thought sadly. Another one gone. Were any left?

She looped *Queequeg*'s painter over the porch banister and splashed up 16 P's steps, towing a child's oversize sailboat behind her. The front door had rusted open and Ethel went inside.

Empty soda and beer squeezebottles floated in the foyer amidst a vaguely disturbing smell. Ethel slogged through soggy newspapers to the kitchen. Maria Cruz had made tea in this kitchen, she recalled, while they had talked about Luisa's chances of getting into Brandeis.

An ancient refrigerator stood in a foot and a half of water. She dragged the door open with a wet creak. Nothing.

The pantry beyond yielded a box of moist taco shells and three cans of tomato paste. Ethel checked the expiration dates, nodded, and tossed them into her makeshift barrow.

What little furniture remained in the living room was rotten and mildewed. The bedroom mattress was green-furred and stank. The bureau's mahogany veneer had curled away from the expanding maple underneath. When Ethel leaned her arm on the dresser, a lion's-claw foot broke. It collapsed slowly into the sawdust-flecked water like an expiring walrus.

Out fell a discolored Polaroid snapshot: Luisa and her brother in graduation cap and gown. I was so proud of her I could have burst, Ethel remembered. Drying the photo carefully, she slipped it into her breast pocket.

On an adjacent high shelf, built into the wall above the attached headboard, were half-a-dozen paperback books, spines frayed and twisted, their covers stripped, and a weathered old hardbound copy of the autobiography of George Roberts Twelve Hughes, a sea captain and legendary talespinner. Luisa had been a good reader, a child who wanted to learn so much it had radiated from her like heat.

Pleased, Ethel took them all.

In the bathroom she found a mirror embossed with the Budweiser logo. With her elbow, Ethel cleaned the glass. The round wrinkled face that grinned back at her had fueled rumors she had been a Marine. The mirror would probably fetch a few dollars at the flea market, maybe more to a memorabilia collector.

Only the front bedroom left to comb, she thought. Good combing. Thank you, Cruz family.

A vulture, Joan Gordon had called her once. "You're just a vulture, eating decay," her friend had said with the certainty of a mainlander.

"I'm a Cobb," Ethel had answered thickly, gripping the phone. "We live on the sea. My grandfather Daniel Endicott was lobstering when he was nine."

"What you're doing isn't fishing. It's theft. Just like the waterkids."

"It's not like the kids!" Ethel had shouted.

"It's stealing," Joan had challenged her.

"No! Just taking what the sea gives. Housecombing is like lobstering." She had clung to her own words for reassurance.

"What you take belongs to other people," her friend had said vehemently.

"Not after they leave," Ethel shot back. "Then it's the ocean's."

Joan switched tacks. "It's dangerous to live in Hull."

"Those folks that left didn't have to go. I'm staying where my roots are."

"Your roots are underwater, Ethel!" Joan entreated. "Your town is disappearing."

"It is not," Ethel insisted. "Don't say that."

"Come live in our building. We have a community here."

"Bunch of old folks. Don't want to live with old folks."

"Plenty of people here younger than you."

"Living in a tower's not for me. Closed in, a prisoner. Afraid to go out. Wouldn't like it."

"How do you know? You've never visited me."

"Anyhow, I can't afford it."

She seldom spoke with Joan now. The subject had worn her feelings raw.

"Damn it, Joan," she said in 16 P's hallway, "why did you have to leave?"

The front bedroom door was ajar in a foot and a half of water. She pushed and heard it butt against something. Slowly she craned her neck around.

The two oriental corpses floated on their faces, backs arched, arms and legs hanging down into muddy brown water swirled with red blood. Ethel gagged at the stench. The youths' long black hair waved like seaweed, their shoulders rocking limply. Catfish and eels nibbled on waving tendrils of human skin and guts.

Retching, Ethel grabbed one of the boys under his armpit and hauled him over onto his back. The bodies had been gutted, bullets gouged out of their chests, leaving no evidence. Periwinkle snails crawled in bloody sockets where the killers had cut out their victims' eyes and sliced off their lips. Each youth's left hand had been amputated. Ethel searched the water until she found one, a bloated white starfish with a Pran gang tattoo on its palm.

She remembered last night's gunshots in Hull Bay. You did not deserve this, she thought to the ruined face, letting it slip back into the water. No one deserved this, not even waterkids.

Of course she knew who did it. Everyone knew who executed waterkids. That was the point. The men on Hog Island wanted you to know. They wanted Hull to themselves. The bodies were reminders. And incentive.

In the distance she heard the chatter of several approaching engines. More Cambodian waterkids coming. Hastily she wiped vomit from her mouth and rushed out of the house.

Jumping into the whaler, she untied *Queequeg*'s painter and turned his key, shoving the throttle down hard as his engine caught. But not quickly enough. Before she could get away, four dark gray whalers surrounded her, Pran gang chop signs airbrushed beautifully onto their fiberglass gunwales.

"Hey, grandma." Their leader, a half-black, half-Cambodian mulatto, stood cockily in the stern of his boat while his helmsman grinned. He wore immaculate brown leather pants and a WWII flight jacket, unmarked by spray or moisture. "What's your hurry? Seen a ghost?"

Queequeg rocked slightly as the waves from their sudden arrival washed underneath him. "Yes," Ethel answered.

"Find anything valuable?"

"Nothing you'd want." Unconsciously she touched her breast pocket. "Nothing you can fence."

"Really? Let's see." His boat drifted up against hers and he leaped across into her stern, landing on sure sea legs. "You keep your stuff here?" He scornfully pointed at the plastic sailboat, mugging for his guffawing friends. He kicked it over with his boot and rummaged around among the floorboards. "Hey, Huang! We got any use for taco shells?" He held them aloft.

"No, man," another Cambodian kid answered gleefully.

"All right, grandma, guess we'll have to look elsewhere." He dropped the box and turned. As she started to relax, he wheeled. "What's in your pocket?"

"I beg your pardon?"

"In your pocket," he snapped.

"A letter and a photograph," she said steadily.

"A naked man, maybe?" the Pran leader chortled. "Let's see it." She opened her sou'wester and handed the picture to him. Waving it like a small fan, he stepped back into his

own boat. "Worthless." He pointed it at her like a prod.
"Pran gang combs *first*, grandma. Understand? Travis Nyo
says so." He thumped his chest. "Otherwise, the next time I
won't just tip over your toy boat. You understand?" He
tossed the photo over his shoulder.

Ethel watched it flutter down onto the water, and nodded. "I understand."

Travis gestured and they started their engines, moving
down P Street toward the empty house.

Ethel debated with herself. Keeping silent was too
risky—they could always find her later. "Check the front
bedroom," she called after them.

He stopped the engine and swung back. "What?" he
asked ominously.

"Check the front bedroom. Your two missing friends are
there."

The teenager's broad face whitened. "Dead?"

She nodded mutely.

"Those bastards," he said softly.

"I'm sorry." She clasped her hands before her.

"*Sorry?*" Travis shrieked in misery, the hurt child suddenly breaking through his tough facade. "What do you
know about sorry?" Their boats leapt away. "What do you
know about sorry?"

The sounds of their engines receded, and Ethel slowly
let out her breath. Hands trembling, she engaged *Queequeg*'s throttle and slowly circled. Sure enough, the snapshot was suspended about three feet below the surface.
Ethel lifted her gaffing net and dragged it by the spot,
scooping up the picture. The water had curled it and she
dried it on her thigh, then returned it to her pocket.

Glancing back at the boats now moored at 16 P, she
quickly cut in the whaler's engine with a roar, carving a
double white plume behind her.

For the rest of the morning Ethel and *Queequeg* combed
the alphabet streets on Hull's submerged flatlands. Nearly

all of these houses had long since been abandoned, and she neither stopped nor slowed. Frequently she twisted to check behind her, but there was no sign of the waterkids.

By eleven she had finished W, X and Y, tiny alleyways that butted against Allerton Hill. Trees at its base were gray and leafless, drowned by the rising seawater. Terry Flaherty had lived on W, she remembered. A short chubby boy with big eyes and a giggle that never stopped, he was someplace in Connecticut now, selling mutual funds. Probably forgotten all the eleventh-grade American history she'd taught him.

As she passed Allerton Point, she looked across the harbor to glass-and-steel Boston. The downtown folks were talking about building walls to hold back the sea that rose as the city sank, but with no money, Hull literally could not afford to save itself. Every storm took more houses, washing out the ground underneath so they fell like sandcastles.

Ethel's house at 22 K was on the far leeward side, as safe as you could be on the flatland, but even it suffered damage and was endangered.

Town government was disintegrating. People no longer paid property taxes, no longer voted. Nobody ran for selectman, nobody cared. For protection, folks relied on themselves or bought it from Hog Island or the Cambodian waterkids. At night, the long black peterborough boats moved sleekly in the harbor, navigating by infrared. Ethel stayed inside then.

Most of Hull High School was submerged, the brick portico columns standing like piers in the shallow water. The football field was a mudflat.

Forty-one years of history students, all gone, all memories.

When she was young, her students had sniggered that Ethel was a dyke. As she aged, firmly single and unromantic, they had claimed she was a transsexual wrestler. When she reached fifty, they had started saying she was eccentric. At sixty, they had called her crazy.

The jibes always hurt, though she concealed it. After each year was over, fortunately, all she could remember were the names and faces of those whose lives she had affected.

Standing at *Queequeg*'s bow, she left a long scimitar of foam as she circled the buildings. The old school was disappearing, windows shattered, corridors full of stagnant water. She had taken *Queequeg* inside once before to her old classroom, but was eventually driven out by the reek of decomposing flesh from a cat that had been trapped inside and starved.

Ethel closed her eyes, hearing once again the clatter of the period bell, the clamor as kids ran through the corridors, talking at the top of their lungs. Mothers whom she taught had sent their daughters to Hull High School. In her last few years, she had even taught a few granddaughters of students. Made you proud.

The high school was shut down, dark, and noiseless. Seagulls perched on its roof were her only companions.

To break her mood, she swung onto the open sea and opened the throttle for the five-mile run to South Boston.

The water, hard as a rock this morning, pounded into her calves and knees as the Boston whaler's flat bottom washboarded across the harbor. *Queequeg* kicked up spray over his teak and chrome bow as she slalomed among day-glo styrofoam lobster buoys, tasting the salt spume on her lips.

Behind and above her, a cawing flock of gulls followed, braiding the air. *Queequeg*'s wake pushed small fish close to the surface, under the sharp eyes of the waiting gray-and-white birds. One after another, the gulls swooped like a line of fighter aircraft. Their flapping wings skimming the waves, they dipped their beaks just enough to catch a fish, then soared back into line.

Hunting and feeding, they escorted her across the harbor until she slowed and docked at the pier.

"Hey, Irving," Ethel said when she entered the store. "Got a letter for you." She unzipped her slicker and pulled it out. "Mail it for me?"

The storekeeper squinted at the address. "Joan Gordon? Doesn't she live in that senior citizen community in Arlington?"

"Old folks' home, you mean."

"Whatever." He suppressed a smile. "You could call her."

"Got no phone."

"No, from here."

"Rather write."

"Okay. What are you writing about?"

Ethel shook her head. "None of your beeswax."

"All right," he laughed, "we've been friends too long for me to complain. How you doing?"

"I get by."

He leaned on the counter. "I worry about you."

"Oh, don't start."

"Sorry." He turned away and began rearranging cans.

"I'm okay," she answered, touched as always.

"Hull gets worse every day." He looked at her over his shoulder. "I see the news."

"Nonsense," Ethel replied with bravado, dismissing his fears with a wave of her hand. "Newsies always exaggerate. Besides, one day Boston will be under water, same as us."

"I know." Irving sighed. "I go down to the bathhouse every Sunday for my swim. It's always higher. Maybe we should move away like Joan did. Chicago or Dallas. Somewhere. Anywhere with no ocean."

She laughed. "What would I do in Dallas, Irv? How would I live?"

"You could teach school. You've taught me more right here in this store than all the history books I ever read."

"Thanks, Irv. But I'm sixty-eight years old. No one would hire me."

He was quiet. "Then I'd take care of you," he said finally, kneading his hands.

She looked through the window at the pier, where *Queequeg* bobbed on the waves. "Couldn't do it, Irv," she said. It was hard to find breath. "Too old to move."

"Yeah. Sure." He wiped his forehead and cleared his throat. "Got your usual all set." He put two orange plastic bags on the counter.

"Did my check come through?" Ethel looked suspicious. "Can't take your credit."

"Of course it did. It always comes through. It's electronic."

She peered inside, shifting cans and boxes. "All right, where is it?"

He scowled and rubbed his balding head. "Hell, you shouldn't eat that stuff. Rots your teeth and wrecks your digestion and I don't know what."

"I want my two-pound box of Whitman's coconut, dammit."

"Ethel, you're carrying too much weight. It'll strain your heart."

"Been eating candy all my life and it hasn't hurt me yet. Wish you'd stop trying to dictate my diet."

"Okay, okay." He sighed and threw up his hands, then pulled down the embossed yellow box. "No charge." He held it out.

"Can't accept your charity, Irv. You know that."

"That's not it." He was hurt and offended. "It's my way of saying I'm sorry I tried to keep it away from you." He gestured with it. "Please?"

Ethel took the chocolates. "Thank you, Irv," she replied somberly, laying her right hand flat on the cover. "You've been a good friend."

"Don't talk like that," the grocer said in exasperation.

"Every time you come in here, you sound like you got one foot in the grave. It's not wholesome."

"Was different this morning." Ethel sat down, the candy held tightly in her lap. Her voice was faint, distant. "This morning I saw it. Saw my future in the water. Sooner or later, I'm going to pass away. No sense denying that." She kicked her right foot aimlessly. "Maybe I should have accepted when you proposed."

"Still could," he said, wistful. "But you won't."

"No." She shook her head just a bit.

"Stubborn."

"Not stubborn." She was gentle. "Wouldn't be fair. You can't live in Hull. You've said so before."

"Ethel." Irving wiped his hands on his apron. "I read the paper. Houses are falling into the ocean or burning down. Dangerous evil kids are running loose."

"I can handle the waterkids," she said defiantly.

"No, you can't," he insisted. "Drugs and crime and I don't know what. Why won't you leave?"

"It's my home," Ethel said in a troubled voice. "My family. Friends." She waved her hands. "My world. What I know."

Irving rubbed his head again. "That world isn't there anymore. The people you knew—they're all gone. It's past. Over."

"Got no place to go," she muttered, biting her thumbnail. "Cobbs and Endicotts have lived in Hull since colonial times. That's something to preserve. Elijah Endicott was a merchant captain. Sailed to China in 1820. Put flowers on his grave every Sunday noon after church. Rain or shine or Cambodian kids. Put flowers on all the Cobbs and Endicotts on Telegraph Hill. Telegraph's an island now, but they will still be in that ground when all the flat is gone. Somebody has to remember them."

"Cripes, don't be so morbid." He came around behind her, put his arm around her shoulder and rubbed it.

"I suppose." She leaned her head in the crook of his elbow.

Cars and buses passed in the street outside, sunlight reflecting off their windshields. He patted her shoulder.

She covered his hand with hers. "Thanks, Irv. You're a good man."

After a moment, she rose and kissed his cheek, then hefted the bags, one to an arm. "Well, that's that," she called with returning jauntiness. "See you next Friday."

Lost in memories, she let *Queequeg* take his return trip more slowly. Islands in the harbor were covered with trees and shrubs, reminding her of great submerged whales. When she neared Hog Island at the entrance to Hull Bay, she kept a respectful distance. The Meagher boys had lived there—Dennis, Douglas, Dana, Donald, and Dapper. Their mother had always shouted for them in the order of their birth. Five rambunctious Boston-Irish hellions in seven years, usually with a black eye or a skinned knee.

No families lived on Hog now. Castellated gray buildings had grown upward from the old Army fortress underneath. Thieves and smugglers and murderers lived in them, men who drove deep-keeled power yachts without finesse, like machetes through a forest.

Tough sentries carrying binoculars stood lookout as she passed, scanning the horizon like big-eyed insects, their rifles out of sight. Ethel shivered. Delinquent waterkids she could evade, but the organized evil on Hog was shrewd and ruthless.

The fish feeding on that poor child's face, Ethel thought. The people who still lived on Hull. The men on Hog. The Cambodian kids. One way or another, all took their livelihoods from the remains of a town whose time was past. Eventually they would extract Hull's last dollar, and they would all leave. And in time, the rising sea would engulf everything.

K Street was falling into shadow when she returned. Her

house needed a coat of paint, but would last long enough without one, she thought wryly. The dark green first-floor shutters were closed and nailed shut as a precaution, but her light was still burning in 22 K's bedroom window. Always leave a light on, so everyone knows you're still on guard.

A gang symbol was sprayed on her front door.

Pran chop, she realized with a sick feeling in her gut, remembering the morning's encounter.

Her padlock was untouched, though the waterkids could have easily forced it.

The chop was a message: this is a Pran house.

Perhaps their form of thanks.

Safely inside, Ethel took off her sou'wester and slicker, shook the wet salt spray off them, and hung them on the pegs. She unloaded her groceries and stacked her day's combings. George Roberts Twelve Hughes would fetch a good price, she thought, for his rarity as much as his age. Tomorrow she would sell everything in the Quincy flea market.

All but the photo. Ethel took it from her pocket and smiled at Luisa's young face. She found a spot on the wall barely large enough and tacked it up, stepping back to admire her work.

As the sun set on the golden bay, she made supper: soup, salad, and cheese sandwiches that she grilled on the wood-burning stove she had installed on the second floor. Seagulls wheeled over the marsh flats, snatching clams in their beaks. Rising high over the coastline, the birds dropped their prey to smash open on the wet shoreline rocks. Then the gulls landed and ate the helpless, exposed animal inside the broken shell.

When she was done, Ethel went onto the upper porch and put down her bowl and plate. The birds converged, jostling for the last scraps, hungry and intense like schoolchildren in gray-and-white uniforms.

Sitting in her rocking chair, her box of Whitman's coconut firmly on her stomach, Ethel thought about the letter she had mailed that morning.

Today the ocean took my ground floor. One day it will take my house. It's going to reclaim South Boston and Dorchester and Back Bay. Folks will go on denying it like I've tried to, but it won't stop until it's through with all of us.

Enclosed is my will. Had a Cohasset lawyer write it up so it's legal. You get everything. You don't have to comb for it, Joan. It's yours.

Except *Queequeg*. The boat goes to Irving. He'll never use it, but he'll care for it, and it's no use to you in your tower.

After I'm gone, burn the place down. With me in it. At high tide so the fire won't spread. Nobody will bother you. Nobody else lives around here anyway. No one else has lived here for years.

22 K is a Cobb house. Always been a Cobb house. No squatters here. Give it all to the sea.

But take the pictures first. Put them on your walls. Remember me.

Should have left years ago. Can't now.

Wish you'd stayed, Joan. Miss you.

Ethel

The houses around her were black hulks, silent like trees. The crescent moon rose, silvering the ocean. Ethel heard the gulls call to one another, smelled the sea as it licked the beach. In the distance, boats moved on the bay, dots of green-and-red light, thin black lines of wake.

"God, I love it here," she said suddenly, full of contentment.

BOSTON IN 2014

By Splashdown Day, Boston is experiencing persistent and severe flooding. The Longfellow and Tobin Bridges are unsafe. The Callahan and Sumner Tunnels, connecting Boston to East Boston, are frequently flooded. A series of small lakes and streams separating Boston and Brookline has become a shallow river.

South Boston, East Boston, the Back Bay, Charlestown, and both banks of the Charles and Mystic rivers have lost land to the water. Revere has been severely flooded. Hull, under water at every high tide, is abandoned except by gangs.

In 2010, the Trenton Endicott Memorial Wall is designed by Jacob Ratjszek to keep the Charles from flooding MIT.

Boston begins its own wall, the City Ring, in 2012.

THE ELEPHANT-ASS THING
JON BURROWES

1

I AM SITTING in the waiting room of the Provincetown police station writing this on a concealed recorder. It is September 1, 2051 A.D.: my eighty-first birthday. Yet they have
found even more ridiculous charges to level against me.
The bureaucracy has decided to start cleaning up the booming Interstellar Port of Boston. But I must not waste time
discussing them; I wish to tell you of the true circumstances
of the arrival of the first aliens on Earth. They did not arrive,
as reported, on August 22, 2014, at 5:05 P.M. in Boston Harbor. They arrived a few hours earlier, on Nantucket Island;
and my sweetheart and I, who were enjoying a tryst on the
dunes, were the first people on Earth to see them.

A young policeman struts down the hall toward me. He
wears the stylish baggy clothes of small-time law officers
the world around. Bedecked with the subtle but elegant
trappings of electronic policery, he sports a tie-clasp antenna, an ear-headset, and a signs-of-life wrist detector.

I gently comb my hair and then smile graciously. He
grimaces; my slicked-back style is long out of date.

He walks up and down for a while, tapping some papers with a pen. His footsteps echo against the pink marble. The building, an architectural murmur in the dusk, is also from my era.

Finally he stops in front of me. "Mr. Boris Nancolm."

"Yes," I answered.

"Residence?"

"I have spent my adult life in the United States and the Far East."

"Currently residing in—?"

"My family and I, originally from Sumatra, have enjoyed a comfortable and obscure life in a beautiful villa overlooking Boston Harbor. What with the rising water washing everything away, we now have considerable oceanfront property. Many fortunes have changed this way. But never mind."

"Currently residing in—?" the policeman repeats.

"Lynn."

"My, my, lifestyles of the rich and famous. You don't look like an aging playboy."

"I do not affect the manners of the rich and famous. I am content to pass unnoticed amid the high and mighty as well as the lowly and downtrodden. It serves my purposes."

"Well, good for you," the policeman sneers. "It seems that the various banks of New England have finally decided to dispense with your services. But before they do, they would like you to explain some of the temptations to which you apparently succumbed some forty years ago." He looks up. "Sound familiar?"

"I have already explained these events in great detail long ago. Why must we replay them now?"

"We have evidence that you may be leaving our administrative district soon; we wish you to stay."

Ah. Well, he was quite right; I *was* planning to leave quite soon, which is why I want to get on with my story. When I leave, I will be resuming my incognito life. Ah well, a brief note about my career: I have been a bank inspector for nearly fifty years. As you might imagine, to do the job properly, one must be discreet. Over the years, I have discovered many interesting facts about the banking community of Greater Boston. I have also developed my own personal style—but that is all another story.

We bicker. We bluff. And finally he goes off again to draw up some more papers.

Outside, three little aliens are capering and hoodling on the sidewalk. They're wearing their usual outrageous garb and carrying on like a tin-pan opera. While they are trying to hawk their popcorn, they happily tickle and pummel each other. As usual, the popcorn spills; as usual, they scoop it up and hold fistfuls out to the frowning inhabitants peeping from their windows. No one buys any, of course, and so they race off down the sidewalk to the next house, tumbling and yelling, and the song-and-dance starts all over again. Commerce and economics completely elude these fellows. I have seen them try to sell the pavement, sometimes to each other, and finally even unscrew pieces of themselves and offer them up for sale.

But enough of them; they will be back. In any case, these little creatures are not even remotely related to the original visitors. My, how those first arrivals have faded into the din of wonders and monstrosities that have since appeared in the City of Boston.

But let me tell you about the first visit.

2

It was one of those hot rainy days on Nantucket—this was August of 2014. The clouds were very low and thick. Lorraine and I were lounging on a sand dune a couple of miles away from the airport. We could see the runway lights, shining up through the fog like a Hollywood premiere, and then the bushes and warm fog filled the rest of our view. What with the water-rise and the storm, there were only a few wistful buildings left on Nantucket. We were blissfully, sexily alone.

"Oh, it's so hot," Lorraine said. "This raincoat is stifling. Do you feel hot?" She threw back her hood and let the fine mist caress her face. For a forensic psychologist she was a true nature lover. The gritty streets of her daily rounds made no dent on her love of foggy glens and quiet hills.

Many years ago, after an unfortunate mix-up on my part while inspecting a bank, we chanced to pass in a corridor, where my employers were attempting to extract me discreetly from the legal system. Instantly we discerned each other's true characters underneath the respective professional masks, and shortly thereafter we conducted a more elaborate investigation of the physical evidence. Which has continued to this day; to this very sand dune, in fact.

As we gazed out over the rolling Atlantic, Lorraine stood up and took off her raincoat and then pulled off her shirt and shorts.

"I'm an Indian," she said.

"Me, too," I said.

"Let's dance." She started prancing around on the dune. "Come on, dance the Salty Dog with me!"

"No," I said.

"No! Who's going to see us?" She waved her arms and began to sing: "Honey, let me be your Salty Dog—!" She is a big billowy woman, a truly beautiful creature. Therefore, I was soon prancing up and down with her, laughing and howling in the summer rain. "You never were very dignified! It's one of the things I like about you!" she yelled. We fell back on the sand and put our arms around each other. She patted me affectionately. "It must have helped you at all those banks. People wouldn't suspect you were an undercover inspector when you looked like an aging quarterback in a bus driver's uniform."

"Now, sweetheart, you know those are complicated opelations. They involve the insurance companies and the government and everything else. I never took any actual money; you know that."

"Yes, dear. But don't you think you could just *not* demolish one little bankie-poo's sense of well-being for *one* weekend? Just for me?"

"Honey, I've got commitments."

"Okay, okay."

While we were kissing, something out of the corner of my eye made me turn my head. I looked out over the dunes to the water beyond. It was smooth except for raindrops and the kelp, but there were large, healthy swells. On the beach, the surf was a white roll of carpet, booming and thudding and rolling shells and pebbles up the beach ahead of it. I stretched out my arms, trying to see through the mist. About a half a mile offshore something was hanging down out of the clouds, a big thing, about a thousand feet across. I couldn't see where it ended because it faded up into the mist. Hanging down from the center of it was a narrow tube; the tube ended in a cluster of lights that trailed just above the waves. All in all, it looked like a gigantic elephant's ass.

When Lorraine saw what I was looking at, she said, "What is that? The Goodyear Blimp?"

"I don't know."

The narrow tube began to shine lights down into the water. The water began to glow a deep red. The lights stuttered like a movie projector. It was kind of pretty out there in the mist.

"What are they doing? Looking for fish?" Lorraine said.

"I don't know," I said again.

There was a huge puff of fog and mist, and then three things were coming across the water toward us.

Now at that time I couldn't see them very well, what with the spray and the fog and the waves. Also, they did not stay on top of the water. Sometimes they would be up to their knees in it, and then sometimes it would be three feet below them. A swell overtook them and rolled over their heads; when it passed, they were in the same position, twiddling with things at their waists. Then they jerked up six feet and tried again. As they came walking onto the beach, we could see them clearly: they were shapeless gray lumps.

Two of them walked purposefully over to a white plastic bleach bottle that had been lying in the sand for who knows how long. They began shining lights on it and lifting it up in the air and turning it over carefully without touching it. The third one remained facing out to sea. It held out a long white box and began sawing squares in the surf with some kind of remote pressure beam. The other two continued working with the bleach bottle. Finally it caught fire. They froze it in midair—flames and all.

A flock of seagulls had wandered up the beach. They froze them, too. The first alien walked over to the gulls and began shining lights on them, shaking their webbed feet, and trying to talk to them. No luck.

Lorraine said, "What are those things?"

"Seagulls," I replied.

"No!" she hit me.

"I don't know. Maybe they're from the CIA."

"Stop it," she said.

"Well maybe they are."

"They can't tell the difference between a bleach bottle and a seagull, dirtbrain."

"So what?"

"Boris, the CIA can tell the difference between a bleach bottle and a seagull."

"How do you know?"

She ignored me. "Look at them, just look at them. They probably think that's the President of the United States there on the sand."

"The bleach bottle, you mean? No, I think it's too small to be the President—"

She hit me again.

"Well, why don't you go down and tell them who the President is?" I said.

"No!"

"Why not?"

"They're—they're wild! They just came out of the sky. You can't just go pet them. Look how fast his hands are moving; does he look like he comes from Nantucket?"

"No—"

"They could be deadly. They could be looking for lunch." She screamed and put her hands on her forehead. "Boris! Boris! What's going on?"

"How should I know? Look—they might not even *eat* lunch, for Christ's sake!"

"*Will you stop yelling at me?*"

"*Okay!*"

The aliens came over the brow of the dune. Standing there in the wet sand, they looked like pieces of pudding-stone, the gray boulders we have in New England which the glaciers kindly left us.

It has been reported many times that the first words the aliens spoke on Earth were, "What profiteth a man to gain riches beyond counting if he lose his soul in the process?" But what really happened was this: in a thin, announcerly voice the biggest one said, "Well, here we are on Earth."

It came up and stood in front of me. Its hands and feet seemed to travel in little blurs.

"Yes," I said, trembling, "we know; this is Earth—do you have some ID?"

"What does ID mean?" the alien responded.

"It shows who you are."

"Who are we?"

"Yes."

"No, I was asking you," the alien replied.

"What do you mean?" Lorraine butted in. "You don't know who you are?"

"We don't understand the word 'who.' It refers to our personality? Our individuality?"

"Yes," Lorraine said, relieved. "Your likes and dislikes, whether you're sociable or like to be by yourself, whether you keep the change when the clerk gives you too much—that kind of thing."

"Ah. Well, our personality is a composite function of two machines, the input of a news beacon, and of course the immediate electrical climate of the surrounding environment."

"Oh," she said.

"Yes. Probably. That is to say, it's a stochastic function."

"Your personality," Lorraine repeated.

"Yes. Isn't yours?"

She looked at me.

I shrugged.

"Twenty years of psychology school," Lorraine said. "Pfft."

"Don't worry, sweetheart," I said, "You can't get everyone on the first bounce."

That's how things went when the first aliens arrived on Earth.

3

From my experience in the banking world, I knew that it was important to firmly establish the identity of a prospective client before proceeding with the actual process of inspection. The inspection of a bank can be a grueling experience; I myself have succumbed to some of the baser motives during the ordeal—and I *perform* the inspections. "So—what's under the suit?" I asked the aliens.

"Our apologies—" the largest one said, "but we cannot show you our bodies at this time. Our suit-control mechanism is not working, as you can see from our clumsy approach." It waved at the ocean.

Up close, they looked like medium-sized industrial machinery with rough, rubbery sheets stretched over them. They did have faces, eyes and mouths; and they had limbs that moved very quickly, although they looked like little puppet feet from a child's toy. Other than that, they were— gray. "Perhaps you have that problem?" the alien said.

"No," I answered. "But these aren't our regular clothes." Lorraine and I weren't wearing any clothes at all; we were soaked from the rain and covered with wet sand from our roll in the dunes.

The word YES flickered for an instant in the air—the alien's hand blurred toward it—and then it nodded briefly and said, "Nodding means 'yes.' True?"

We nodded.

The aliens, all three, nodded.

We laughed. The aliens nodded some more.

"Is there a place where we could dispose of some atomic waste?" the first alien said calmly.

"*Atomic waste? Are you kidding?*" yelled Lorraine.

"No," the alien said.

"Are you sure they're not from the CIA?" Lorraine said severely to me.

"They wouldn't tell us if they were," I said.

"That's what I mean!"

"As opposed to *molecular* waste," the alien continued.

"—What?"

"They are just some atoms we've reassembled and wish to discard. Medium weight, nothing dangerous."

"You mean—you want to dump some *atoms?* Some used *atoms?*" I said.

"Yes. Our personal life systems have finished with them." The alien hesitated. "Bathroom. Do you have a bathroom?"

"Oh, *bathroom!*" Lorraine began to laugh. "Ha ha! Not out here!"

The alien looked at us and finally said, "Is personal waste disposal a problem?"

"No! Er—how much were you planning to dispose of?" I asked.

The alien hesitated again. "Which is better—much or little?"

We stared at each other. "How much is much?"

"Twenty mfplthsks," the alien said quickly. "Sixty grams."

"Just go over there—behind those bushes," Lorraine said. "Just go! Oh, I don't believe it!" She had started laughing again and finally and had to hang on to me for support to keep from falling in the sand.

The aliens nodded.

I nodded. And then they left.

"What's so funny, my darling?" I said.

"Oh, shut up you big oaf!" she yelled and pulled me down on top of her. "Oh, Boris," she said, "Something always happens on our dates. If it's not the court or the car, it's—" She burst into wild laughter again.

The aliens were now busy behind the bushes.

Lorraine stopped laughing and sat up. "Come on," she whispered to me, "Let's go watch."

We tiptoed over to the clump of evergreen bushes and peeked through.

From around their heads the aliens were unrolling long threads—hairs—of fine silvery metal. Pretty soon there were three little piles that you might have mistaken for tangled fishline if you hadn't noticed how regularly they were coiled and how cleanly they shone.

"They're finished! Hurry!" said Lorraine. We ran back to where we had been standing and tried to act as if we hadn't moved.

The rain was still coming down and we raised our faces to the dark sky. The aliens' ship was now nearly overhead. It was a huge thing, complex, convoluted, covered with incomprehensible structures—and gray. And we could only see the part that stuck down from the clouds. The long elephant's-tail thing was now staring fixedly at a dolphin. The dolphin was about six feet above the waves, wagging its flippers, and making unhappy and obscene-sounding screeches and buzz-saw sounds.

The aliens returned. The medium-sized one gingerly put its foot on the ground and then looked up. "What is this place called?" it said in a rich basso.

"The beach," I said.

"He means: where are we?" Lorraine corrected.

"Oh. Massachusetts."

"Massachusetts," the alien repeated. "Are there any small groups of buildings where people gather to perform commercial tasks together, such as advertisement, parking, and federal regulation?"

"You mean—like cities?" Lorraine said warily.

"Yes. Cities. Are there any open at this hour?"

"Yeah, I think New York's still open," I put in.

"Don't listen to him," Lorraine said. "You don't want to go there anyway. Why don't you go up to Boston?"

"They can't park—"

"But it's much nicer than New York," Lorraine said, covering my face with her arms. "Classier bunch of people; better restaurants; and cheaper, much cheaper! You'll love it."

"Ball team's no good, either—"

"By the way, what is Charles Laquidara?" the alien continued.

"He's a big star—" Lorraine began.

"—You have a star here on Earth?" the alien said quickly. "How do you control the radiation?"

The other alien's hands began to blur at something at its waist.

"No, no, I mean—he's a big attraction," said Lorraine reassuringly.

"He can't be very big," the alien said. "We detect no ul-
tramass in this region."

"What I meant to say was, he's a famous person."

"Famous?"

"Everybody knows him."

"Oh." The alien seemed to relax. "Like God?"

"Ah—no. Look—"

The aliens began looking around. "Where?"

"No, no," Lorraine waved her hands and then began to
giggle. "Christ, you guys don't know anything."

I nodded.

The aliens nodded.

We all nodded.

"Where is Boston?" the largest alien said.

"Will you be walking, or taking the—ship?" I said.

"Both."

"I—"

"Never mind him," said Lorraine. "You go north until
you hit the P-town light, then hang a left and keep walking
until you see the jets landing. That's the airport."

"Thank you," the alien said.

"They'll probably want to know what that thing is up
there," I mused.

"Let them go!" said Lorraine to me. "Don't ask!"

The fine September mist was blowing steadily up from
the beach and swirling over our heads. "By the way, is there
any way to get this rain to stop?" the announcer-voiced
alien said.

"Not that we know of," said Lorraine.

"God can't do it?"

"Oh sure. He can," she sighed. "But we just don't know
how to—I don't know."

"Ah. You must feel terribly sad."

"I don't think we know what we're missing," I said.

They nodded.

We nodded.

"Speaking of water—" I said. But the alien stopped me. "Wait. You mean rain is water?"

"Yes," I said.

"Very clever." They all nodded. "And the clouds. Water, too?"

"Yes, clouds too."

"Lovely."

"We like it," said Lorraine.

"You certainly have a lot of it here on Earth. You just use it for landscaping?"

"Oh, no," Lorraine said. "Sometimes we drink it."

"But not all at once," I said. "In any case—can you walk on it, whenever you like?"

"Oh, yes, we can walk on it. Would you like to?"

"I—why—"

"Here." The largest alien handed me a tube of what looked like suntan lotion. "This will enable you to walk on water by yourself."

I took the tube. "What is it?"

"Rub it on an upper region of your body," said the alien. "Otherwise, you will become upside down."

"Good stuff," the middle-sized alien boomed.

"Gojwoo," the largest one added.

They nodded.

"Gojwoo," I said. "Thanks."

Lorraine and I put our arms around each other. "Can you say something in your native language?" Lorraine asked.

The largest alien waved its left hand solemnly and made a sound like a tin can being flattened.

She nodded.

"Ask him what it means," I whispered.

"What does it mean?"

"It's the Pledge of Allegiance to Electromagnetism," it answered proudly.

We nodded.

They nodded.

And then they walked off up the Atlantic Ocean.

Lorraine and I looked at each other. "Gee," Lorraine sighed. "We could have been famous."

"I know," I said. But as a bank inspector, I had to protect my anonymity in order to perform my job. And Lorraine had no interest in becoming a celebrity herself. Her subjects, otherwise confined to the Massachusetts legal system, could do all sorts of creative things with her real name and address.

"But let's not," she said. "Let's just send them on their way and stay here and enjoy the rest of our holiday. I mean, I want to take this all in—but just with you. Do you want Nancy Golub from Channel Five asking you how it felt?"

"I'd get to look down her dress."

"Forget it," she grabbed me. "Besides, it's none of her damned business."

I felt a wave of intense relief. We'd lived through something incredible. Later, mile-long silver snakes, art-crazed beavers, and a bishop with rules of engagement would fall form the sky. Some of us would learn from them; some of us would not. I put my arm around Lorraine and squeezed her back. She kissed me; I was getting excited; our bodies were starting to murmur their ancient language to each other.

One of the aliens turned back. "Why is that thing, which has been hanging down between your legs, now sticking out straight?" its deep basso boomed across the water.

I looked down: I was sticking out straight. I looked up. "It's because—because I'm attracted to my girlfriend."

Lorraine blushed and squeezed me tighter.

"You mean, she has control over a part of your body?"

"Not exactly," I called back. "It's—I just get a feeling, because she's near me—"

"I don't understand."

"Well—"

"That's why you were dancing around on the beach

when we first arrived, wasn't it?" the deep voice echoed.

"*You saw us?*" Lorraine turned bright red.

I waved. "When you get to Boston, they'll be able to explain everything. Try Harvard. They used to be pretty good."

4

So off they went to Boston, striding across the rolling ocean as though it were a basketball court. Behind them they towed the big elephant-ass thing like a balloon. In a few minutes they had disappeared into the mist. I wondered what the Logan Airport tower would say when it saw them, not to mention the poor whales and fishes on the Stelwagen Bank. And, of course, the good people of Boston.

Lorraine and I sat on a dune and let the rain soak us through. She leaned into me and said, "Honey, you know this was quite a bit different for our usual holiday."

"Yes, it was," I agreed.

"You know, I wasn't afraid of any of it. Were you?"

"Yes, I was scared shitless," I said.

"You were? Oh, sweetie, but you were so brave." She hugged me. "Ooh!" She jumped up.

"What?"

"Come on!" She pulled me up.

We ran along the dunes to where aliens had made their deposits of "atomic waste." There in the sand three piles of silvery wire lay in a neat triangle. They were now covered with condensation; they seemed to be sagging, compressing already with just the weight of the water.

"Pick one up," said Lorraine.

But I didn't feel like it. They could be coated with poison. Or they could be radioactive (my watch said no). They might be connected to a mine. Or perhaps the aliens were somehow still watching them to see they were not disturbed. I considered these possibilities of sabotage as I noticed that they looked a great deal like fine platinum. But the taboo against poop-touching was mighty indeed. "Why ruin a perfectly nice day at the beach," I said, "by picking up—?"

Lorraine gingerly lifted a coil with her fingernails. "Oh, my God," she said, "Feel this."

I should have known: after years teasing motives out of the hardest of hardened murderers, a little beachcombing was hardly a high-risk activity for her. "It's like wool," she said. "But heavy."

I put my palm under it. "Maybe we could make a scarf out of it," I said. We gazed at the coils. Native Americans had probably stood here, I thought. A thousand years ago, Tom Nevers Head was probably the center for romance, seafood, and good-timing for the entire Iroquois Nation. Teenage prehistorians probably paddled out here all the time to discuss the concerns of the day (each other, I would guess) and chase those same concerns through the laughing seagrass. I know I would have. They might have even caught a glimpse of long boats filled with blond sailors bashing their way through the whitecaps on the horizon: hungry Vikings looking for fish.

And here *we* were, a thousand years later, still hanging around on the beach.

Lorraine looked at me and put her arms around my neck. "I love you," she said. "My big Sumatran bank whatever. I don't want an alien-poop scarf. I want you."

We embraced and she began to cry. I held her close. "Don't cry, sweetheart," I said. "At least we didn't run out of gas."

5

That was thirty-seven years ago.

We made love and thereafter we parted. By 5:05 P.M. I was far away on a ConnBank speedboat, heading for Bermuda. Lorraine was back in Charlestown, shaking out her bathing suit. It has been too painful for me to recall even one detail of our last moment together on the beach, for it turned out to be the last time I ever saw my beloved Lorraine.

Now, here in the Provincetown police station thirty-seven years later, I am hastily setting down the last snatches of this tale before my time runs out. Perhaps in its socio-sanitary wisdom the Interstellar Port of Boston will be better off without me; perhaps I will be better off without it. I suppose time will tell.

The three little popcorn aliens are still outside on the curb. God only knows why they go through this sham of earning a living. They don't need to eat; they don't need sleep; they can exist on air quite comfortably. They have absolutely no need of money; and they haven't the faintest idea what to do with it when they get it. But they're harmless; and I suppose we all have a lesson to learn there.

One came eagerly up to the window and said to me, "R U BOPROIS NANCIOOLM?"

"Yes," I said. "What about it?"

"U R BOHRESE NAKINOM!"

"Yes, yes; how did you know my name?"

"U SAYED IT EIN YOUR MI-EEND!" the alien squealed with glee. A telepath; I should have known. "HEYRE! DIES EE FOR U!" It fumbled in its absurd garments with great energy and then brought forth an orange, which it handed to me.

The orange unrolled itself in my palm, and a little frowzy creature stood up and said in a piping voice, "I-am-a-VOICE-BRIDGE-response-letter. You-may-talk-to-me-as-you-would-a-telephone-call. I-will-respond-to-the-extent-of-my-recorded-ability."

"Yes, yes," I said. "Who are you from?"

"Belmont hotel, Navtar, Iran."

"Navtar?" I said. "Where is that? I never heard of it."

"It's a fancy resort on the gulf," the little letter sneered.

"All right, all right—get on with it."

"Sweetheart," the creature said in an astounding imitation, "remember when you brought me those wonderful rubber clothes from Romania?"

"Yes," I said eagerly. "What a weekend that was!" I could hardly contain myself.

"I can still remember the feel of that sheer latex," she said. "So soft, so rich."

"If that chambermaid hadn't seen you slipping out of the swimming pool at dawn—" I answered excitedly.

"We might still be able to get visas."

It was Lorraine; there was no doubt about it. I was beside myself with joy.

The little creature rubbed its eyes and coughed. "Are you gonna let me finish or what?" it peeped.

"Go on, go on," I urged, but I couldn't stop. "Where are you, my dear?"

"I'm—I'm working in a halfway house," the creature's uncanny imitation said again. "A bar by the marina. These people are very nice—but they're pretty boring; they always were." She hesitated. "I'm telling fortunes."

"Fortunes?"

"Yes, you know: fertile crescent, birth of civilization, all that. But it's terrible. All they ever ask for is stupid boy-girl problems; and all I can tell them is the truth. They're not going to like it when they get back on the street. I hate it!"

"Where are you living? Do you live in a nice place?"

There was no answer.

"She wants you to come and get her," the little creature said sleepily.

"Where is she living?" I demanded.

"That's all I got," the creature said.

"Is she all right?"

"I-don't-know-I-don't-know-I-don't-know," the creature chanted.

"Okay! All right. How much do I owe you?"

"Nothing," the creature snapped. "How do I get out of here?"

"Just a minute." I rolled the thing back into a little ball, leaned out the window, and waved to the popcorn aliens.

They were up the street trying to sell a woman to her baby carriage; the baby was squealing with glee and pulling at their clothes. Two of the aliens raced back to my window, spraying cascades of popcorn across sidewalk. "POP-CHON?" They yelled. "POPPA-POPPA?"

"No, no," I said, "Just take this little messenger back—wherever he wants to go." I handed them the little orange.

"POP-CONE!!" They yelled together at the tops of their lungs and emptied their pockets in wild fountains into the air. "POPCORN! POPCORN! POPCORN!" They danced around the street in mad ecstasy; I suppose I was their first sale.

The young policeman came up behind me. His footsteps echoed on the pink marble; he was tapping his papers again. The sort of tap a statute of limitations might make as it was about to run out.

I ran the comb through my hair.

He stared at me.

I rubbed a little more gojwoo on my comb and ran it through my hair one more time. My hair had now taken on the sheen of a light, silvery mackerel.

"Do you mind?" said the policeman.

"Please," I said. I could feel myself rising; I hung on to the bench. "I'm an old man; my dignity."

He snorted.

"Could we go somewhere else?" I said meekly. "It is offensive to have these charges read out in the hall here; people can hear them." I nodded to the piazza outside. It overlooked the Atlantic Ocean, which now rings the little islands we still call Cape Cod.

The officer glared at me for a moment, and then, hitching up his stylishly baggy pants, he strutted outside, slapping the papers rhythmically against his thigh.

I hardly needed to rise out of my seat in order to follow him.

Facing the water, he read the charges against me without looking up: conveying financial instruments in an unauthorized manner, becoming physically intimate with currency, throwing live things at a bank officer (those were at an alien bank, don't forget), and offering the bank for sale under multiple names. What can I say? Run-of-the-mill, routine scenarios. You have to get pretty obtuse with some of these financial people, you know. Nothing close to what I've actually done, of course. Well, it was a living. Forty years later, I can hardly remember it at all.

A swell rolled toward the police station and broke over the edge of the piazza; a thin puddle of foam slid across the granite floor toward us.

The young officer instinctively turned back from the encroaching water and walked away without looking up.

I, on the other hand, combed my hair one last time and strolled in the other direction—out onto the dull green water.

A harbor seal poked its head up and sniffed at my pants cuff. I leaned down to pet it, but it fled. I continued walking.

The sun went behind a cloud, and it began to drizzle. I marched on. My hair stood up of its own accord now; my feet were a foot above the waves.

A lost rowboat floated past, its painter trailing in the rain-speckled waves.

"Hey! Where are you going?" the policeman yelled faintly. "Come back . . ."

They'll probably send a launch after me, bounding out through the downpour. They might even confiscate my gojwoo. But I think I'm safe; they won't know what to look for. But then, it's never what you look for that's the most fun, is it?

THE PARADE
STEVEN POPKES

HERBERT MAXWELL IS coming back from New York on the train, across the marshes from the hulking towers of Manhattan, past the bomb shelters of Co-op City. It is unseasonably cold and the sun over the marshes looks anemic. He has just finished visiting his family, a collection of poor Polish Catholics living in Queens. They have been crying out to him not to leave MIT. Herbert is on his way back to school—on scholarship; his family is poor, remember?—to study physics. This is a compromise between him and his family: it was better than the priesthood. He could be a lawyer who wanted to study drama, a receptionist who wanted to be a writer. Instead he is a student of physics who wishes he were a student of music. Herbert's love is not the intricacies of particle physics but the complexities of Gershwin, not Reimann Space but Baroque fugues. Herbert loves the oboe.

He has, however, a talent for physics.

The instrument case is above his seat, as it is never far from him. The train is empty. He looks guiltily around him, and takes down the case. The way he opens and fits together the ebony pieces can only be described as stealthy.

He looks around him again. Nobody. He fits the reed inside his mouth and begins to play.

A moment later the conductor slams open the door to his car, holding his hands to his ears. "Christ Almighty! Put that goddamn thing away. This is a train, not a circus!"

But there is no instrument here. Herbert is carefully studying a text on General Relativity with the intensity of the guilty.

It is August 14, 2014.

The scholarship covers his tuition and fees and an assistantship will cover living expenses throughout the school year. But the school year begins in September and he has to be able to cover the rent by the first of the month.

The weather has changed again and now it is deep summer, dog days—the only real heat Boston ever experiences. The air is thick, wet and salty. It smells of people, cotton candy, burned food—tourist smells. Boston is sinking, gradually slipping foot by greasy foot into the sea. People come to bear witness: the tallest buildings in the Boston skyline are hotels. The puddling streets are thick with tourists, along the Freedom Trail, past the Old North Church, the Old Burial Ground, the Old Customs House, all safely sealed against the rising water. Drowning Boston's biggest industry is tourism. People wear USS *Constitution* T-shirts and the streets are littered with brochures from the Aquarium and the Constitution Museum.

Disasters always draw a crowd.

Herbert goes to confession on orders from his mother. The booth is hot and smells of seasoned wood. He tries to think of a list of sins but beyond the reflex litany of how many months it has been since his last confession, he stops and can think of nothing. The priest prompts him and they speak of music and physics and how Herbert is to pay his rent. The priest sends him to an address downtown.

There Herbert is able to rent a popcorn cart. From eight-thirty in the morning to nine o'clock at night, Herbert is out selling popcorn to a family from Omaha, newlyweds from Huntsville, Alabama, a retired grandmother from Butte, Montana.

At first he moves the cart around from one area to another, but soon he realizes that it is better to remain in one location for a while before he moves on. Then he tries various hawking methods. One day, in front of the Aquarium, he points out that popcorn is the preferred food of the seals. He is asked politely to leave. Outside Faneuil Hall, he tells customers that popcorn was one of the favorite foods of George Washington and Thomas Jefferson. (That this might be true does not occur to him.) He is not believed and this hurts both his sales and his pride. In the pseudo-Italian North End, he hits on a winning combination: he mentions casually that Betsy Ross used to sew popcorn on the stars of her flags as Christmas ornaments. Sales pick up.

He takes a break in the afternoon in Waterfront Park. He holds his oboe case next to him in case the park empties out enough for him to play it. It, of course, never empties in August. On his first day on the job, in a mistaken mood of exuberance, he tried to play the opening measures of *Rhapsody in Blue*. He was pelted with popcorn. Now he just sits and waits. To pass the time, he throws popcorn at the seagulls, but to his annoyance, the seagulls eat them in midair.

It is a hot day, August 18, 2014.

Herbert has a roommate, Willy Bernard, a fat computer freak who has only two subjects about which he speaks: operating systems and Tolstoy. It is his roommate's opinion that the world has been denied reams of great literature because Tolstoy was born before word processors. Willy occupies his free time trying to write a program which will reconstruct what Tolstoy might have written if only he'd had access to the world of computers. So far Willy has only managed to discover two poems and a scrap of what might have been *Anna Karenina* as written by Ernest Hemingway:

"We must throw ourselves in front of the train, my dear."
They did.
It was good.

Willy finds this intensely promising. "It's got to be a rough draft. Something he did in his peasant period. Primitive. Strong."

Herbert disagrees but is too polite to say anything.

It is Willy who tells Herbert that he has an ex-lover. Before this, Herbert thought her perfectly current.

He had met Beverly the previous semester in a class on Newtonian Mechanics. Finding Beverly made him resolve to look at physics in a new light: nothing he considered good had ever come out of it before. True, she was no beauty. She outweighed Herbert and her complexion had a sheen that resembled shellac. In her dorm room was a sign that read, Physics Spoken Here. Even in their most romantic moments, somehow a discussion of bubble chambers or Partial Field Theory would come up. Even so, she was more than Herbert felt he deserved and if he wasn't in love, he still had someone to cuddle up with on Saturday night. He considered her an unlooked-for gift given to him by a capricious, Heisenbergian universe. They pledged undying love over the summer during an emotional moment behind the mainframe printroom. Beverly said the earth moved. Considering the accounting reports that were coming out at the time, this did not surprise Herbert at all.

But barely a week into his job, Willy is waiting for him in his room with a letter. The letter is opened.

"I did that," says Willy. "I thought it was mine."

Written in large block letters across the front is Herbert's name. Herbert nods.

"You better sit down," continues Willy.

Herbert looks at him.

"It might be bad news," says Willy defensively.

Herbert sits down and opens the letter.

"I have some rum. Do you want a drink?" Willy is right behind him. "She can't spell 'forever.' "

"Willy, go get me a drink."

Herbert reads the letter hurriedly while Willy is in the kitchen. There is a slow grinding sensation in his stomach. Beverly has been in France this summer and has fallen in love with a CERN technician. "It's not the best technology anymore," she writes. "But what is computer power next to love?" Herbert drops the letter to the floor, unable to read further. It is not love, he realizes again. That doesn't change the way he feels.

Willy comes back with rum and Coca-Cola. Herbert doesn't like Coke, but drinks it down in a rush out of a sense of duty. When one loses one's woman, he thinks, one gets drunk. All the best writers say so. He would mention this to Willy, but Willy would talk for twenty minutes about how it relates to *War and Peace* and Herbert doesn't feel up to it.

"Did you get to the part about where she's going to live?" Willy picks up the letter and looks at it. "France. Wow." He shakes his head. "She's not for you anyway. Too much brains. I like a woman that's not too smart. Who can appreciate a real man."

Herbert just stares at him.

Herbert realizes Willy *wants* Beverly. He offers Willy Beverly's phone number but when he does, Willy begins to talk again about Tolstoy's peasant period. "He went barefoot. All the time. Barefoot in the snow. He was a demon for consistency."

Herbert considers that there might be a girl in Willy's past whose memory still stirs up bad blood. But Willy begins to talk about Czarist Russia and Herbert concludes this must not be the case.

They finish the rum and a leftover six-pack of Haffen-reffer beer. Not feeling drunk enough, they share a pint of tequila between them. Soon they cannot stand. They attempt to drink sitting in chairs but fall down anyway. With a sly grin, Herbert fits together the pieces of his oboe and begins to play. Willy is too drunk to object and Herbert is too drunk to care. For a moment, he is happy.

It is August 20, 2014.

The next morning, neither is able to leave his bed without throwing up. Lost in a sort of nauseous glow, Herbert feels a weak satisfaction that he has mourned Beverly properly.

It is nearly noon when he is able to drag his cart out to the edge of Boston Common. WalkMan, a street person of indeterminate origin, stands at the fountain for most of the day just watching him. Business has never been better. It is all Herbert can do to stand straight without falling over. Fortunately, this is all that is required of him and he manages to rake in money. The smell of popcorn makes him ill and the ever-present stare of WalkMan makes him nervous.

"Hey," he finally yells at WalkMan. "What the hell you looking at?"

WalkMan seems to take his time in answering. "I don't know, man. Something feels about to happen and I was looking for it." WalkMan shakes his head slowly and walks away. The encounter makes Herbert irritable. He longs for the beginning of the semester. He will not enjoy it, but at least he will be occupied.

It is August 21, 2014.

The weather makes him feel itchy inside.

The sky has scratchy gray clouds shot through with blue patches. The breezes buffet him as he drags his cart down to the Aquarium. First cold gusts freeze him, then hot gusts warm him again, then the two together. He remembers reading in *The Wizard of Oz* that this signifies tornado weather. Or was that where he read it? He is glum, thinking about Emerald Cities, whirlwinds and dead witches.

The water slops over the edge of the pier, the docks, the wind blowing it over the crowd in a mist. Like the mist, the crowd is a strange chancy thing. One minute he cannot keep from selling out the current batch of popcorn. the next several minutes he is not noticed. Even the seagulls are flying in tight circles over the water. He throws popcorn at them. They ignore him. He wonders if it's the full moon, but can't remember the calendar. A trick of the wind brings the weather report to him from a car radio a hundred yards away:

"—sudden gusts of rain and occasional sleet have been reported over Provincetown. Possibly this is another effect of the unseasonal El Niño current that was discovered earlier in the year. Strong sudden winds have been noted all the way from Nantucket across the Cape. In Quincy—"

And just as suddenly, the wind blows the broadcast away. The snatch of news has an unsettling effect on him. He brings out his oboe and puts it together, fingering the notes but not blowing.

"Hey, mister?"

It's a kid, maybe ten years old, standing next to him. He hadn't seen him before, hadn't noticed him before. "Yeah," he says shortly.

"You can play that thing?" the kid asks.

He shakes his head. "Not really."

"Is it really hard?"

The kid is small for his age, redheaded, blue-eyed. It is as if he has just stepped off the canvas of a Norman Rockwell painting. He is missing one of his front teeth and he's wearing a baseball cap. Under his arm is a baseball glove and Herbert can see bubble gum in his shirt pocket. Herbert looks around the plaza in front of the Aquarium. There are other kids there the same age as this kid, but they look normal: wearing wet-look shirts and bermuda shorts, sleek, glittering tennis shoes, writhing plastic bracelets made of charm-sized hands and feet. Herbert looks back at the kid.

"What's your name?"

The kid grins again. There is not one tooth missing, but two. A moment before Herbert could have sworn the kid was missing only one tooth. "My friends call me Paulie."

"Glad to meet you, Paulie."

The wind picks up a breeze now from off the water. It's not cold, but there is a kind of cold annealed to its underside. Herbert shakes his head again. There is something . . .

Paulie takes the oboe out of his hand and fingers it as Herbert did. He blows through it. There's a faint bleat. Herbert wonders if his own playing sounds like that.

"So. Is there a trick to it?" Paulie produces another bleat.

"Not really. I'm not very good. But you put the whole reed in your mouth and blow."

Paulie shakes his head and hands it back to Herbert. "Show me."

Herbert sighs resignedly. The wind is blowing steadily from over the water. It's cold, but Herbert does not feel cold. He holds the oboe, wishing he could play it. He looks at Paulie but Paulie looks implacable: Herbert must play.

He grimaces as he blows through the mouthpiece. From the oboe comes the sweetest sound Herbert has ever heard. He stops immediately and looks at the instrument.

"And you said you couldn't play!" says Paulie and punches him playfully on the arm.

Wordlessly, Herbert plays the opening glissando to *Rhapsody in Blue.* It slides effortlessly into the upper register with a poignancy and strength no clarinet could ever reach. Two bars after that he slips into the beginning of the *New World Symphony,* then "Sheep May Safely Graze." His eyes are closed and tears stream down his face. He looks down at Paulie. Paulie gently turns him seaward and points.

Floating hundreds of feet over the harbor is something as grand and magnificent and natural as a mountain. The sounds die in Herbert's oboe. The mountain comes slowly in toward half-drowned Long Wharf. Herbert hears the crowd muttering behind him, close to panic. He feels a touch on his arm.

"Play, Herbert," whispers Paulie intensely. "Play!"

Herbert turns back to the thing in the sky. He can see now how huge it is. Most of it is blocked by the clouds. There is a long tube or trunk or tail or snake hanging down nearly to the water. It quests over the harbor, dipping into the water, splashing. It is too big to be seen, too big to be understood.

"Play," urges Paulie.

Hesitantly, he places the mouthpiece in his mouth. He is playing for it. He has been given by it the gift of music—by what? A mountain? God? A ten-year-old? He looks down at Paulie and Paulie is gone. There is nobody near him but the crowd that presses in, staring at the sky. He starts again with Gershwin, that long moaning glissando that sounds like a cat in heat. This time, he hears an orchestra backing him up at the top of the run—from where? He can't tell—holding him there with tympani and trumpet.

He breathes, looks around. The crowd has parted in front of him. It follows him as he harmonizes with the piano solo. Both he and his orchestra are breathless and ready by the time he is before the Expressway. They launch into the *giusto* together, echoing off the walls of the Expressway like the laughter of spirits. He is laughing with them. They march up State Street together, the crowd behind him now, dancing. Old grandmothers who could barely move without pain, young and clumsy children, fat smug tourists dancing with a sudden unknown grace. In his breaks in the music, he dances with one partner, then the next. It is his whole life he dances, his whole life he plays. They walk up the steps along Government Center where he is joined by the Mayor, over Beacon Hill past the State House where the

Governor follows him outside. He has been sent. He is the herald. He has been touched.

As they all descend from the steps of the State House, he sees there are more than just people in the crowd. He is dancing now, is playing now, with great heavy-bodied things like young dancing whales. They change around him and he can't keep track. They are one moment like elephants, as shapeless as seals, the hard edge of rhinoceri. It doesn't matter: his whole life he has been fettered, now he is free. His whole life he has been muffled, but now he rings.

They lead up through the *grandioso* into the *molto* and finish. There is a hush, then applause. Still crying, he bows to them along with the elephants, the seals, the whales. He sees above him this thing, this altar where he has been freed. An angel cries out and asks who he is.

"Herbert!" he answers. "Herbert Maxwell!"

And for that moment alone, it is enough.

It is August 22, 2014, 5:05 P.M., Eastern Standard Time.

The aliens have landed.

He finds himself that night in a church. He has wandered the city, unable to play again just yet for fear that the gift was merely temporary. He looks up at the pictures of the saints, the different figures of crucified agony and compassion. He finds himself wondering where God is in all of this—and wonders at the thought. Is this not the Heisenberg universe? He holds his oboe. It is warm to his touch.

He is not alone in the church: it is full to bursting. All evening the news services have been showing the dancing and music in Boston Common. But there is fear now. The euphoria is disappearing. The aliens—for that is what they are, is what they claim to be—are speaking with the state and city officials. The Secretary of State of the United States has just flown into Hanscom Field and is being rushed to the Common by helicopter. Herbert has heard rumors Boston has been quarantined, that flights in and out of the entire United States have been cancelled. He has listened carefully as a man in a business suit is shouting at a crowd near the Old Customs House that aliens driving large, fuzzy Cadillacs have already landed in San Francisco and Los Angeles.

Here in the church, people are praying, for their lives, for profit, for deliverance from an uncertain future.

Herbert does not pray for deliverance. He has been touched—by God, he decides. The aliens used him. This he knows. But the choice is God's. If God comes to him by aliens, so be it. What has happened to him could have come from nothing less. Herbert prays to keep the gift. It is enough, he prays, to have been the herald for this day. But please, let it stay with me.

The city is alive with people, eating, drinking, speaking with a soft, boisterous awe. He wanders among them down to a small park in the North End. It is still quiet enough to have lovers and children playing, still soft, still relatively untouched. He sits down on the bench and Paulie sits next to him.

"Nicely done, Herbert. Nicely done." Paulie rubs his hands together.

Herbert is staring at his oboe. "I can't do it."

"Do what?"

"Play. I can't do it."

"Why not?"

"I don't have the courage. It might be gone."

Paulie holds up his hands in an elaborate shrug. "Sure you can."

Herbert doesn't move.

"Come on, Herbert. You can do it."

He tries something simple: "Jesu, Joy of Man's Desiring." And the music comes out of him. He can still play. He stops, too filled to play more.

"There, you see?"

"Thank you."

Paulie slaps his hands on his lap. "No problem."

"I will serve God the rest of my life."

"As you wish." Paulie snaps his fingers.

Herbert looks up from his oboe. Paulie is gone.

Herbert finds himself in the park next to the Charles River locks. There he holds his oboe, looks at it closely. His face is reflected at him split across its levers, tabs and rods on the outside. Herbert holds it closely and as he looks at it, it comes to him that the world is contained inside. It is not his reflection staring solemnly back at him; it is himself, watching his own consternation, the city behind him, breathing, as this city breathes, the stars lit behind the buildings were these stars shining down on him. Onward and forever, as it was in the beginning, is now and ever shall be. World without end—

He looks up and sees the oboe and his music reflected in the world.

"I will sing me a hymn," he says quietly. And deep within him now there is a faith. A sense of awakening. This is the most important thing that has ever happened to us, he wants to shout. Nothing else will ever be the same.

At that moment, he conceives of what he will do: he will build a monastery.

It is August 23, 2014, 2:00 A.M.

He climbs to the top of the old Route 1/I-93 interchange, now broken and abandoned. From here he can see the base of the high buildings. The ship—for he now knows it is the aliens' ship, and that what it is does not matter—still floats over the city. Parts of it shimmer like trembling mercury and reflect back Boston's distorted image.

During the night, by judicious thievery, he brings to the bridge loads of food, an equipment shack, a dumptruck or two of dirt, seeds. No one notices. Their eyes are on the heavens. Afterwards he replaces the truck. He stands in the

Boston Common a long time, staring up. The ship is so huge that there is always something new to look at.

Then he walks back slowly, finding himself by sunrise on his bridge, next to his shack. He looks down at the city, the sea that built the city and is now reclaiming it, the river that cleaves the two apart. This is his city, his world. And the world he has now left behind, for now he is convinced. He is committed. He is dedicated. Where will he get water? Where will he get a thousand perishable things that he needs? He does not know. He does not care. He will do what is needed and the rest the Lord will provide.

He prays alongside us, the city, the world. He prays for us as we wait to see what happens next. And we listen to him and our hearts are glad.

Herbert prays by playing his oboe, singing.

SEATING ARRANGEMENT
ALEXANDER JABLOKOV

DAMN IT, KRISHENA Carlyle decided, looking at the sketch-book in her lap, it was true—almost provable mathemati-cally. There was no way to seat everyone at her upcoming wedding reception without violating one or another of her mother's inviolable rules. Krishena could just hear it: "Kri-shie, darling, don't you know that Frederick once slept with Arnold's wife Steffie? Long before Arnold and Steffie be-came engaged, of course, but it might come up. A natural topic of conversation at a wedding, don't you think?" No, Krishena *didn't* think, but arguing with her mother was like arguing with the Pythagorean Theorem.

She leaned back in her chair. The aides' pen was silent, the paper-covered desks all around her like glaciers in the penetrating fluorescent light. Krishena had come into the State House offices to escape her personal life, but it had somehow followed her in, refusing to be distracted by the zoning regulations she was analyzing for her boss, State Senator Merwin. Let's zone it NO WEDDINGS, Krishena thought, and tugged at her hair. The seating arrangement. *It could not be done.* Eloping, as Jerry had once half-jokingly suggested, started to make more and more sense. And he wasn't even home to talk to, off on one of his after-hours water plant inspections. She shrugged and, gritting her teeth, forwarded the seating plan to her mother. She'd be hearing about it soon enough.

Her friend Jaganthir Nasil poked her head through the door. "You're back," she said. "Alien update. They took a walk on the beach. A long walk. Twittered to each other the whole time. I caught a glimpse of Merwin just before a commercial for hair spray. He was pouring sand out of his Italian shoes."

"Don't be so unfeeling, Jag," Krishena said. "He *loves* those shoes."

"The aliens put silver things on their heads and stared out at the ocean."

"Italian silver things?"

"Hah! They don't seem too fashion-conscious, do they? But who knows? Glad you're here. It's been quiet." She gestured around the empty desks, which were normally occupied by a contingent of late-working senatorial aides. "Everybody important is tromping around Nantucket with the space cases."

Jag had grown up in an Indian family in New Jersey. She had the beautiful elongated features of a temple goddess. She had dyed her long black hair blond, contrasting oddly with her burnt-caramel skin.

"Getting sand in their shoes."

"Let's hope." Jag leaned against the doorjamb. Idly, she wound a thick strand of hair around a finger. "Oh, damn!" The distant beep of a phone, and Jag ran out of the room.

Krishena finally turned her attention to the documents she had to explain to Merwin tomorrow. They were mostly city matters, but since he represented a Boston district, his voters tended to be concerned with them. Massport had sucked the Port of Boston into its bureaucratic maw. Something in its technocratic control fascinated Merwin: the compulsive, never-satisfied *orality* of the Port, its nebulous lines of ancestral authority representing long-fallen patriarchs, slain by Oedipal subcommittees. Krishena smiled at herself. She had once wanted to be an English professor, but she'd been glad to take any job she could find.

Her own phone beeped. Mother, ready to discuss more wedding minutiae. She hesitated. "I'm sorry I was so crabby before, Mother, but it's just impossible—hello?"

A sound like wind sweeping across a great plain, and the distant chanting of incomprehensible words. She clicked off, and shivered. It had sounded like an obscene phone call from beyond the grave.

A moment later, it beeped again. She hesitated, and finally answered. "Have I reached a government entity?" an uninflected voice said.

"Krishena Carlyle, aide to State Senator Trent Merwin. May I help you?"

"I must communicate with a recognized entity."

"Well, Senator Merwin is certainly a recognized entity." What was she saying? She had no idea who this was. It was most likely some new immigrant looking for the Department of Motor Vehicles. The numbers were similar. "If you need a driver's license you should call—"

"I am . . . the term best translates as . . . Protocol Interpreter. Is that a recognized, titled office? Do you comprehend?"

"Are you at one of the consulates?" Krishena was trying to place the accent. "I'm not up on diplomatic language . . ."

"We will not establish a consulate. It does not intersect with our level of instrumentality. I need to convey an explanation. To a recognized entity. I do not have much time." Despite the tonelessness, the voice managed to convey impatience. Peevish impatience, Krishena thought.

Another beep and an ID appeared: her mother was trying to call her. Something about the napkin rings at the reception, no doubt. Krishena sighed at her own unfairness.

Her mother had already saved her from a couple of serious blunders, like spending several thousand dollars for out-of-season flowers. "Get married in the fall and live with the consequences, dearest." Thanks, Mom.

But Krishena couldn't talk now. Something about the Protocol Interpreter's cold tones was utterly convincing. He didn't represent anyone on Earth. Aliens walked the autumn sands of Nantucket, but countless others were shooting out of that nozzle in solar orbit, the Loophole. This looked to be one of them.

"Can you give some indication of your *bona fides?*" she asked, in precise, legalistic tones. "Whom do you represent?"

"What is important is not whom I represent, but whom you represent. Are you a recognized entity? I must state that time is short. I have other commitments."

"I am—" She thought about it. She was an aide to a State Senator of the Commonwealth of Massachusetts. And she sat in on her local Neighborhood Watch meetings in Jamaica Plain. She was talking to a being from another star. However he had gotten on the phone line, he could just as easily call someone else. And she could go back to worrying about zoning restrictions and napkin rings. "I represent *both* state and local . . . entities." Joy zinged up her spine.

"The Contact Zone is a circle approximately fifteen kilometers in radius centered on the point of first contact. According to your simplistic nomenclature, this is in Boston Harbor, several hundred meters off your shoreline. All trade contact will occur within these geographic limits. Do your territorial entites contain this zone?"

Krishena rummaged in her desk and pulled out a map of the Boston metropolitan area. She put her fingernail over the scale on the bottom and marked off distances. "All parts of the circle fall within entities I represent."

"Excellent. Then we can negotiate the operations of the Contact Zone and I can be on my way."

"What is this Contact Zone?"

"Is the term not comprehensible? It is the standard legal term in Galactic Space. I had hoped that a simple fifteen-kilometer circle would be within the limits of your simple mental patterns. Perhaps I should speak with someone with greater access to mentation."

This was worse than dealing with Merwin. "And that's our legal trade zone?"

"Your laws are irrelevant. That's *our* legal trade zone. Spacecraft can land nowhere else. Cannot you get this clear?"

"Is this for, like, good luck, or something?"

A long pause before the Protocol Interpreter finally spoke again. "I did not have to come here. It is quite a distance out of my way. I merely thought it polite to inform you about some of the rules, since your ignorance is quite astounding. I do not have much time. If there is no agreement at this point, there will be no trade with the stars, until another representative arrives in . . . your year would be 2089."

"2089? Seventy-five years from now? Why are you in such a big hurry now?"

"Sincere apologies. I have an appointment at van Maanen's star to which I am already late."

"An appointment? What's so important? We have a complex agreement to negotiate and you want to take off?"

"I don't believe you understand. Van Maanen's is a tedious diplomatic function, true, but compared to your affairs . . . but there's no need to insult you. I have another five minutes in Earth orbit."

"That's not enough time for any serious—"

"Five minutes." Whoever he was, the alien was enjoying this. She could tell. But what sort of diplomat took so much pleasure in pushing ignorant natives around? She knew the answer from long experience. Not a powerful plenipotentiary. A low-level bureaucrat, much like herself. Now, a low-level bureaucrat from an interstellar civilization was not necessarily the same as a low-level bureaucrat from the Massachusetts Department of Internal Revenue, but she would bet that the similarities outweighed the differences.

A beep: her mother was calling again. "Excuse me," Krishena said. "I have a call on another line."

"But—" Her finger cut him off.

"Mom. What is it?" Krishena tried to slow her breathing.

"Oh, dear, I'm sorry to bother you at work."

"That's all right. I'm not doing anything very important. What is it?"

"Well, it's this seating chart you just sent me. We can't put Uncle Arnold next to that terrible Phoebe from your friend's law firm. Arnold's been unemployed for three years and thinks lawyers should be ground up for cat food. And Arnold hates cats . . . which brings up the problem of that lady with the Abyssinian who's just three seats away . . ."

"That's all right. Phoebe hates cats too. She could tell him which of her partners would make the best vittles." Krishena's mother, of course, had found the seating flashpoint. Last week it had been a Zoroastrian hairdresser and a Shi'ite turban maker. Blame it on Jerry's family. They had odd friends. Krishena knew; she was one of them.

"Oh dear, you didn't tell me *that*, Krishena. That changes the whole room structure—"

"It's okay, Mom. Let's just make sure the caterer serves one thing that's so bad that everyone gets together to criticize the food and forgets their differences. How about cheese balls in ginger sauce?"

A long pause. "You know, Krishena, you're not taking any of this at all seriously."

"You know that's not true at all." Krishena felt a sudden surge of temper she felt with no one else. Her mother continually increased the complexity of the wedding and then blamed Krishena for the consequences. Instead of snapping at her mother, she took a deep breath and resolved to stick her with Jerry's Uncle Jed, who was desperately looking for a woman his own age to retire to Alaska with him.

"I have to get back to work now," Krishena said.

"Bye."

She clicked lines. "Protocol Interpreter?" She held her breath.

"Here." He sounded sulky.

"Cancel that pesky van Maanen's star engagement?"

A long pause. The Protocol Interpreter should have a conversation with her mother, Krishena thought. They had a similar pattern of eloquent silence. "I was compelled to reschedule."

"Great." At least she had some power over this outer-space paper-pusher, if no one else. "So we have a good long time to negotiate this contract?"

"An hour at least. I must leave geosynchronous orbit by—"

"An hour is plenty for a basis. The details will have to be worked out by committee—"

"There are no details. What we agree is what the agreement is. Its operations will determine the details."

"Great. I like running things that way." When this came out, where was her career? Screw it, she would take her chances. What would the Protocol Interpreter's superiors make of his willingness to negotiate with an unknown government operative? Nothing, she suspected. An agreement had to be reached. Once it was, no one on Earth could affect it. It would be what it was. It would be what she, Krishena Carlyle, *said* it was.

"All right. We need an entity to control the contact."

"Wait, wait." She raised her voice. "Jag! Do you have that Massport stuff in your desk?"

"Huh?" Jag sounded startled, distracted from her TV. "Yeah, sure. What about it?"

"Bring the Boston Port stuff in here, will you? I need it, pronto."

Jag muttered beyond the partition, then appeared with a sheaf of documents. "What do you need this for? The aliens have stopped at the end of the beach at Madaket and are staring up at the sky. They haven't moved for half an hour. The escorts are starting to worry that they're dead, and the news announcers ran out of things to say ten minutes ago, even with a lecture on whaling ships and beach ecology."

"That might well have some connection with my call. I'm negotiating with an emissary from outer space. Sit down and help me. You have a degree in International Relations, don't you?"

Jag sat down limply in the chair and stared at her. "Weddings are a big strain, Krish. Maybe you better—"

"Don't screw around. This is important." Krishena turned back to the phone. "Name of entity . . . how about Interstellar Port of Boston?"

"Not the most imaginative name for the most important organization on your world."

"Hey, we're in a hurry, remember? Don't get wise. IPOB it is. I'll just cross out 'nation of origin' and write in 'planet of origin' on this stuff . . ."

"I believe we will enjoy working with you."

"Don't try to get friendly."

She listed IPOB as a Boston city agency, not a Massachusetts or U.S. one. Boston had been as good to her as it could be in a black-hole depression, and there was really no better reason for it than that. Jerry was from New York, and kept crowing about how much better things were down there. If this worked out, he'd have to move up here, and NYC would become a city whose harbor had silted up. So that was that.

"And the physical structure. Where should it be?" The Protocol Interpreter had a series of questions, each of which demanded a specific answer before he would proceed to the next.

"Stick it in Weston, Wayland, somewhere like that," Jag demanded. "Piss all those fat asses off, put a spaceport on their golf course."

"Jag, this is no time to pay off grudges."

"Oh yeah? What better time?"

"You're right," Krishena laughed, dizzy with possibility. "But they're outside the Contact Zone." She looked at the map on her desk. "Put it in the harbor. Right in the water. Can you do that, Protocol Interpreter?"

"We can do anything."

"Yeah," Jag said. "I've had guys tell me that before." She giggled.

"Calm down," Krishena said severely, then laughed herself. "Your traders won't be bringing cars, will they? There won't be a damn place to park."

"No, no cars. We have moved beyond such primitive means of—"

"Stop bragging," Krishena said. "It's annoying. You should move beyond such primitive emotional responses."

Jag sucked in a startled breath, but the Protocol Interpreter did not respond to the sally. "Careful where you put things," Jag cautioned. "We don't want buildings to end up underwater."

"Why do you think I put IPOB headquarters out in the harbor? Might as well face the water issue straight on. Did you know Boston was sinking?" she asked the Protocol Interpreter.

"We are aware. It is not important in this context. We have materials. Now about the distressed traveler relations . . ."

Like first settlers on a deserted island, they set up rules. Regardless of what they were, someone's ox would always get gored. Gored oxen were not the responsibility of IPOB.

That should probably be written in big letters over the entrance.

"All Loophole travelers will abide by these regulations," the Protocol Interpreter said suddenly. A printer in another part of the offices hummed and started spitting out documentation. "Any questions of interpretation will be referred to you, Krishena Carlyle."

"You mean the office of—"

"I mean *you*, personally. Thank you for your attention." Just like that, the line went dead.

The two women sat there for a long while, saying nothing whatsoever, just looking at each other in the cold fluorescent light.

"Well, Krish," Jag said. "This changes the whole game, doesn't it?"

"You bet. This'll will piss Merwin off, big time."

"Oh, don't worry about it." Jag waved a hand dismissively. "He'll be sucking up to you soon enough. He's a flexible guy, you know. His strength as a politician."

"Right, right."

Jag wandered back out into the other room to look at the TV. "Hey, they're walking around again, knocking their silver headgear together. Something's got them real excited."

The phone rang. Krishena felt a flare of panic. What if the alien beachcombers were, in a rage, denouncing the Protocol Interpreter's dealings, and Krishena's temerity in participating in them? Were they ready to haul her off to some interstellar tribunal? Or—much worse thought—what if had been just one of her sister's practical jokes? Luwanda loved that kind of thing. There had been times when she'd even successfully imitated Jerry's voice on the phone. That, at any rate, would solve the reception seating problem. Everyone would talk about what a bubble-brain the bride was. With a gulp, Krishena finally activated the phone.

"Krish! What the hell are you doing still at work?"

"Jerry! Something unexpected came up."

"Sorry I wasn't home to answer your call about the seating arrangements." Jerry was exceedingly patient about the intergenerational war in the Carlyle family. "Water treatment plant inspections in the middle of the night are becoming one of my favorite things. Now, this business about Uncle Arnold—"

"Jerry." Krishena's voice was suddenly crisp. "Pack up. Now. And get your ass up to Boston."

"What? Why?"

"In a couple of weeks there's going to be more work up here than anyone can handle." She leafed through the documentation on her desk and found the specifications for life-support systems for a dozen different planetary environments, all to be packed into the proposed IPOB structure. "Can you handle halogens, steam, and liquid oxygen?"

"Multiphase vortex stuff? Sure. You know I've done industrial work . . . not that anyone's paying for that these days."

"They will be! How soon can you be here?"

Now he paused. It was easier to tolerate than her mother's, because there was a legitimate reason for it. "All right, Krishena. I can be in Boston by noon tomorrow." He took a deep breath. "I love you, sweetheart. You better not be psychotic."

"I'm not." She kissed the air. "I'll explain when you get here. I'll pick you up at the airport. Bye." They could buy a bigger place in Jamaica Plain. She'd always liked it there. The houses were old and big. Not like Jerry's Manhattan apartment.

Krishena turned a page in her sketchbook and started working on another seating arrangement. In ink. Maybe the excitement of seeing her and Jerry get married would overcome any personality conflicts and confine the conversation to the beauty of the bride, the elegant simplicity of the floral arrangements, and the fine quality of the food.

Stranger things had happened.

THE UPRISING
JON BURROWES

From the memoirs of Robert Reynaud, freelance journalist in Boston:

In August of 2016—two years after the first aliens arrive—a
band of "action squads" from all over the world sneaks into
the city of Boston and unloads hundreds of canisters of ancient nerve gases into the narrow streets of the Financial
District. People pay no attention to them at first because
they drive plain commercial trucks and wear water-masks
and black pressure suits. They look like the rest of the workers in the harbor area who are reclaiming the city from the
"advancing" sea.

The groups include grizzled white-power professionals
from hate groups in Idaho and Alabama, dry old fanatics
from Austria and the Caucasus, weirdos from the Carib-
bean and South America, and even some junketers from the
Far East.

Upon the opening the canisters that contain the poison
gases in the middle of downtown Boston, the sequence of
events now known as the Uprising is set in motion. The first
few clouds, floating up State Street that day, cause no panic

whatsoever. Bodies drop; pedestrians continue on their way. But the bodies stay where they are. More gas floats up. It begins to be clear to the remaining pedestrians that they, too, will get only a few more steps before they have to kiss the pavement, probably good-bye—and in the name of their fellow pedestrians, they begin to complain.

But this plaintive protest is ignored. "Hey! Hey! Hey!" the few people shout. And then they die.

At this point, the Uprising begins to hose the gases up the sides of buildings and down the neighboring streets as far as their guns can reach. Within seconds—seconds—a twenty-five-block area of the downtown city is dying *en masse.* And remember that this is a three-dimensional space, not simply a phenomenon occurring at street level. The gases are sucked into air-conditioning systems, splashed up across windows and over doorways, tossed up to rooftops and over alleyways. With no wind to blow it away, the gas gets into business—

Office workers tumble out of doorways and pitch senseless into gutters. Bodies writhe in the streets.

Sorry dear, I won't be home tonight. We mistook a bunch of terrorists for construction workers, heh heh. Film at eleven; bye now.

People try to cover their heads with their clothing. They choke and scream as the loudspeakers bellow, "COME OUT! COME OUT! ALIENS COME OUT! SEE THE PEACE AND HARMONY YOU HAVE SOWED AMONG THE COMPLACENT PEOPLE OF EARTH!"

And only the humans die from the gas; none of the aliens get it.

The sirens begin to pick up now; and health units from all over the city dash into the downtown area, only to be met with gas, spray-guns, and the hundred-megawatt loudspeakers: "SEE HOW YOUR EARTH-FRIENDS ARE FARING NOW!" they scream. "ALIENS COME OUT! COME OUT! COME OUT! THIS IS HOW WE GET ALONG WITH

EACH OTHER NOW THAT YOU'RE HERE!" It goes on and on, into the night.

No one can get near the Uprising commandos. They dart behind clouds of fumes, race through towers choked with bodies, clamber down streets jammed with empty cars, a collective raging animal soul, rearing its mad head from the wreckage of the drowned harbor. Soon, Boston looks as if a graveyard has been emptied over it—agonized bodies are strewn everywhere. They lie across the curbs, up against the sides of buildings, under cars; they hang from windows, poke out of sewers. Finally the National Guard brings out the beam weapons. Building by building, stone by stone, they clear the streets of the Uprising, forcing them down to the water and leaving the city a shambles.

But they only catch eleven of them. The rest of them disappear.

Where do they go? Have only eleven black-suited, greasy maniacs kept the City of Boston at bay for an entire day and night? No. Have the gas-sprayers dressed their dead as civilians and left them among the crowds of bodies, so that no one will know how many actually died? How many escaped? They have pressure suits, breathers, even submarines. They can scramble away across the harbor floor and regroup somewhere else. . . .

There follows two months of martial law. Nothing comes of them. The Uprising has left. All that remains are old letter-to-the-editor writer types and young nonviolent try-hards. There is a brief resurgence of interest when the police bomb Hull in 2019. Drug dealing is the putative reason for the bombing, but the real reason is that HALO gets word Hull might be the staging ground for another Uprising. This is never confirmed or denied. The city succeeds in scaring all the would-be commandos underground. Even the heretofore moderate/liberal anti-alienists—tolerated, respected, articulate—quietly disappear.

The aliens are upset but not surprised. To abolish dissent in the City of Boston has been the furthest thing from their minds. Yet they know the first city on Earth to welcome aliens will have problems more complex than anyone can dream of. But there is no longer any illusion that every last man, woman, and deranged loon on Earth is pleased as punch that the marvelous old aliens are here on little old Earth. Some of us obviously aren't.

FENNARIO
RESA NELSON AND SARAH SMITH

When we marched down to Fennario,
When we marched down to Fennario,
Our captain fell in love
*   With a lady like a dove*
Her name it was pretty Peggy-O.

"TELL US ABOUT meeting your first alien," you say.

I was nine when I met my Phner. Boston was still in quarantine and he ought to have been out in the harbor with the rest of the aliens, all those aliens we'd never seen. He must have been a stowaway on one of the first ships through the Loophole, a refugee, running away before the end of the last Phneri war with the Sh'k. He was some sort of soldier, I guess, and maybe he knew already how it would end.

But how am I going to tell you? In what language? If I made a naming story in Phner, with my translator box, the story would be about structures that deform and the flow of one structure into another. But you don't know Phner and after thirty years I can't speak it well enough to say an *esfn*. When I tell you in English, it has to be about me, a little girl.

And I won't be able to tell you all of it, even if we two had every word of Phner and every human language, because the story's still stuck in no language, somewhere between the two of us, human and alien. . . .

* * *

What I remember of Houston is what you remember of a place you lived before you started to grow up. There were the three of us, Dad-and-Mom-and-Jennifer, and we lived in a suburb called Pioneer Ridge. There weren't any pioneers and there wasn't any ridge—it was mostly NASA families in split-levels—but I played baseball for the Junior Girls' All-Stars and I went to Brownies and 4F. I had a best friend named Althea and we used to catch grasshoppers down in the long grass behind the school, under the big blue sky. I loved my mother and father. I had never seen the sea.

I came home one day and found my parents sitting one on either side of the kitchen table, calling each other Tom and Margaret the way they did when they weren't sure of their welcome with each other. "It's your big chance, Tom." Mom always said everything was for Dad's sake. That night Mom started packing. We left most of our clothes there and our furniture and all my toys, as if we were going to go back.

We came to Boston the summer of 2016 and lived in one room in what had been a student dorm at Boston University. In our room there was a bunk bed and two dressers and two desks and one closet, in a space half the size of my room at home. Do you remember how it was then? Everyone in the world had come to Boston. People lived on basketball courts and in churches, and a friend of mine lived with all her family in the closed-in mall on Washington Street, right in front of Filene's.

There wasn't anything to see yet, but we still came. There were black men in skirts and yellow men in yellow robes. I think people had already begun to dress like their idea of alien. I remember huge red-haired women in enormous geometrical dresses with crowns of light round their heads.

Nothing was stable in Boston. The city changed all the time, like the sea, sucking away the ground right under our feet. One day there'd be a crack down the bedroom wall and the next I'd have no place to play because the school grounds had suddenly turned soft and marshy, starting to be a pond. Boston smelled like sea and mildew. Some people said the aliens were making Boston sink. I didn't believe that, but I never went outside in the rain. It rained a lot more in Boston than down South, and I had my suspicions.

I decided that when I met the aliens I would be a heroine. They would be eight feet tall—ten!—and purple all over except where they were green and slick and shiny, and their eyes would glow in the dark. I would be real scared but I wouldn't look it. I'd stare them down until they ran away. Then everything would be normal again, and Dad and Mom and me would go back to Houston.

Way down deep where I didn't think about it I was scared all over, pretty much all the time. I knew something was going to happen. We were all alien-crazy in Boston, dressing like aliens and thinking about aliens, as if living like rats in the crannies of a drowning city, as if just being different, was going to help somehow. But we knew when the actual meeting came, it wouldn't.

One wet night I dreamed that all the streets had turned into canals. I woke up and looked out my window, and Commonwealth Avenue was wet and shining in the streetlights like the surface of water. I knew if I went outside I'd be sucked under the surface of the street, down into the water with *them*, with the aliens.

I don't remember if my parents still loved each other before we came to Boston. Whatever it was, they sort of lost track of each other. Dad began hanging around with this woman named RoseAnn who was always changing the color of her eyes and hair. A little bit later Mom met Gerald.

They started losing track of me.

I remember one evening at Gerald's construction site. His crew was building a building around another building.

This job was exciting because it was an experiment, using a special thing that the aliens had invented. Five Cambodian men were fitting waffled silver ribbons into a kind of orange goo, pressing it around the building. When they shone a special light on the orange goo—*prock* was its name—it got hard. Nobody was really supposed to have any alien stuff yet but Gerald laughed and said he knew people. The Cambodians fitted and stretched the ribbons between the hunks of goo, moving all together that way like bees or some animals have, like they knew how to work together without thinking about it. Like they belonged together and knew where they were.

When I looked around, Gerald and Mom were gone, and I was all alone in Boston.

Boston policemen wore armor in those days—they had to be responsible for a lot of things they hadn't prepared for. I told the big shining man the things you're supposed to tell a policeman. "I'm lost. My name is Jennifer. I live at the BU dorms—"

"What do your parents look like?" he asked.

"*He's* not—" Suddenly I didn't want to tell the man in armor that Gerald wasn't my father, or who Gerald was, or anything. I felt really bad, I felt so scared I could die.

I sat down on the edge of the curb, that was still like a curb in any city, but damp. Everybody's knees pressed all around me, men's knees in skirts and knobby knees in green pants and the policeman's hard steel tin-can knees. He lifted me up like a little girl, but I was too big for that, and when he held me up on his shoulder, I cried and then I was afraid to cry.

I saw Mom and Gerald, hand in hand, peering into a storefront window full of little talking manikins. Mom was laughing. The policeman put me down and I buried my face in Mom's skirt.

"What's up, Peggy-O?" Mom said.

I looked up at her. She just looked puzzled. Gerald put

his fat arm around me. I backed away and rubbed the feeling off my skin.

"Nothing. Nothing's wrong."

They'd just lost me and they hadn't minded. They had each other and I had no one at all.

In a carriage you will ride, pretty Peggy-O,
In a carriage you will ride, pretty Peggy-O,
In a carriage you will ride,
    With your soldier by your side,
As fair as any lady in the are-O.

Mom spent more time with Gerald. By then she must have figured out that her doctoral thesis on alien communications wasn't good for much except getting invitations to parties. But she liked the parties.

I was in our room watching my homework on the terminal one day when she came in.

"Can we go to the Common this weekend?" I asked her.

She was wearing a white silk suit and carried a shopping bag. She was beautiful in a kind of way that made me want her to love me as much as she loved Gerald.

"This weekend there's going to be a kite festival," I said. "At the Common. Please, Momma, let's go there."

Mom had keyed the terminal to Mail and was scanning the menu in the cafeteria. "This weekend . . ." Mom looked up from the terminal at me. "I don't think so, Jen. Dad and RoseAnn are going to take you this weekend."

"He took me last weekend. I want to be with you."

Mom looked up at me, down at the terminal again, pressed the Return key. It was like she wanted to pay more attention to her mail than she did to me. She sat there running her hands over the keyboard and not looking up. When she looked at me, her eyes were sad like they'd been just before we moved.

"I'm going to marry Gerald," she said. I saw she had a

big ring on her finger. She turned it around as if she wasn't sure about it.

"We'll all be very happy," she kept telling me. I began to cry. She said I was going to live with them but I knew I was going to be all alone in the city. She had bought a doll for me that day, one of the new neural dolls that acted almost like a baby. She unwrapped it and laid it in my lap, I remember, and she made me say something to activate it. I said "Hello, Peggy." It was the most frightening thing when I talked to it, this piece of plastic opened its eyes, and they were shiny like water, like that doll had real eyes with real tears. It gurgled and reached out to me. I screamed and dropped it and ran out of the room.

I thought it was an alien.

That Saturday, Gerald and Mom went to Schenectady to meet his parents, and I was supposed to go visit Dad but I didn't. I was angry with both of them and I went to the kite festival alone.

It was October but warm and windy. I could smell hot peanuts and cider, like a circus. There were vendors moving through the crowd. I got a hot pretzel, one of those big hot doughy ones that make a whole meal, and then while I was eating it a girl set up a vendor's stand right next to me and she was selling those pretty-looking shimmershift metal ornaments that girls were putting in their hair. So I bought one, a silver-and-blue mesh that reminded me of the sky over Texas.

I went up near the top of the hill on the Common, by the old bandstand, where the kite people were setting up. Most of the crowd was down below, on the other side of the big light-green patch that was the Common marsh. In the bandstand a Jamaican bluehair band was playing some kind of Oriental-sounding music on steel drums and handbells and gongs, real nice, all rhythmic. I sat down where I wouldn't be noticed or get in the way and I watched the men and women setting up their kites, fitting the struts together and the kite-fabric over the struts. There were more kites than I'd ever imagined. Japanese kites shaped like stop signs with a big angry man's face. Stunt kites, bright triangles zipping from side to side in the big blue sky. Little diamond-shaped fighter kites. The kite flyers jerked on the strings and the kites sprang into the air on the updraft and danced and spun in the sky.

From here I could see everything from the kite making to the kites in the air, like a whole story from beginning to end. The way the kites were being put together reminded me of the construction workers on Gerald's site, how they moved all together, like they knew each other and liked each other, how they fit with the city. Maybe it would be like that with Mom and Gerald and me. The music was playing and the wind blew out of a blue Texas sky, and the men ran down the hill with their kites and the kites were leaping into the air and dancing. I suddenly felt like I had to be happy right then or cry. I had to do something. I jumped up and I spun myself around with my arms flung wide, and I sang my song Mom had taught me, and the tears stayed in my eyes and they didn't fall down.

Come tripping down the stair, pretty Peggy-O,
Come tripping down the stair, pretty Peggy-O,
Come tripping down the stair,
   Brushing back your yellow hair,
And bid farewell to your soldier O.

A strange man was watching me. His skin was tanned golden brown and there was curly black hair on him everywhere, not just on his head but on his chest, arms, legs. He wore banana yellow shorts and black high-top canvas basketball shoes and nothing else at all.

A new kite was going up. It wasn't like any other I had seen; it was like a box kite but it had wings, sharp-pointed and curved, and it was shiny black. It was like a box kite that was turning into an animal. Like a bird or a bat or one of the aliens out in the harbor, that no one in Boston had seen since the quarantine.

"Hello," he said, nodding his head slightly and smiling. "What's *that* kite?"

"A Cody." He smiled.

Cody. I knew that name, I was sure of it. It was a Texas name. "That's the prettiest kite I've ever seen." I watched it wing its way into the blue Texas sky. I wanted to throw my arms around the man who said a Texas name and bury my face in all that curly hair. —I knew it was a crazy idea, but I wanted to be with somebody I wasn't angry with. I gave him a big artificial smile because I didn't want him to get scared when I felt like crying.

Someone called to him. He ran off down the hill, laughing.

I was so disappointed. I couldn't watch him go away. I walked down the hill the other way, not looking where I was going. This side of the hill wasn't so warm; the shadow of the hill stretched all the way down deep into the Public Garden.

The Public Garden is the other half of Boston's downtown. The Common is an open space with lots of trees but the Public Garden has flower gardens and there's what used to be a little pond with swanboats—I'd read about it in *Make Way for Ducklings* when I was a kid, but the pond was bigger now and the ducks' island was gone.

It felt weird somehow in the park, with the long shadows and the middle of the bridge poking up out of the water. It took me a moment to figure out what was wrong. Everybody had gone to see the kite festival. It must have been as empty as before the aliens came, and I was the only person near the pond at all.

In the middle of the pond, some kind of animal poked a triangular head out of the water. He looked around and then at the shore. I held real still and I guess he didn't see me because he pointed his head straight at the shore. I watched a V of water trailing behind him, and a moment later he ducked and scrabbled up onto the bank and shook himself.

I guess I knew right away he wasn't a puppy chasing sticks, or a beaver or anything, though he looked something like a wet cocker spaniel but slick like an otter or maybe a beaver. He had something in his mouth, one of those little trash fish you saw in every street-corner pond. I figured then he was some kind of Boston animal, I just didn't know what kind. His fish was still alive. He laid one paw on it and bit out the throat delicately and began to eat.

Right then he saw me.

He flattened his body like I was going to hit him. I didn't move an inch. I didn't want him to go away. He looked real hungry, and besides, he was somebody, he was there, even if he wasn't anything but an animal. I just thought my thoughts at him. It's all right, I thought to him. I won't hurt you, I don't want your fish. You just sit there and eat. After a minute or so he took one quick bite out of his fish, moving so fast his head was a blur, then looked up at me, real still, as if I'd hurt him while his attention was somewhere else. But I hadn't moved. Then he took another bite and looked up at me again.

The fish was almost gone and I knew when it was done he'd be back in that water and I'd never see him again.

Real soft and slow, so I could hardly hear myself at first, I began to sing.

> "What will your mother say, pretty Peggy-O?
> What will your mother say, pretty Peggy-O?
> What will your mother say
>   When she finds you gone away,
> To places far and strange to Fennario?"

He whistled, and it was high and sweet and shrill, and it was no sound I had ever heard before.

It wasn't whistling. It was a warbling and a sort of sound high up where you can barely hear it, the kind of sound electronics make. He was looking at me and trembling all over, the way you might if you heard something you couldn't believe. I kept on singing. "—Your soldier is dead, and he died for a maid, the fairest maid in Fennario—"

He still looked scared, but he crept across the grass to me.

He wasn't a puppy at all.

He was heavy, solid. I knelt down and he climbed onto my lap, and I hugged him, nice and easy so he wouldn't be scared. He was a little wet, I didn't mind. He was trembling just like a purring cat, and for all he was thin, he had some muscle weight and big heavy bones. I felt like I hadn't really had anything or anyone to hold since Houston, and my hands could melt right into his fur, it was that thick. He put his hand against my throat—he had a hand, a little hand, leathery like a monkey's, with sharp long nails like claws. His eyes were round, bright, the color of old pennies, and I knew he was a real someone, just like me.

I said, "Do you want to feel my voice? I'll sing to you some more." I sang more songs I knew, but the only one he wanted was "Fennario." When I sang "As we marched down," he didn't do a thing, but when I sang "to Fennario" he trilled and slapped his tail against my lap.

"All right, you're Fennario," I said, and he nearly went crazy; he wriggled and slapped his tail and sniffed at my face, all the time making his warbling and chirping sounds. My face buzzed from the vibrations. He hugged himself up into my arms and I couldn't stop holding him. I sang his song over and over until my voice was hoarse.

I took him to see the kites. I carried him in my arms with my jacket over him, trying to hide his tail. Here goes the little Boston girl with her pet beaver. Don't anybody bother noticing, this happens all the time. We watched the kites with the Texas name, the Cody kites, and I didn't miss anyone. I wasn't scared. I was with my friend.

I carried him all the way home. At the university we lived on the third floor, and when I got there my arms and legs were so tired I just sat down on the linoleum. He started in right away exploring, scrabbling around looking at the linoleum and the concrete blocks and the wood the bunk bed was made out of and my old shoes. I wondered if he was hungry.

"I've got to get you some food."

Downstairs in the cafeteria they had tuna fish sandwiches for dinner, so I got all the tuna fish I could get and some potato chips and a squeeze bottle of Coke for me, and wrapped them all up in a napkin and brought them back upstairs. He ate the tuna fish, all but one sandwich which I got, and then a couple of the potato chips, but he didn't like them. He explored them though. He sniffed them all over, quick and sharp.

Then for a while I watched him exploring the room. He looked at everything, shortsighted, making his strange purr-whistling sound, getting his claws caught in the curtain over the window. He found the silver-color mesh in my jacket pocket. He turned it around in his hands and suddenly started bending it. His hands were quick and almost human-looking, though they had claws, strange hands like they didn't belong with the rest of his big thick body. A moment later he gave me what he had made.

It was a Cody kite, a perfect little one, an inch or so across. It just fit in my hand and it was the color of the Texas sky.

I couldn't believe that he had done something for me that I wanted. I was so happy and so bewildered that someone knew who I was. I cried and he sniffed my tears, quick and sharp, then slow. I looked at the kite and I thought,

This'll help me remember. I'll remember this day forever. This kite will be my lucky thing.

It was time to go to bed. I turned off all the lights but one, a dim one, sort of a night light. I hung the Cody kite real carefully on a piece of thread from the springs of the top bunk where I could see it. The metal sent off little shimmers of light.

I put my jacket and a sweater and the pillows from the top bunk down on the floor for a bed for him, and I got into bed and took off my socks and most of my clothes. I'd kind of hoped he didn't want to stay on the floor, and I was glad when, a moment after I'd turned off the light, he jumped onto the bed so heavily the bedsprings creaked. I patted the bed next me. "You can lie here, Fennario."

But that wasn't what he wanted. He wanted to explore me.

I leaned back on my pillow. It was dark and still warm, that warm October night. I turned up the dimmer on the light so I could watch him. He began sniffing at me. He poked his head with its little stiff whiskers right into my armpit and over my face and purr-whistled at me so it tickled, like the electronic sound had tickled my face in the Public Garden. Not a tickling, a vibration, but so delicate it was just like getting warm, so slowly you hardly noticed, as slow and delicate as growing. He snuffed at the soles of my feet, all around my hair and behind my ears, all the unimportant places I didn't even know or think about, he touched them all and explored them. So when finally he got to the place Mom told me never to touch, it seemed like it was just one more place to him. He lay with his head close to that secret place, not touching it even, but giving off that buzzing that was like language and eyes to him, it tickled me and made me happy and wanted, giggling, feeling some way I hadn't any words for, until I was laughing and sighing both at once. Somebody loved me—and I gave up everything else, because nothing mattered in comparison with having somebody love me. I took off all my clothes, right down past my T-shirt and underpants, so I was skin-naked, and I hugged Fennario and got him to lie next to me, and it was like my whole body was fingers to touch his fur with.

Somebody loved me.

I know what you're thinking, but it was innocent enough. Do you want me to say nothing happened? Nothing happened. Don't worry, you don't have to feel uncomfortable. I didn't feel alone or afraid, that was what happened. That was all.

But he and I were two of one kind, the way Gerald and Mom and I weren't, and that was what happened, and it happened forever.

He thumped down next to me again, sighing into my neck under my ears, and Fennario and I just lay next to each other and we just went to sleep, innocent as two babies, with the Cody kite glittering over us like a star.

When I woke up, the police had found him.

They woke me with their shouting. The light was in my eyes and there were people in my room, as many as could fit, steel policemen clumsy in big germproof suits. One of them held Fennario and he was wrapped in a plastic bag. I could see him through it, he was struggling and his fur was all pressed down over his body because of the bag. I don't know how he could breathe. He reached out, either his hand wasn't really in the bag, or he clawed it out, but he reached out his hand with the webs and the claws, and he snatched the Cody kite. He was looking at me, so desperate, I remember. He wanted me to see everything and to know.

"He's an alien!" someone screamed at me. And they were looking at me just the way they looked at him, bug-eyed, like I was some kind of monster and it was catching.

And it came to me all I had done, how I hadn't known, how he had come out of the water to me and I still hadn't known, how wrong I'd been and how I'd let him get close to all my secret places. "Alien!" I screamed too. I pointed my finger at him. "Alien!"

He reached out and took the Cody kite, and he crumpled it up in his hand, and he broke it beyond any hope of fixing.

When we went down to Fennario,
When we went down to Fennario,
Our captain fell in love
*   With a lady like a dove,*
Her name it was pretty Peggy-O.

Everything I remember is wrong. He couldn't have breathed in the germ-bag; he couldn't have reached out of it. Other people must have been in the Public Garden. Somebody must have seen me walking home with an alien. It must have been different. I've made all this up.

He was some sort of soldier, I guess, or a refugee, looking for someplace to hide in this little new-discovered watery harbor on the outside of nowhere. Afterward a whole lot of them came. Now I have a construction crew of Phneri. Three hundred of us, and we rebuild all those dissolving old brick houses in the Back Bay, not with orange prock and ribbons the way they do it in the Boston Cube, but with Phner handwork that looks like human, reshaping the bricks to the old structures the Phneri see. We help remember Boston the way it used to be, before we ever knew it.

The Phneri don't think like you and I do. Other people's structures are their memory. They buzz at a half-ruined piece of brickwork and can describe the person's hand that made it and the kiln it was fired in. They tell each other *esfnai* about structures like we tell stories about humans. But they don't have stories about themselves.

Once I asked them to tell me my story. I showed them my little broken piece of shimmershift and they said that it was broken by a Phner. They said it was hanging above his head and described the structure of his hand, but they couldn't tell what he was thinking. That's how they remember him and me, parts of a structure, bits and pieces, like broken bricks in Boston.

Phneri don't understand about time, so they don't know he was the first. I ask them, What was his name? They don't know that. Phneri don't have names until they're dead. " 'He Was Sung,' " they tell me for a name, but I know they're making it up because I want it. Then they dive back into the water. They're polite but they find me alien.

What happened? I ask. Who were we? Do you know what he thought? I don't know what he meant. Did he love me? Did I betray him? Did he forgive me?

The Phneri have only just one word for "know" and "understand" and "structure". It also means history, memory, and life, and it isn't what I mean. The word I mean is the one for a girl alone in Boston, who met someone new, a pet, a friend, someone to be hers, who fed him and took him home. Who knew that everything would be all right now that he was there. Who left a trail—because I must have left a trail—that led the police to him. Who shouted "Alien" at him.

Do I remember being the first child to meet an alien? I have memories. I tell them to you and I remember blue sky over Texas, wet fur, tuna fish sandwiches. You hear it and—I don't know what you hear, perhaps a story with a little shock in it, a dirty story, something to make you laugh and wish you hadn't. The Phneri remember metal being broken.

I keep trying to say what it was like to be first. I keep telling it, but I don't know.

The first holo movie I ever saw was about alien monsters. There were a hero and a heroine in it, but when the pictures came out of the screen and started getting too close to me, I rushed out of the theater just like the grown-ups did. It was different and I was frightened. The first people never can explain how frightening the difference is.

That's what it's like to meet the aliens: not to know. Not to understand. To scream and cry and run even though it was the first and special time and you were special and it's never going to be like that again. And never to be able to explain how it was good.

To be alien, to be alien too.

TOPOLOGY OF THE LOOPHOLE
GEOFFREY A. LANDIS

(DRAFT OF PAPER FOR SUBMISSION TO
PHYSICAL REVIEW A, JUNE 2021)

PRELIMINARY RESULTS OF THE CANADIAN AIR
FORCE/ESA/NATIONAL GEOGRAPHICAL SOCIETY JOINT EXPEDITION
TO INVESTIGATE ANOMALOUS SPACETIME REGIONS NEAR JUPITER

S.A. FFOEG, Z. HLOUSEK, E. HOLUPKA, V. O'DELL, K.H. O'BRIEN,
H. STODDART, K. DE, P. DE, M.J. MOELTER, J. SHERTZER,
A. JAGANATHAN, R.V. MULKERN, AND B. MING-CHAO.

ABSTRACT

THE MULTIPLY-CONNECTED SPACETIME topological anomalous region (MCSTAR), popularly but inaccurately referred to as a "loophole," was investigated in detail by a joint scientific expedition sponsored by the National Geographical Society (USA) and the European Space Agency. Transportation to the MCSTAR was provided by the Canadian Air Force spacecraft *Maple Leaf.* Spacetime curvature measurements were made using both a conventional Forward gravity gradiometer and a Kozak-Cho strain-gauge bridge. A long-wavelength spectrometer was used to look for spontaneous emission due to vacuum polarization effects, and a maser calibration standard measured relativistic time dilation in the vicinity of the MCSTAR. Null results obtained by these experiments are compared with the predictions of General Relativity and seven alternative gauge theories of spacetime topology. In addition to the prime observations, several secondary experiments were . . .

REFEREE'S COMMENTS:

In the opinion of the reviewer, this paper should be (check one):
[ ] Accepted as is for *Phys. Rev.*
[ ] Accepted in shortened form for *Phys. Rev. Letters*
[ ] Accepted with minor revisions as noted
[ ] May be acceptable after major revisions (see comments)
[X] Rejected

Comments: These guys didn't learn a damn thing about the Loophole. Throw this one back

The Amateur Scientist: Topology of Loopholes and Christmas Ornaments

BY BENJAMIN R. TARNE

SCIENTIFIC AMERICAN, JULY 2033

Ever since the famous "Splashdown Day" arrival of aliens in Boston Harbor on August 22, 2014, there has been much discussion among physicists of the loopholes the aliens use to cross interstellar distances without encountering the well-known difficulties described by Einstein. According to the famous story, the Theory of Relativity was explained to one alien visitor, who was then asked whether the star drive they used means that the theory was false. The alien reputedly replied, "No, we greenly pass camels through the loopholes." While the story is likely apocryphal, the name "loophole" stuck to the twists in spacetime used for shortcuts across interstellar distances.

As we now know, a loophole is a multiply-connected region of space which a spaceship can traverse to travel from one place to another without crossing the intervening distance. The term "loophole" is misleading: a loophole is shaped neither like a loop, nor a hole, but is instead spherical. Loopholes always come in pairs, with an "in" loophole corresponding to an "out" loophole somewhere else. More precisely, the "pair" of loopholes is actually only one physical object, with an "outside" in one place and the "inside," turned inside out, elsewhere. As we shall discuss shortly, this leads to several very interesting phenomena, quite aside from the obvious one of using a loophole for travel.

The "Earth" loophole is actually located at a position slightly outside the orbit of Jupiter, and leads to a "transport nexus" consisting of seven loopholes placed moderately close together in empty space about half a light-year from Beta Triangulum, a star otherwise of no particular interest.

Loopholes, as it turns out, cannot be placed on the surface of a planet, nor in close orbit to a planet. If two loopholes are not stationary with respect to each other, the physical structure of any object passing between them is randomized by an amount roughly proportional to the mismatch in velocity. This is not good if you want to travel (you wouldn't like to be randomized!), but allows the aliens to fine-tune the loophole.

A loophole cannot be passed through another loophole—if it were tried, both loopholes would vanish, leaving the far ends connected to each other. Since loopholes are apparently extremely difficult to manufacture (though nobody knows just how hard), this would be a very bad thing to happen. To bring a loophole to a new place, it has to be towed to position at slower-than-light speeds.

What would a loophole look like if you could bring one to Earth and look inside it? Suppose you had one loophole placed in Harvard Square and another one on a houseboat in the Boston Common. As you look into the Harvard loophole, you will see Boston turned inside out about the center of the loophole. This is known mathematically as an $1/R$ Transformation. The entire universe would appear to be compressed into the center of the loophole you are peering into. In its exact center is the edge of the universe, with very tiny galaxies just barely away from the center, the nearby stars slightly farther out, the solar system farther from the center yet, and close to the edge of the sphere Harvard Square (quite a bit distorted, of course).

In fact, this is not just an illusion: the entire universe actually *is* inside the loophole you're looking into. Paradoxically, the universe includes the loophole you're looking into, with the universe also inside of that, which includes the loophole, and so on.

Looking into the loophole, you might be tempted to think that you could reach in and touch distant planets, stars, and such. If you tried this, you would be surprised. As your arm reached into the loophole, it would appear to shrink and foreshorten in direct proportion to how far you reach. You would find that you can only touch things that are no farther than an arm's reach away from the loophole. This should come as no surprise.

The topology of the loophole illusion is in many ways similar to the view one sees by looking at the reflection of the world in a shiny sphere such as a Christmas ornament. For our experiments, you will need two or more shiny spheres. If Christmas-tree balls are not available, two large (at least one inch in diameter) ball bearings will also be adequate. . . .

Not for Broadcast
Steven Popkes

Excerpt from transcript of interview with Bishop 24

Joel McCracken Show

12 August 2020

>>>>>>>>>>>>NOT FOR BROADCAST<<<<<<<<<<<<<
>>>>>>>>>>>>NOT FOR BROADCAST<<<<<<<<<<<<<
>>>>>>>>>>>>NOT FOR BROADCAST<<<<<<<<<<<<<

McC: Ladies and gentlemen, for the first time anywhere, I would like to introduce to you Bishop 24, the sole representative of the Centaur species on Earth. Bishop, it's good to have you on the show.

Bishop: Thank you, Joel McCracken.

McC: Just Joel, please. Bishop, since you landed here, IPOB has been very secretive about you. Does your being here on the show tonight mean the silence is finally going to break?

Bishop: I will answer any question you ask, Joel McCracken.

McC:	Just Joel. Let's start with the more personal questions. Is 24 your name? I have a brother-in-law named Doctor. He gets a great referral service.

<audience laughter>

BISHOP:	My reference is Bishop 24. This has significance. There are other bishops in this section.
McC:	Are all of them Centaurs?
BISHOP:	How could it be otherwise?
McC:	Yes, of course. So, what church are you a bishop of? Will you be giving underwater sermons at the Mother Church?
BISHOP:	Pardon?
McC:	A bishop is a leader in the faith. What faith do Centaurs believe in?
BISHOP:	Faith. *<pause.>* A bishop—to us—is one who recognizes kinship with those not yet sentient.
McC:	Meaning us?
BISHOP:	Meaning the inhabitants of the earth, yes.
McC:	The Centaurs don't really think we're that bright, eh?
BISHOP:	It is not a matter of intelligence, but sentience. You, and other humans, are fah*!kder.

<*denotes mandible snap; ! indicates a head-shaking gesture.>

McC: Did you say farkakdah?

BISHOP: *<in German> Nein. Das ist ein gauz vershie-
denes wort.* *<in English>* You are not yet full members of the community, but you cannot be ignored.

McC: New kids on the block. You don't know what to make of us, then.

BISHOP: Exactly.

McC: Tell me, Bishop—

BISHOP.   Yes, Joel McCracken.

McC: Just Joel. Tell me, this word, sentient, has nothing to do with intelligence, right?

BISHOP: Only a correlation.

McC: What do you mean?

BISHOP: Just that species which are sentient are usually intelligent as well.

McC: There are some that aren't?

BISHOP: There's a kind of sea slug that grows deep in the intestinal waste of—

McC: Just a minute, Bishop. We'll be right back, folks, after this word from our sponsor.

McC: We have the honorable Bishop 24, the only
            Centaur on the Earth, as our guest today.
            So, Bishop, we're the new kids on the
            block. Are we going through some kind of
            test, then?

BISHOP: It is too early to test you. You would not
            let a child fly a plane. The child has not the
            skill. You would not let an untrained per-
            son manage your government—

McC: Why not? We've done it before.

<laughter>

BISHOP: —He has not the skill. Consider this a
            training period.

McC: So, what happens if we don't pass the
            test? We get F's on our report cards? Papa
            spank?

BISHOP: I don't know.

McC: What do you mean?

BISHOP: You would be on your own. There would
            be no law or sponsor to protect you.

McC: Do we need this protection?

BISHOP: IPOB thinks you do.

McC: Bishop—

BISHOP: Yes, Joel McCracken?

McC: Just Joel. Right folks?

CROWD: Right, Joel!

McC: There must be planets that have failed. What's happened to them?

BISHOP: I am not allowed to say.

McC: You make it sound positively threatening. *<pause>* Look, do you have any kids?

BISHOP: I have two pupae with me. At home, I have several offspring.

McC: Do they have to have tests? I mean some places here have big exams for kids, to get into high school or college. Do you have something like that?

BISHOP: A juvenile must pass a sentience test before it can become an adult.

McC: I got two kids, too. We sweated bullets to get them into college. One of them didn't make it. Instead, he went into the Army. So, if one of your kids failed his—sentience test? Is that what you said?

BISHOP: Yes.

McC: If one of your kids failed, what would happen to him?

BISHOP: He would be eaten.

McC: WHAT? YOU'D EAT YOUR OWN KID?

BISHOP: He would not be my child if he failed this test. He would be food.

McC: CHRIST! BISHOP—

BISHOP: Yes, Joel McCracken.

McC: JUST JOEL, GODDAMMIT! FOR CHRIST'S SAKE—

<commercial>

{end of transcript}

>>>>>>>>>>>>NOT FOR BROADCAST<<<<<<<<<<<<
>>>>>>>>>>>>NOT FOR BROADCAST<<<<<<<<<<<<
>>>>>>>>>>>>NOT FOR BROADCAST<<<<<<<<<<<<

WHEN THE PHNERI FELL
DAVID ALEXANDER SMITH

EVERY BOSTONIAN KNOWS where he was on December 4, 2022, for that was the night the Phneri fell from the sky.

Of course we had met some Phneri: the scouts who were looking for a home for their people. Some time, who knows how long ago, the Phneri fought an offplanet war with the Sh'k. The Sh'k are a waldo-building supercilious race, none of whose members have been seen in Boston. Little is known about them, and the Phneri aren't talking.

With their ability to *esfn*, the Phneri discovered that their planet was unstable and was going to destroy itself, so they set out on a great diaspora. Did the Sh'k fracture the Phneri planet? Did the Phneri, realizing their world must die, hasten its end themselves, so as to mourn it properly? Your guess is as good as mine.

All we know is that, very soon after the Boston Loophole was opened, the Sh'k won the war and killed most of the Phneri. Perhaps seeing Earth as an "uninhabited" planet (only a few aliens had followed the Gray Glubs here), the Sh'k decided to dump the Phneri in Boston. Whether they did this out of kindness, or just because it was convenient, the Phneri aren't saying.

The Sh'k built a huge combination ark and rabbit warren, a sphere almost a kilometer in diameter, and sent it through the Loophole into Solspace. Once here, the ship (it had no crew, being operated by Sh'k high-quality robots) oriented itself, made a course for Earth, took up orbit until it was over Boston Harbor, and . . . blew itself to pieces, scattering several million Phneri into the air.

The Phneri fell almost five kilometers down through the high atmosphere. Although they can accelerate their time-sense at moments of stress, their terminal velocity was so great (several hundred klicks an hour) that most of them—the old, the infirm, the babies, the unlucky—died when they crashed into the water.

With their exquisite sense of the structure of things, they could *see* their deaths coming as the earth rose like a giant blue fist. Because they have a strong race consciousness and a diminished sense of individuality, they *all* felt like they were *all* dying. As they fell, they mourned their deaths before they died, a huge symphony of trilling and clicking voices like a squadron of bees, until they hit the water.

About one-tenth of them—several hundred thousand brown-and-gold creatures, half-mad with pain and fear—survived impact. Those lucky few immediately started swimming (they swim like seals) for the nearest shore—South Boston.

To the few human beings awake to see it, the sky seemed to have opened up and rained cats and dogs. The Phneri poured in a steady torrent for several minutes, while people gathered along the shoreline, watching.

The splashes from so many bodies landing created a small tidal wave that washed over Logan Airport (it didn't get submerged until a few years later) and flooded many houses along the shoreline. Children sleeping on first floors drowned in their beds.

The Phneri swam closer and emerged from the water. To us, they resembled a new breed of rabid, oversize alien rats—the typical Bostonian's psyche was wobbly then. People panicked. Some got weapons and tried to kill the vermin. The Phneri defended themselves. Blood was shed. Both people and Phneri died—many more of them than us, of course. Some people fled, grabbing their children and vacating their houses. Desperate to find a place to recover, the Phneri moved in, dozens to a room.

Most settled in the waterfront houses and warehouse buildings. A few intrepid explorers ventured into Boston, so that by nightfall, there were small Phneri enclaves in any dark, moist, contained place within the Boston peninsula.

Any Phner, regardless of its status and generation, has a memory of that day: they call it the Endless Fall. Even sixty years later, Phneri have nightmares of falling through the clouds into Boston Harbor.

The event seared public consciousness. Nobody knew about the Sh'k, but everyone saw and smelled the millions of bedraggled corpses lining the harbor. The pervasive stink drove the smell of Phneri into the soul of everyone who lived here. By the time the city fished out the broken Sh'k drone remains, public sentiment had hardened. It's taken the Phneri at least sixty years to live down the damage to their reputation in Boston.

Anyone alive at the time knows where he was when it rained Phneri. It's one of those watersheds like the assassination of John Kennedy, the Apollo 11 landing, or the Bombing of Hull, that marks you for life. Any Irishman, whether or not he lived in South Boston, holds a deep-seated resentment of the Phneri, who drove us from our homes.

I was watching a late movie when I heard a hammering like a distant battle. Had the Loophole brought us a new war? I went to the window.

The sky was black with glistening hairy bodies that fell so fast and so heavily that you couldn't distinguish individuals, just shapes falling into the harbor with a sound like the thrumming of tom-toms. A few were landing on the streets in a staccato rhythm of splats and thuds. I looked up but could see no stars, only a torrent of small animals.

To this day, if someone drums his fingers idly on a tabletop, it summons back that strange night when the sky rained Phneri, when I wept without knowing why.

BOSTON IN 2030

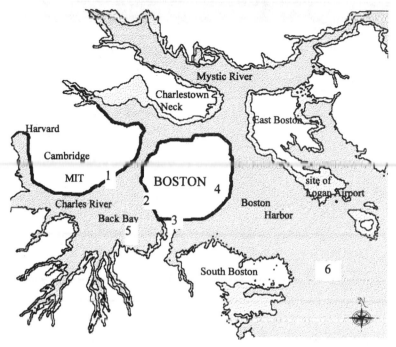

Fifteen years after the aliens' arrival, water has reclaimed Boston almost back to its Revolutionary War land contours. Most land near water is marshy and flooded. The shoreline changes constantly.

The Cambridge Wall (1) and the Boston Ring (2) are virtually complete. The Washington Street Gate (3) guards Boston's only land bridge to the outside.

Inside the Ring, Bostonians and aliens are jammed together in crowded confusion. Many of Boston's existing buildings are now encased in prock and connected to each other; Boston is well on the way to becoming a single huge warren.

In 2029 construction is begun on Miller's Hall (4), a showplace of alien technology and the center of alien life in Boston.

The Back Bay is partially submerged, and the Copley Mall, in the ruins of Copley Square, has become a semi-aquatic street market (5).

In the harbor, the headquarters of the Interstellar Port of Boston rises like a huge black needle (6).

Playing Chess with the Bishop
Steven Popkes and David Alexander Smith

Playing Chess with the Bishop:
An Analysis of Centaur Perception and Motivation

by Thomas Ryle

Natural History, June 2035

THROUGH HIS CONTROL of the Loophole, Bishop 24 wields enormous influence of over Bostonian (and thus Terrestrial) affairs. Understanding and predicting the Bishop's behavior is crucial to Earth's survival.

Unfortunately, Bishop 24 is the only Centaur on Earth; indeed, as far as we know, the only Centaur ever to visit Solspace. So what little we know of the Bishop's perception and motivation is built up only by observing him, and we have no way of knowing whether Bishop 24 is typical of his race or unusual, even insane.

Of course, even if the Bishop *is* insane, this knowledge can do us little good, since insane or not, he is the only Centaur we have and he shows no signs of leaving.

Understand the five ways the Bishop's perceptions and motivations differ from those of a human being and you will understand him. No one knows how to do that. But we can make some educated guesses.

Context-dependent definition. To human beings, the world consists of causes and effects; an effect without a cause is a paradox fully great enough to make us found a religion. To a Centaur, the universe has neither causes nor effects, only contexts, shifting from moment to moment.

A man drops a ball and it falls to the ground. He sees an object (the ball) and an action (falling), links them, and concludes that *if* he releases the ball, it *will* fall to the ground.

A Centaur drops a ball and it falls to the ground. The action (falling) and its context (ball in midair) are a contextual state which links two other states: ball in hand, being released; and ball on ground. He does not extract a logical conclusion; he notes a linkage, a change.

Context-dependent definition apparently makes it easy for the Bishop to learn human knowledge. By count verified from IPOB transcripts, he knows forty-two languages, and he appears to learn them nearly as fast as a human speaks them.

Arbitrary sense of time. The mental machinery whereby humans gain the ability to perceive cause-and-effect locks us into the assumption that time moves at a steady pace. The Centaur, on the other hand, appears to perceive time passing at whatever rate is appropriate to the context he is observing.

This can best be seen in conversation. Talk with the Bishop and he will respond at your pace. Speed up and so will he; slow down and he will too. When the Bishop speaks with a Gray Glub or a Phner, his time sense will change accordingly. In fact, it may be disconcerting to a human for the Bishop to carry on two or three simultaneous nonsynchronous conversations. We find nothing surprising that white light may contain waves of many different lengths; the Bishop finds nothing surprising that a particular instant contains many different paces at which time flows.

Arbitrary definition of friend and prey. Human beings tend to make judgments and then sustain them even in the face of contrary evidence: this person is my friend, that one is my enemy. Humans are not emotionally flexible. In part this arises from our mental machinery (cause-and-effect again), and in part because our relationships with other species are constant: tigers are predators whom we must fear, chickens are prey whom we may eat.

To the Bishop, however, these definitions can change in an instant, usually based on a contextual change. The Bishop can digest almost any carbon-based molecule. Food value depends primarily on the time the food spends in the Bishop's gut. Some foods are not worth digesting; others are worth digesting if the Bishop is not very hungry.

The Bishop has been known, for instance, to define an animal as food one moment and then, having been fed in another way, define the same animal as a pet. The Bishop sees no contradiction in this; the definition depends on context: I am hungry, and Fluffy the cat is food. I am no longer hungry, and Fluffy is my pet.

The Bishop appears perplexed when this behavior upsets human beings.

Clan Rules. The Bishop applies the friend/prey/food definitions to Centaurs, even its own offspring when they are not judged sentient.

The Centaur life cycle resembles invertebrates more than vertebrates:

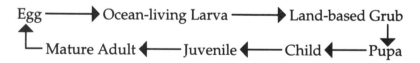

Starting with the egg, each phase begins with a large number and reduces that number. A Centaur may cast ten thousand eggs into the sea. Of these, a thousand survive to become larvae, and a hundred larvae become grubs. Each clan claims ancestral rights over a part of the sea; eggs or larvae from other clans which wander into that harvest area are defined as food and are eaten.

Centaurs eat even the land-based grubs as a matter of course, although the Bishop has expressed ambivalence which suggests a mild cultural taboo, similar for example to vegetarianism among some humans. Once the offspring reach pupa stage, the cultural taboos are strong, and when the young becomes a child, eating is forbidden.

Children are defined as *fah*kder* (the asterisk denotes a mandible snap), which is loosely translated into English as "potential for sentience." The word should not be confused with *fah*!kder* (the ! denotes a head-shake accompanied by the rustle of legs against one another), which, loosely translated, means, "inedible by reason of insanity." The Bishop uses this word when referring to all of humanity.

Children have the potential for sentience, which is determined via what the Bishop refers to as a "sentience test." What constitutes this test, how it is administered, and when, are unknown. Children who pass their sentience tests are defined to be adults. Children who do not pass are defined to be food and are eaten, apparently without a second chance.

To a Centaur, these changes are instantaneous and dramatic. A child becomes an adult or food in an eyeblink. A pupa becomes a child at a similar precise instant.

The Centaur knows intellectually that a pupa can become a child, but until the instant this occurs the pupa is not, never was, and cannot be a child. It is perfectly proper for a Centaur to realize that a pupa is going to become a child and to eat the pupa seconds before this would have occurred, thus eliminating any potential ethical dilemma.

Religion. Humans use religion to explain man's place in the cosmos. Man is greater than some creatures, less than others. Humans make their god human; he is a benevolent, powerful, stern father, or a nurturing, all-embracing mother goddess. Chimpanzees confronted with a thunderstorm perform a thunder dance where they shake their limbs and roar back at the storm. Humans pray to a god to give them rain or eternal life.

Centaurs let the sea rear their young into childhood. They perceive the world in context. Their religion does not involve faith; it involves seeing. It is a description of Centaur reality, not Centaur hope. It is the ability to see the entire universe in its context, to see every connection to every other context. Holiness, then, is seeing further than others.

Thus, the Bishop seeks to see the context of humanity, and to judge, via a sentience test which still lies before us, if we are sentient, and therefore defined as adults. If we can be adults, then we are kin, but we may not be clan.

The Bishop will design, create, or observe the sentience test most appropriate for humanity.

If we are kin, we have the responsibilities of kin. The Bishop brings us toward the sentience test to determine this. Delivery and management of the Loophole may be, indeed almost certainly is, part of the Centaur's preparation for humanity's sentience test.

By Centaur definition, sentients are capable of choosing their own best interests. This is not an altruistic statement. Being holy, and thereby being able to see further than others, the Bishop perceives when humanity can best see its own interest.

Pre-sentients may have the ability to recognize their best interests; the Centaur waits by observing and testing. Non-sentients lack the ability. By failing the appropriate test, pre-sentients can become non-sentients. Non-sentients can be food.

How the Bishop might carry out his threat, if indeed a threat is implied by any of the foregoing, is unknown. All attempts to extract even the slightest clue from the Bishop have been deftly rebuffed. We speculate, in fact, that the Centaurs have limited themselves to only one member per species so as to prevent any possibility of information contamination which might invalidate our sentience test. This is, of course, pure (and possibly dangerous) speculation.

The Bishop has told us that we are pre-sentients. He has not told us what our sentience test is, when it will occur, how we might pass it, or what will happen to us if we do not.

We can be forgiven, I think, if we choose not to challenge the Bishop's control over the Loophole and thus remain, at least for the present, inedible by reason of insanity.

LETTER TO THE EDITOR
ALEXANDER JABLOKOV

FOUND IN THE FILES OF THE *BOSTON BUSINESS LEADER* AFTER ITS
2037 PURCHASE AND DISSOLUTION BY NYO ENTERPRISES

LETTER DATED 20 SEPTEMBER 2035
ADDRESSED TO STANLEY KALMBACH, EDITOR

Dear Mr. Kalmbach:

I am writing in response to your rather intemperate
editorial of September 18. While it is not normally the
practice of my employer to respond to even the most
slanderous of journalistic accusations, since such are
part and parcel of your sordid business of satisfying the
baser appetites of your readers, we believe that in this
case you have gone so far beyond the bounds of truth
that you need to be reined in.

First and foremost, your so-called "Bar Harbor
Compact" is a chimera and a delusion. It is true that
certain key figures in the Boston business community
were vacationing on Mount Desert Island in June of
2031, but this is scarcely unusual. Bar Harbor is a well-
known summer resort. Nor would it be unusual if they
had dinner together and spoke, since they have many
mutual interests. Some interim business agreements
may have been reached. This is normal business practice. To see in this some sort of sinister cabal is sheerest
paranoia.

Second, you seem to see the civic activities of the Boston Chamber of Commerce as some sort of cover for the greed of this cabal. The BCC is an association of community-minded businessmen. Its operations are open to any scrutiny you care to give. It has hundreds of members, many of whom are insulted by your derogatory references to them as "tools of the cartel."

Finally, there is your use of the term "cartel" itself. While there are natural divisions of business interest, defined solely in the interest of economic efficiency, there is no massive conspiracy in restraint of trade. Decisions on which business organization is dominant in what area of trade is a result of the basic efficiency of the market.

We do not intend any legal action at this time. We feel that, properly informed, you will cease these ridiculous accusations. Since you are a business paper, we are sure that you will soon understand the flow of business here in Boston.

Sincerely,

Edward Stone
for Mi Nyo,
Nyo Enterprises

WHO IS VENTURE CAPITAL?
DAVID ALEXANDER SMITH

WHO IS VENTURE CAPITAL?

Venture Capital Limited Partnership is a company
owned and operated by humans in a joint venture
with Bishop 24. Under our ninety-nine-year
Loophole Lease from Bishop Holding Company,
Venture Capital makes investments to benefit
humanity through the services and wonders
brought to Earth through the Loophole.

Venture Capital has three main businesses:

Venture Travel and Shipping provides transit across
the Loophole to people of every race, color, creed,
or place of planetary origin. The Loophole Lease
requires us to be non-discriminatory.
*Warning: bringing prohibited materials (consult
your ticket for details) through the Loophole will not
only cancel your ticket, but also expose you to criminal
prosecution and probable physical harm.*

Venture Investments provides startup funding for
dozens of Earth businesses capitalizing on the

investment opportunities brought through
the Loophole.

Venture Targive, which we own equally with Earth
Targive Products Inc., is the exclusive franchisee
for dequarantined Targive technology.

Shares in Venture Capital are traded on every
major world stock exchange and are owned by
millions of people just like you. Over the last
twenty years, they have produced a combined
annual compound yield of 16.4%.*

Come join the future! Invest in Venture Capital.

*After-inflation pre-tax buying power, measured in the standard OECD basket of
currencies, after dividends, capital gains, stock dividends, international tax adjust-
ments, and currency revaluations are taken into consideration.

IPOB DINING HALL PROCEDURES
ALEXANDER JABLOKOV

MEMORANDUM

Date: 20 January 2038

From: Siegried Altona, Assistant Director, Food Services

To: Maria Miatse, Under Director, Public Relations

Re: Recent controversy surrounding proposed integration of thirty-seventh-level dining area

It has been recently proposed that the dining area on level 37 of the IPOB Needle be integrated so that all sentient member and associated species of IPOB will be permitted to be served there, and expect to have their metabolic needs met. It is felt in some quarters that it is high time that separate but equal facilities—which are discriminatory, derogatory, and insulting to our fellow sentient species—be eliminated in favor of a common facility.

This proposal has cogent social, moral, and economic arguments in favor of it. It will improve the image of IPOB as forward-looking in the alien relations area, always something we have always been on the cutting edge of. It is morally and ethically dubious to separate different species by style of alimentation, particularly as they are integrated in a variety of other ways, such as conference facilities, audio-visual aids, and some toilets, though, of course, not all. It is expensive to maintain seven separate dining areas, with separate cooking/preservation/maintenance facilities. All arguments are in favor of it.

Except for one, which I must mention. It is insane.

Sh'k use as a food source a variety of live hopping rodent. That is, they don't actually eat the rodent itself, but the particular species of body lice that infest it. They have bred both rodent and louse to a symbiotic relationship, so that the unfortunate rodent is literally dripping with a mass of lice equal to half its body weight. Its body is invisible beneath the crawling mass. A Sh'k's method of eating resembles the way you or I would eat corn on the cob. The leftover rodents are left on the floor to run around, scavenge, and develop a fresh crop of lice. As a complete ecological food system, it has its merits.

Rezz, from Xi Puppis VI, do not eat still-living things. They eat dead things, like humans do. Unlike humans, they prefer *long*-dead things. *Large,* long-dead things. Rezz evolved as scavengers on the vicious predators of their low-g home planet. These predators hunted herbivores resembling blue whales with dozens of legs, massing 30,000–80,000 kg. Rezz still prefer food killed by these predators, which have razor-sharp claws a meter long, but shipping the multilegged blue whales to Earth has, fortunately, proved impossible, so they don't bring the predators either, saving us a nasty security problem. They accept deliveries of killed meat. Chunks of meat massing 2000–5000 kg. are left in the dining area until spoilage is complete. The heat generated by the decay bacteria typically raises the center of the meat to a temperature of 300–400° Celsius. Ignition has been known to occur. The smell has been defined as "aggressive" and "vile" by people with little interest in pursuing interplanetary amity.

Gliuksk, from Beta Hydri X, eat what we would consider a more normal style of food: harvested plants and newly-dead flesh, prepared with a variety of sauces and condiments. It is in the sauces and condiments that the drawbacks lie. Gal, a favorite sauce, is made up of a fulminant compound of arsenic with a piquant hint of beryllium. Mnkrob powder, used in an otherwise inoffensive dish of lentils and root vegetables, contains various tasty oxides of plutonium, cerium, uranium, and neptunium. The dish warms without cooking, and is popular on Gliuksk picnics. A fizzy children's drink gives off clouds of chlorine gas.

If, as proposed, we go forward with the integration of the dining areas, I will, of course, do my best to see that everything proceeds smoothly, with minimum disturbance. Then I will bring my lunch, and eat in my office.

Siegried Altona

So You Want to Meet the Bishop?
Steven Popkes

For approval: Draft of pamphlet, IPOB Pub. #2040–39a
Main head: So You Want to Meet the Bishop?
Subhead: IPOB Alien Etiquette Guide #30

LIKE MOST OF us, you probably have met only the most
common aliens in Boston. You've probably walked around
the North End and had the popcorn aliens try to sell you
your own name, or watched the Phneri at play along the
Back Bay ruins. Maybe you've taken a whaler tour into the
harbor around the IPOB Tower, hoping to get a glimpse of
the exotic and the strange, the misshapen and the ugly. All
of the aliens are strange to us, from the ugly-beautiful
Koltsoi to the never-seen Targives. Bostonians, and
humans in general, are excited and attracted to the exotic
and the strange.

Bishop 24 of Boston is not only exotic and strange, but
unique! He is the only Centaur ever to have visited
Boston.

The Bishop is the head of Venture Capital, the firm
which manages Boston's Loophole, and as such is a very
busy and important alien indeed. This pamphlet is
intended to help humans who wish to speak with our
unique and distinguished guest.

BISHOP 24: The small, tapering part of the Bishop, with the large eyes and the mandibles, is his head. Midway down the body, or *thorax,* are the Bishop's claws. The smooth rounded base has several hundred small limbs. The Bishop can run faster than a cheetah and catch a fly by its wings.

The Bishop speaks forty-two human languages. If your language is one of those listed, please feel free to speak as quickly or as slowly as you wish. The Bishop will understand you and will be able to speak in return.

THE BISHOP'S OFFICE: The round object with the corrugated surface is the Bishop's desk. Do not be intimidated by any small animals that move along it. The Bishop keeps a few pets as a part of his religion. You may remark on these animals as you wish.

DO NOT AT ANY TIME OR IN ANY MANNER AT-TEMPT TO TOUCH OR FONDLE OR REACH OUT TO ANY OF THE BISHOP'S ANIMALS. IF YOU ARE INVITED TO DO SO BY THE BISHOP, POLITELY DECLINE.

Protocol demands that the Bishop speak second to you. Therefore, enter the room, stand in front of the desk, and announce yourself. You may use any name you wish, but you must be forewarned that whatever you name yourself to the Bishop will be how the Bishop refers to you from then on. Many visitors prefer strict formality.

The Bishop will then rise and announce himself and

snap his mandibles. This is a harmless gesture and should
not be intimidating.

From this point until the interview is concluded, the
protocol is very flexible and comfortable. You may stand
or sit, smoke or not smoke. We suggest you move slowly.
The Bishop will determine the pace of your discussion
from the cues you give him. If you move or speak quickly,
the Bishop will move or speak quickly with you. This has
been known to make some people uneasy.

**IF THE BISHOP OFFERS TO TEST YOU, OR SEEMS
TO FEEL YOU HAVE ASKED TO BE TESTED, IM-
MEDIATELY ASK THE NATURE OF THE TEST. IF
THE TEST IS REFERRED TO AS A SENTIENCE
TEST, IMMEDIATELY DECLINE, POLITELY BUT
FIRMLY.**

The Bishop has a habit of moving in a quick, jerky
fashion when his attention is distracted. This is unnerving
to some people and has been known to cause epileptic
seizures.

**IF YOU KNOW YOURSELF TO BE AN EPILEPTIC,
PLEASE NOTIFY THE RECEPTIONIST ON DUTY.**

Either you or the Bishop may request that the interview
be ended by the extension of an open hand in the
handshake manner. The Bishop will then shake your hand.
It is considered bad form to faint at this time. The
interview will then be over and you may leave.

Bathrooms are provided adjacent to the doors of the
Bishop's office. If you require either tranquilizers or
motion sickness medicine, these will be provided for you

before or after the interview by the receptionist and will be courtesy of IPOB.

We at IPOB hope you will enjoy your visit with the Bishop.

> **IPOB ASSUMES NO RESPONSIBILITY FOR ACCIDENTS RESULTING FROM FAILURE TO FOLLOW THESE INSTRUCTIONS.**

Camomile and Crimson; or, The Tale of the Brahmin's Wife
Geoffrey A. Landis

1. *A Morning of Onyx and Pearl*

WISPY FOG, LIKE an air of age and mystery, hangs over the city. Tendrils of mist rise from the canals like uncertain wraiths, to hesitate for a moment in the air, then spin away on urgent business in silent eddies behind speeding waterstriders. Overhead, glass-filament bridges like spiderwebs spun of metallic candy arch across the canals. It is a baroque and jaded city, a city where you can get anything if you know where to ask: love philtres of guaranteed efficacy, amulets of power crafted by forgotten alien hands, strange sensual pleasures to titillate the jaded, or silent death for those more jaded still. It is a city of the very rich, and of the desperate poor.

It is all this and more.

It is Boston, in the autumn of 2039.

The water taxi coasted to a stop, settling into the dirty green water. Elliot Sheridan Endicott spoke a word to the driver and stepped out into the Back Bay fog. It was, perhaps, a sleazier part of town than the Beacon Hill clubs and brownstones he was normally used to.

The breeze was damp, and he wrapped his cape tighter around his body. The jewel at his throat glistened for a moment in a vagrant beam of sunlight as he hesitated for a moment, then entered the discreetly marked storefront office.

The 'eye spread the photos out for him. Elliot bent over to look closer. Anne eating lunch at a trendy canalside restaurant, alone. Anne reading a book elegantly bound in gold-embossed plastic. Anne wandering through the Gardner Museum, her eyes wide and quizzical. Anne at the Copley Cube, indecisive over a selection. Anne taking a bath, half-hidden in a fairyland of bubbles. Alone. Alone, alone, alone.

"She's clean, Mr. Endicott."

He shook his head. "You haven't looked hard enough."

"We're the best in the business, sir."

He knew that. If they hadn't been the best, he wouldn't have hired them. "She's fooling you."

The detective frowned. "If you could give us even a hint of reason *why* you suspect she's deceiving you, then maybe we could . . ."

The pale blue stones on Endicott's bracelet shimmered in tones of orchid. He paused, concentrating on slowing and deepening his breathing until it returned to a quiet milky blue. "I don't *suspect*. I *know*. And if you can't find out who it is, then I will go somewhere else. Good day."

"That, of course, is your choice, sir. Our courier will bring your final bill in the morning. But if we can't find him, then nobody can."

Elliot knows he cannot be satisfying her, though she may pretend otherwise. A young woman like her, ripe body, full of life. She will have a lover, he knows, someone who will give her what he cannot. When he confronts her with the evidence, she will tearfully confess, say how she couldn't help herself. They will have a joyous reconciliation. After, he will give her his blessing, warning her never again to attempt lying to him. He has no need to fear any young studs. They could give her physically what he could not, but in the end, he would hold her with his poetry, his culture, his conversation; areas in which no upstart water-rat could possibly compete. She will always return to him. This he also knows.

But who? *Who?*

Perhaps she has corrupted the detective, he thought, striding purposefully into the mist-entwined air. Perhaps they are in collusion, laughing at his foolishness.

With a sudden impulse he tossed the folder of information the detective had given him into the Marlborough Street canal. A single still of Anne slipped out and hovered just under the water, staring up at him with a wide-eyed look of faint surprise.

The morning haze had burned away. Windows glistened in iridescent colors, staring down at Elliot like strange insectile eyes.

The sign on the shop says simply *Artisan*. It means jeweler, technician, craftsman, engineer: artificer. The artisan subcontracts for Boston University, hand-crafting micro-electronic circuits for arcane research projects. In his spare time he grows gems in hand-blown glass bottles and crafts jewelry and trinkets for the few who can both appreciate and afford handmade ornaments. His shop is never busy, but he does not work cheaply.

The shop smells of orange and cinnamon. The artisan is a skinny, twisted black man, his eyes too large and too far apart, his fingers misshapen as if they had long ago been caught in a vise and smashed, mending *wrong*. It takes a moment to notice that he is not human at all. Then the wrong angles take on proper perspective; the subtle shadings on his skin are seen as a delicate patterning, not a hideous disease; his stature and shape seen as an almost fragile beauty. His voice is unexpected, soft and sensual, almost caressing the ears.

"My good Doctor Endicott. How nice again to see you, how nice indeed. Have you work for me, some assignment to challenge these clever hands, or are today you just browsing?"

Endicott paused, examining an exquisitely carved eighteenth-century ship. Sculpted out of superconductor, she floated in the air, the tip of her keel almost brushing the surface of what must be a magnet. With each puff of air, she bobbed and dipped. Elliot frowns; it is the Nyo chip

He puts the ship down, brushing the tips of his fingers against his cape. "I would have an assignment, if I thought your hands would take interest, but I now realize it could hardly challenge hands such as yours, so justly famous. I will not bother you with mentioning it."

"Ah, such a pity. I have been here hoping for some challenge for these hands. Surely, there is ever beauty to be created in even the most common crafting, but from time to time they long for something more . . . unusual."

"Of course. Such hands as yours deserve only the most difficult projects."

"Indeed. Alas, though, patrons who can appreciate such work are rare."

"Alas." He examined one of the gems, a rose crystal with tiny flecks of gold glittering inside. "This one is quite interesting. What is it?"

The artisan—Endicott never knew his name, nor even if he had one—glanced up. "Yes, isn't it? It's a crystal of my own devising. A variation on chromium-doped aluminosilicate, with traces of manganese and beryllium. Do try the magnet, please."

Next to the jar sat a metal rod that he guessed to be the magnet. He waved it by the jar, and the gold flecks turned greenish, then deep blue, and seemed to sparkle and swirl. "Beautiful."

"This project of yours, what would it be?"

190 ■ GEOFFREY A. LANDIS

"Purely to satisfy your curiosity, I have been thinking of having a ring made to give my wife for our anniversary."

"To be sure, more than a ring merely?"

"To be sure. But it must be beautiful. Unique, ornate, cultured."

"A pity that your project will so lack interest, since these hands have been waiting for just exactly such a work. But tell me more about this work you will be having some other artisan to do. If you wish, perhaps I can give you some advice."

Endicott smiled.

The ring was magnificent. As Anne put it on, it shrank to fit her finger. The jewel took on color, deepening from gray to a pale opalescent turquoise as it picked up heat from her hand. "Oh! It's marvelous!"

She is beautiful, beautiful; and it makes his heart break that she could lie with such an innocent, childlike smile.

Or perhaps his suspicions are baseless. When he sees her smile, Elliot believes anything she tells him. He cannot believe it, that she would be, could be, so true to him—to him!—and yet . . .

The doubt is tearing him apart. He has to know for sure.

2. *AFTERNOONS OF DUSKY JADE*

She had been to all the right schools, and there was nothing there she wanted. Earnest young men of good families had sought her; she had only laughed. Football players tried to mount her as another triumph they deserved for merely existing; she hardly even bothered to laugh. None of them had even tempted her. And then, an hour after she'd met Elliot, in a Harvard Square bookstore, she'd fallen. Later, they had both stopped to watch a street musician play saxophone while juggling, and she saw that they'd both bought the same book. She loved him for everything he was—cultured, poetic, smooth; and for everything he wasn't—rough, shallow, unsophisticated. He brought her roses and champagne; a dozen violets in blown-glass goblets; midnight gondola rides through the canals under the full moon. She treasured his lovemaking, his tenderness, imagination, attention. She loved the way his mustache tickles her, the pungent aroma of his pipe, which he always lit to draw no more than one or two puffs of, after dinner, his soft warm voice as he whispered poetry for her alone.

The corner store was just close enough from their Commonwealth Avenue townhouse to walk to, just far enough not to intrude its commerciality into their lives. It sold beans, milk, tomatoes and cocaine hand-cultivated in Boston roof gardens, bootleg electronics and vid, Targive dust-suckers, replica scrimshaw, alien geegaws and trinkets. Above the counter a hand-lettered sign said Appliances Repaired. It smelled of spices and baked beans.

He was rough. His arms were strong and hairy. He wore an old-style biocling shirt, the patterns faded and stained, inferior merchandise bought wholesale at the Back Bay end of Copley Mall. A name badge over the pocket labelled him "Rick."

The shop was full of calico kittens. The mother cat dozed patiently in a corner, while two kittens stalked and attacked Anne's ankles. She smiled and picked one up. "He's so cute. What's his name?"

"That little one's Sally McGiddykitty." He nudged the other one with a toe, which the kitten promptly attacked. "This one here's Martha." He paused. "Gotta have cats in a place like this, otherwise the rats would get too forward, you know?"

"Oh! You have *rats* here?"

"Lady, this is Boston, you know? There's rats everywhere."

Rich bitch, he thought, but then she smiled and he forgot everything else.

She wandered through the store, occasionally pausing to look at something, but not buying. At last she ordered half a pound of tea, a blend of camomile and vargaspice that was one of the shop's specialties. He bagged it for her, and she turned to leave.

He touched her arm, and she turned back to him questioningly. "Hey. What's your name?"

She paused. "Anne."

"Anne. You live around here?"

She jerked her head. "Toward the hill."

"Do you know just how beautiful you are?" His words were hushed.

She laughed. "Thank you. I'm also married."

He shrugged helplessly. "I'm Rick."

"Oh." She dropped a bill on the counter and walked out. Her fingers were long and slender. On her right hand was a single ring, an elaborately carved braid of gold, copper, and iridium, coiled around a stone which speckled with crimson and azure that seemed to swirl and dance. He looked up just as the door shut. Her voice seemed to linger in the spice-scented air. *"Au revoir,* Rick."

Rick pays the gangs for the right to operate. He sells things in sealed boxes from his back dock, and doesn't ask what they are. One man sells them to him, another man buys. In turn, nobody else competes in his territory.

She was not drop-dead gorgeous, but rather had a beauty that showed in her poise, her self-confidence, the correctness of her dress, the slightest hint of Boston accent. She was so far above him that he could barely imagine her talking to him. He was captivated. While waiting on customers he would suddenly think of her and lose his train of thought, have to ask the customer again what they wanted. His heart pounded when she came in the door.

* * *

She is faithful, she is faithful. Endicott's heart sings. She loves only me, I know it, the ring does not lie. How, how could I ever have been so lucky?

When next she went into the shop, Anne's gaze wandered everywhere, across the shelves, down at the floor, but never met Rick's eyes. As she left, he pressed something into her hands. She didn't look at it until she was well clear of the shop, then she glanced down and laughed. It was a water lily. He could not possibly have known that such a gift would be considered an insult in polite society. He'd meant well; in its own way, the gesture was rather sweet, and the flower was quite pretty. She held it awhile as she walked, and then dropped it into a canal.

Rick caught her in the corner and held her wrists in one hand. Like a small animal in a trap, she was caught. Her hair smelled like the first snowstorm of winter. The Brahmin, he thought, they can afford those exotic scents. He too was trapped, captured. He tried to say something, but suddenly realized that he knew no words to express what he felt. He started to kiss her, and she turned her head, so he kissed the side of her throat. He rested his cheek against hers. She softened for a moment, then broke free with a peculiar noise that was half a sigh, half a protest.

"That was uncalled-for."

"I'm sorry." His eyes did not look sorry.

The colors in the ring swirled and danced. "I'm sorry too," she said. "But I'm faithful to my husband." The ring remained blue. "I'm not interested."

The blue of the ring swirled with pink.

He was out of line, way out of line, and Anne knew she had to put him back in his place with a few well-chosen words, but the words she needed would not come to mind.

Her head was fuzzy; her heart pounded. But what could she do? She knew that to avoid the nearby store altogether would excite Elliot's suspicions even more. Could she just tell him that she had had a passing infatuation with a store clerk, but it was nothing, she was faithful still? He would never believe it.

And she couldn't put off shopping forever. Already they were almost out of fresh tea. Surely if they ran out, Elliot would notice something?

3. *Evening in Crinoline and Camomile*

Rick pictured her face, and the ring flashed into his mind. The ring. It had to be biodesign crystal; nothing else would change with her moods so quickly. Alien, expensive. She was out of his class, he thought. Forget her. But didn't the high-caste get lonely too?

The ring. Funny how his thoughts kept coming back to it. What did it react to? Blood pressure? Something more complicated?

What was it trying to tell him?

She walked with hesitation, looking every direction except toward the store. He ran to catch her, leaving the shop open behind him. She turned her back.

"Listen, I'm sorry." She was silent. "Really."

He stared at her back as she walked away.

It was a week later before he saw her again. He explained himself to her, hopeless, helpless.

"My mother was Brazilian. Is this a crime? If so, I am guilty, though you charge me with something I had no control over. She was very beautiful, my mother. That I can remember. She used to play maracas in the Samba band, at Carnival. She was tall, and stood with her back absolutely straight. She died when I was eight, in the riots.

"I never had a chance to go to college. Is this a crime? I longed to go; but the expense, it was impossible. We barely scraped by; times were not good. We put together all the money we had or could borrow to send my younger sister Elise to college, to music school in New York. She left, and never returned. But I have no regrets. She deserved her chance. What did she have to return to?

"I aspire to greater things, to arts and literature and love that they say is above my station. Is this a crime? And I aspire to love you. Is this a crime? If it is, I must plead guilty, guilty in the highest degree, and throw myself on your mercy."

When he finally caught up to her all his words deserted him.

She looked at him, though—so much better than her looking away!—but still silent. Approval? Disapproval? The ring was muddy, no help in fathoming her emotions. He sighed. "I'm sorry, I should apologize."

"Your apology accepted," she said, quickly. The ring speckled vermilion and blue. A half-truth, he thought. What does that mean?

The day was cold with the preparations for winter. She walked without thinking and gave a tiny jerk when she looked up and saw where she was. She tried desperately to picture Elliot's face, remember his voice, his words. All she could see was Rick. She had to break free. With a huge effort, she stepped back and walked past the shop.

When next she entered the shop the canals were glazed over with the first ice of winter. Down the canal, people were out fixing ice-blades on their 'foils. The mood was gay and festive.

The shop was warm and cozy. Rick lifted her hand, admiring the ring. She avoided his eyes, but could not summon the strength to pull her hand away. "He gave you that ring?"

"Elliot. Yes. Isn't it beautiful?"

"And I bet he holds your hand, looks you deep into the eye, and asks if you're faithful to him."

"Surely that is no business of yours?"

"And then when you assure him that you are, he drops his eyes, ashamed to have ever doubted you, and stares at your ring."

"Why—how did you—"

"He doesn't trust you, Anne. Watch the ring. Now say something untrue. Come on, anything."

"I, I—" She laughed softly. "The moon is a huge ball made of bright blue cheese." The ring was a contemptuous red. She stared at it, her laughter fading. "No."

"It is."

"He wouldn't . . . he couldn't violate my trust like that."

"Tell me you don't find me interesting." She shook her head, tried to pull her hand free. But she didn't pull very hard.

"Come in back." She hesitated. "I won't hurt you. I just want to show you something." In the back room were appliances in various stages of repair, coffeemakers, vid cartridges, biochips opened up with gleaming crystals exposed, micromanipulators poised to the side. He put her hand on the image stage of a zoom viewer. An enlarged vid image floated in front of her, gaudy with the bright falsecolor of elemental identification. He zoomed and focused, found a particular spot, zoomed in until it filled the air. "Here. Biosensors. Skin conductivity, heart rate." Arcane patterns, thin-film circuitry revealed in green falsecolor glow against the gold. He rotated the ring, zoomed out. "There. Muscular microtremor sensor, synaptic firing pattern analyzer. Beautiful piece of workmanship. Made by an artist. But it's a lie detector, without doubt."

"Oh," she said. She pulled away her hand. How could Elliot have done this to her? He had violated their trust.

Worse, he had given her over—unintentionally perhaps, but no less completely—to a stranger.

No, she thought. Not a stranger. She was lost, adrift. She didn't know how to feel.

"Tell me you don't find me interesting." He watched the ring. She said nothing.

"I'm not a poet. I know. I've never had the chance to be. I'm rough, uncultured, all the things you despise. I can't help the way I am, my love. Quote poetry to me, Lady Anne. I will listen to you. Teach me, sculpt me, make of me what you will. Am I the less for being rough? I am a diamond, for you alone to carve."

"I . . . I have to go. Someone is waiting for me. A, a girl-friend. We're meeting this afternoon to go shopping."

He held her hand and brought it up between their faces, turning the ring so they could both see it. "Say you are going to meet a girlfriend this afternoon. Say it."

She was silent.

"Just say that you aren't excited by the idea of letting me make love to you." She shook her head. "*Say* it."

"I don't want to go to bed with you," she gasped.

The ring blazed with the intensity of her lie.

He stroked her hand, slowly, gently. "My love."

"He will be suspicious."

"My love, he will be suspicious of you no matter what you do. He will be suspicious of you until his dying day."

"What will I say?"

He reached into a cup behind him, pulled out an ice cube, pressed it to her finger. She jerked back, startled, but he held her hand firm. In a moment the ring loosened. He pulled it off her finger, looked at it for a moment, then put it on his own finger. "I've loved you from the moment I first laid eyes on you," he said. "I will never hurt you, I will never lie to you, I will never try to make you into something you are not. I love you." The ring was a deep, magnificent azure.

She trembled. "What can I do? What could I tell Elliot?"
He smiled. "I know a jeweler . . ."

With a scent of—musk? Camomile?—her shift fell away.
They made love in his apartment above the shop, in the
clutter of kittens and houseplants. After the storm, a kitten
hopped up on the bed and licked her nose. She giggled. The
kitten held her down with both paws, and resolutely began
to wash her face.

When she leaves it is already early night. The sky is open
here, and snow is gently falling. She is calm; for the moment
at peace with herself, with the world, her passion stilled.
The snow falls in large clusters, dyed garish colors in the
lights of the city, the eddying winds blowing it upward as
often as it falls down. In the distance children scream and
shout as their sleds glide by, pushed by silent puffs of air
across the snow-covered canals.

The new ring feels strange for a moment, then adjusts to
her finger. She looks at it, marveling at how perfect a dupli-
cate it is.

Perhaps someday she will have to make a choice. Perhaps one day Elliot's sleeping suspicions will again awake.
But for now she walks calmly, peacefully in the eye of the
storm.

She smiles, and walks slowly into the snowswept night.

THE TEST
STEVEN POPKES

BOSTON CAST A long shadow over the water when Ira turned into the last leg of his trip. He dipped and turned in one motion over to the crumbled spires of Marriott Towers. The kayak barely made an extra ripple. He leaned hard into his strokes now, breathing in great, deep gasps. His boat cut through the water cleanly, silent but for the slight rasp of salt against the hull. He looked up and saw where he was— beneath the Boston Promenade, a wide walking park atop the seawall leading into the mouth of the Charles River— and tried to get a little more power out of each stroke.

He passed the corner of Hanover Street Pier, slapped the clock on the instrument array, and leaned back, choking for breath. The kayak coasted past the pier and he eased it into a long arc under the bridge and into the lilies. For a long time after he had stopped he just leaned back, inhaling the cold September air mixed with the light mist that came from the warm water.

The sky had the violet tinge of New England fall days and contrasted with the partially enclosed hulk of Boston and the impossibly high spire of IPOB. Ira looked down at a sound in the water. Large reptilian eyes peered back.

"Hey, fella," he said to the sea turtle. "I have something for you." He rummaged behind the seat and pulled out a strip of thick, dried seaweed. "You like this?"

The turtle said nothing as it took the proffered gift, but chewed it and watched him placidly.

"Give it to Tommy," came a voice behind him. "He'll eat it."

Ira scratched Tommy's nose. "Hey, Pete," he said without turning around.

Pete's kayak glided to a stop across from Ira's and the motion must have startled the turtle, for it made a low grunt and disappeared.

"Hell of a note to come in second," growled Pete. "If you tie him to the back of your boat, maybe he'll slow you down."

"Could be." Ira leaned back and closed his eyes.

"Was it a good time?"

"Eleven minutes, forty seconds. I lost a bit on the Fort Point Channel turn."

Pete shrugged. "It's still a qualifying time. You'll make the nationals on it—then it's the Olympics for sure."

"Yeah," Ira said, his eyes still closed. In his mind, he could see beyond the sky to a single ship in orbit. The 2048 Olympics seemed very far away. Pete, for all his familiarity of the past few years, kayaking around Boston, up in Maine, down the coast, seemed no closer.

"Another round of the city," asked Pete.

"No, I've got an appointment." Ira sat up.

"Later, then. I'll see you at the game."

Ira shook his head. "I don't think I'll be at Fenway."

Pete looked aghast. "Come on, Ira. You've been wanting to see that new catcher—Marty Weeden—"

"—Marty Warden—"

"—for weeks now. What's going on?"

Ira looked at him. "Family problems."

* * *

When I think of Gray, I always remember how my father described him to someone else: fingers of a spider, skin of rhino, nose of a small elephant. But I did not know Gray as he did. He met Gray when he was in his twenties. I met Gray when I was two. He is part of my first, vague memories. I remember him more than I remember my dead parents. And that was true even before they died. I remember spiders because they are like Gray's fingers. I remember rhinos and elephants because they resemble Gray's skin and face. Gray was never alien to me. It was all the rest of you.

You people here don't understand them, locked into your own minds as you are. Gray and the other Spatiens are creatures of definition. The Phneri are creatures of moment—events without the structural pegboards of time. Even the Bishop is a product of context.

What are you?

Perhaps your specialness is that overvalued and ill-conceived thing called consciousness. Certainly, it is not something highly considered by the others and is, therefore, left for you to cling to. Some of my classmates at Harvard think the aliens feel this way out of contempt. Not so. It is like a cat looking at a king. From the king's point of view, he is so above the cat he can allow the cat this singular honor. The cat, on the other hand, though he can probably perceive the king's power and intellect, is not much impressed by it. The king is merely furniture. Which is correct? And are you cat or king?

I was eleven when I met the Bishop. My parents had died in the union riots on Maxwell Station—America's last abortive attempt to gain something of value from the Interstellar Port of Boston. I had never known anything but the swamps and marsh of the station. And I had been brought "home" to a relative—my aunt—here in Boston. This supplies the context suitable for a Centaur. The only person I trusted then was Gray; he was all the home or parents I had.

This supplies the definition necessary for a Spatien. For reasons of his own, Gray asked me along to Miller's Hall, the recreational area of the aliens, where I found that the Bishop's people had murdered Gray's family. This would suffice to be a Phneri moment. What was left for me?

Gray didn't get off shift until six o'clock. Ira picked up a hardcopy of the news and sat in Durgin Park reading.

"There's a press release about the new ship today," said the bartender conversationally. "They said the Bishop won't let them land—funny, huh?"

Ira grunted and looked through the sports news. The Yankees had lost this afternoon—this put the Red Sox a half game ahead.

"It's weird how this ship didn't come through the Loophole at all," continued the bartender, shaking his head.

"Have you heard how the Twins are doing?" asked Ira. "They don't have the national news in this edition."

"No, I'm a minority: I don't follow major league. Too slow—the new open ball clubs are better. Anybody can play: modified humans, aliens. It's more exciting. Faster play."

"I suppose," Ira said idly.

A Phner came in and took the stool next to him and asked for a beer.

The bartender served him coldly and moved to the other end of the bar.

"Arrogant slime," whistled the Phner under his breath.

"Careful, careful," whistled Ira back softly. "All can listen."

The Phner jerked and stared at him, took his beer and slipped to the floor. Standing before Ira, he bobbed his head once. "Chastised, I am. I do not like his smell."

Ira waved him away. "He does not understand tradition. Drink in peace."

"You are in Gray's family. I recognize you from Miller's Hall."

Ira nodded and the Phner scuttled into one of the booths.

Sometime later, Ira saw Gray through the door windows and went outside to meet him.

Outside of Boston it was early evening, the sunset shining across thin, high clouds. Here in Quincy Market, in the interior of Boston, time had stopped in mid-afternoon. Pigeons flew over and roosted in the eaves of the old buildings, and there was a shadow of the Old Customs House across the cobblestones.

Gray stood rock-still beneath an elm tree. He was covered with mortar dust and splotches of paint.

"What's Iris got you doing now?"

"The City Manager has my team laying the foundations for the improved mover lines." Gray looked at Ira, then at himself. "I am filthy—I should have hosed down before I came here."

"It's not important," Ira said, suddenly fiercely protective. "Who cares?"

"Several humans have given me looks like yours—I didn't take notice of them until now."

"It's not *important.*" Ira took his hand and led him toward the market entrance. "Where do you want to eat?"

"Anywhere is all right. I must go up to the family ship tonight. You will be coming, correct?"

Ira looked away from him. "Not tonight."

Gray didn't answer immediately. "I had hoped to introduce you to the rest of your family."

"I met them when they got here."

"This would be a formal introduction. So that you know them."

"I know who my family is." Ira led him to a street vendor selling baby lobsters. He bought each of them a bag and they sat down near the Customs House.

Gray held the bag, not opening it. "I don't understand. It is important—"

"Not tonight. That's all I said."

Gray was still, then nodded and opened the bag. "We'll be here a bit longer—a week, perhaps. Do not wait over-long."

"I won't." Ira touched one of Gray's lower arms and it held his hand in a firm grip. Rather than release it, Ira ate one-handed.

"How about that catcher, eh?" Ira said at last. "You think the Sox have a chance this year?

Gray shook his head. "I don't know. I don't understand baseball."

"Sure you do. I dragged you to enough games."

Gray looked at him. "There are many things you dragged me to that I didn't understand. Should I not have gray hairs? I understand the rules and the strategy, but I don't understand its purpose."

"It's a game."

"Games are a mammalian exercise. I don't have to understand it."

Ira leaned forward on his knees. "My kayaking is a game."

"That is something I understand—you are pursuing excellence in an antique skill. Such skills can be useful under some circumstances." Gray stopped and seemed to ponder. "You are considering something?"

"Nothing much. I did the course in eleven-forty."

"A qualifying time. You do not seem excited."

Ira rubbed his hands together vigorously and stood up. "The Olympics are in forty-eight, Gray. Harvard Law School wants me. So does IPOB. I can't do everything."

Gray hesitated for a long moment. "That is not it—the time is good, but it is only a qualifying time. And you have known about Harvard and IPOB for some time. It is something else."

"Nothing else. Nothing but my family might go to war with the Bishop."

"Ah." Gray seemed satisfied. "A difference of opinion."

"Yeah," said Ira bitterly. "The Bishop kills everyone in your family but a handful and when the survivors reach here, he tells them to move on."

"That's enough."

Ira studied the cobblestones for a moment. "Would he really have eaten me, that day in Miller's Hall?"

"The Bishop?"

"Yes."

"I don't know." Gray stood and placed the now-empty bag into the open trunk of a trash tree. He watched as the bag and leftover lobsters were eaten and disposed of. "We are products of our nature, he and I. We Spatiens were made, not evolved, so long ago. We are free-floating willful machines in the world. The Bishop is circumscribed by duty. If you know his goals and his duty, you can tell what he will do. I've never mastered this." His words did not seem to be musing. They were dry, as casual as statements dealing with bath temperature, countertops, and shoes. Gray looked up at Ira suddenly. "Perhaps humans have more options than we do. They are not any brighter, certainly. Nor more creative. Perhaps there is something of freedom in their vagueness. Something that enables them to make a choice with conviction, but without certainty."

I remember the subway, the underground lights flashing by like a succession of days, the thick urine smell and the companion smell of the sea. We left the subway in Haymarket, in the shadow of the seawall and Monastery Bridge.

Miller's Hall was a disorganized concrete-and-brick sculpture melted on one end. The aliens had built it themselves—the windows all looked out on the same place. Why this was so I never understood, though Gray explained it to me.

We waited in a great lounge overlooking the harbor. You could see the water, the hovercraft and the boats floating in and out of the Back Bay archipelago. Mostly I remember the smell of all the aliens: pepper and milk, benzene and charcoal. One of them had the largest, bluest eyes I'd ever seen: octopus eyes, cartoon eyes. The lounge was carpeted and strewn with large, soft pillows. I fell asleep for a while and dreamed of a great, white forest surrounding a red lake.

When I awoke, the room was buzzing. At one corner, *he* had entered.

You've seen the pictures: the chest and head of a praying mantis stuck on the body of a pill bug. But the pictures don't show you how he moves—looking here one moment, the next moved a few steps, stop stare at you, move on—a life spent in freeze-frame motion. He was waiting for us— all of us, not just humans—to catch up.

He moved toward us and we waited for him.

From the monastery balcony Ira looked down on the mouth of the Charles River. The bulk of Boston loomed over both monastery and river, but neither seemed intimidated. Like the river, the monastery was a green and growing thing. Its bedrock was the remains of the old Interstate 93 and U.S. Route 1 interchange. Thick, woody vines covered the old bridge columns that sank into the river and the great trees that had grown up to support them. The bridge itself was lost in a jungle of terrestrial and extraterrestrial plants. Within the jungle was the monastery.

Set against the air and water traffic of the harbor was the traffic of the animals of the bridge: lyrebird and monkey, dragonfly and parrot. While the jungle was of mixed parentage, the animals of the monastery seemed to be of mainly Earth stock. Ira listened to the birds and behind them he could hear the faint sound of someone playing music.

"Ira Bloom!" came a voice behind him.

Ira turned and faced an old man in a cassock walking quickly down the stairs. "It's good to meet you. I've been watching you for several years now."

"Your Grace." Ira started to kneel before him but the Abbot stopped him.

"Don't bother. You're not Catholic and I'm not much of an abbot. Call me Herbert." As Ira rose, the Abbot leaned toward him. "So: are you going to the Olympics? What was your time this morning?"

"Eleven-forty, Your Grace."

"Herbert, I said." The Abbot shook his head. "A good time—not as good as you did at Acadia in the spring. You'll have to do better than that to win."

Ira was nonplussed. "I'm gratified you've taken such an interest in this—"

"—but you're wondering why, eh?" The Abbot chuckled. "I've walked this balcony every morning for twenty years. Don't you think I'd take an interest in what goes on beneath it? Besides, I read the sports news."

"I see."

"And you came to me, not I to you." The Abbot waved his hand at the monastery. "Or rather, you came and asked for advice about alien religion—something that happens fairly often and is usually dealt with by one of the brethren. And didn't expect to talk to me, I think. Eh?"

Ira nodded. "A great honor—"

"I know they teach you to be polite at Harvard. Don't bother. I confess, Ira," he leaned forward and winked. "I would have known who you were even if you weren't Olympic material."

"Because of Gray." Ira smiled wryly.

"Of course. That and your record at Harvard. There are a few other such adoptions—true adoptions, I mean. The artificial creation of families. Not the empty formal ceremony that's becoming popular." The Abbot nodded. "And none at all like you. Knowing that, it must be important and must have something to do with the Spatien ship. So tell me: how can I help you?"

"You know the situation: the Spatiens have nowhere else to go and the Bishop won't let them land." Ira took a deep breath. "But these particular Spatiens are the last remains of the clan wiped out by the Centaurs. And they *are* my family. I need to convince the Bishop to let them stay. I had hoped that my special position might give me some extra credibility when I spoke to him."

"Why should he let them down?" the Abbot asked.

Ira was taken aback. "They have nowhere else to go."

"A naive answer. Try again."

"They'll fight to stay—"

The Abbot shook his head. "And be destroyed. Nobody knows what the Bishop has in reserve, but he'd be stupid not to have something amazing. Neither the Spatiens nor the Bishop are stupid. They will not fight—at least they won't fight to stay."

"Are you telling me what my family will do?"

The Abbot laughed. "Of course not. I'm looking at it from the outside. Let's think again. What will they do?"

"They'll settle somewhere else in the system—Mars, maybe. Spatiens could live almost anywhere. And then they'll die out."

"Eh?" The Abbot seemed surprised. "That's not an option I'd have considered. I would have thought Spatiens far tougher. Why do you say that?"

"Because they were built," Ira said tiredly, "not made. They were designed to work for *someone else.* Their family groups gradually disintegrate over time without that. In large numbers, they manage because they can trade work between families. But here they have only each other."

"Have you discussed this with Gray?"

"I've tried—he won't talk about it. But I've been hearing stories about the Spatiens since before I can remember and this theme keeps coming back: you have to work to live. Literally."

"And what do you want the Bishop to do?"

"Let them come down and work. Probably for Boston, since Gray is already working for the City Manager. There are only a few dozen of them."

"Why should he?"

"Because he must."

"Wrong." The Abbot pointed at him. "Naive again. You're assuming that because the Bishop is here in an altruistic cause—our assimilation into a larger culture—that he has a 'higher nature.' He doesn't operate that way."

"Then how does he operate?"

The Abbot grinned. "The original question you came here to ask, eh? Think it through: the Bishop doesn't know if we'll make the grade or not, right? But he *does* know if he directs us appropriately—by his definition—we *may* make the grade. Remember the Venture Capital announcement? It's been twenty years, but I think they still show a copy in the Alien Studies course at Harvard."

"Of course I've seen it."

"Then you remember how the Bishop defined sentience: 'the ability of a species to see its own best interest.' How do we deal with the Sh'k? With the Targives? With the Phneri? According to our own best interest. What's that? We don't know—that's been our problem for generations. That is the quality he's attempting to discover in us."

"I don't understand."

"Alien Studies 101. You took the course—I saw your transcript. Remember the Ryle article in *Nature*? It's on the reading list. The Bishop operates in context: a given situation falls into one of several contextual categories. Clearly, the Spatien ship falls into one now. You have to change that in order to change his mind."

"What do you mean?"

"Come in from the side—you're going to him as a

Human pleading for the survival of a species about which the Bishop does not appear to be concerned. The goal is clear: determine the sentience of the human species. That is his duty, and duty is always the center of the Bishop's behavior. The context is defined, and therefore *so is the Bishop's response.* It's necessary to redefine the context."

"How do I do that?"

"I have no idea."

"That doesn't do me much good."

"True." The Abbot shrugged. "Look, given the situation, the Bishop has made a decision. He's smarter than we are—we've had that drummed into us more than once. When it comes to the pursuit of his own goals, nobody can match him. He's already thought through the arguments that concern his goals and if you have other arguments with other goals, they are not arguments he'll find worth considering. Again, the context of the argument must be changed."

Ira smiled grimly and nodded. "I can't appeal to his good side."

"He hasn't got one."

"Yeah." He was silent a moment. "Thank you for your time. I'd best be going."

The Abbot peered closely at him. "You've already got an appointment, don't you?"

"Yes. Later this evening."

The Abbot took both his hands. "Have faith, boy. It can move mountains."

"I'll try." Ira released the Abbot's hands. "But I don't need to move mountains." He turned to go.

"Good luck."

Ira stopped. "Does it bother you what the Bishop can do? The power of a creature like that?"

The Abbot shook his head. "Not at all. The Bishop's been my good friend for years. I'd trust no one else to do what he must."

* * *

There was a kind of beauty and grace in the way he sat, folded across his back like a dignified old man sitting down. And he was huge: he towered over me, like Gray towered over me. Large, fast, his eyes as big as dinner plates and slitted like a cat's.

"I have not seen you for years," he said to Gray, ignoring me. "Not since we cleaned out your nest perhaps a cycle ago. Are you the last?"

"No, Your Grace," said Gray softly. "I don't think so. But I am alone—I estivated until I was found by humans."

"Of course," said the Bishop. "And this is your pet?" He indicated me with one of his mandibles.

I tried hard not to flinch. He reached down and touched the crown of my head, gently, like a man might test with a knife the shell of an egg before eating it. I think I may have been shaking, but I don't remember. I only recall trying to hold still, listening to the Bishop talking casually about killing Gray's family, talking about me in the same breath. I felt—I knew—if I so much as said one word, I'd be scooped up and eaten in the same moment. I was standing blind on the edge of a cliff, trying hard not to tip over.

"No," said Gray. "He is no pet. He is my nephew."

Family is where they have to take you in when you have nowhere else to go. At that moment, I knew the meaning of those words. Gray was there. Gray would protect me.

"Are you certain?" The Bishop crossed his arms, looking cross and ready for action.

"I am certain, Holy One." Gray made an obscure gesture, a nuance in Lingua I did not know at the time. It meant: this is certain; let us speak of something else. "How are your offspring?"

The Centaur looked nonplussed for a moment. "Fine. I brought two pupae with me and they will be molting soon. No eggs as yet. Pity, as I have been hungering for the delicacy a great deal. But it would be unfortunate to return home with no children so I have restrained myself. Soon they will molt and of course become children—if they pass the test. Tell me: do you think I would be too embarrassed by returning with only one child instead of two?"

"You have no eggs, Your Grace?" Gray seemed eager to find the answer to this question, eager beyond what I understood then.

"None as yet. I have tried several times but my flesh will not obey me." The Bishop turned his head all the way around and looked behind him, then whipped it back toward us. It clicked like a machine. The sound and the speed of it made me nauseous and I tried hard not to throw up.

"Give me the pet," he said suddenly. "I would cook it well. Look." He pointed at me. "It does not even know language."

I felt very alone. Very cold. There was a deep, blank disbelief that this was really happening to me. I wanted to run but I knew he would catch me before I could even take a step.

"I cannot, Holy One," said Gray.

"Come. Give it to me as an offering." He stiffened somehow, like a whip in midair, ready to strike.

I heard a sound from Gray and turned toward him. Every finger was extended and every finger was a glittering knife. All of them were made of points.

"I cannot, Holy One," he said softly. "Forgive me."

They stared at each other an interminable time. I felt like a rag hanging in the wind, holding on by threads.

Finally the Bishop relaxed. "This is a very great sin. Perhaps the fault is mine. I encourage my appetites as much as I can. That is not always a virtue." His head snapped around and back again. "I must go, my friend. Until we meet again."

He turned and left as smoothly as if he'd been on wheels.

Gray helped me sit down. I sat, shaking. He waited for

THE TEST ■ 213

half an hour before he led me out and I was grateful for every minute.

"Jesus," I said when we were outside. "What was that all about?"

Gray thought for a moment before speaking. "His people and my family disputed over some territory. My family was defeated. I don't know where they are. Your parents found me in the asteroids about a thousand years later. I needed to know if the Bishop was without family as I am."

"Why was I here at all, then?"

"I did not want the Bishop to think I had come for revenge. If I brought my family, he would know for certain I had not come for war. I don't want to die either, Ira."

We walked a little farther and I reached up and took his hand. "I'm sorry about your family, Gray."

Gray was quiet for a block or two. "You're my family now."

Spatiens are born knowing what they need to know, as self-sufficient and complete as reptiles. Centaurs are cast out and must swim through the sea, migrating and changing until they return home to become pupae. One final metamorphosis and they are Centaur adolescents. Of the aliens I know best, only the Phneri rear their young as we do: from formless infant to volatile adult.

I was eleven and, like all children, selfishly thought that Gray's words and actions always related to me and had no meaning beyond that. Over ten years later, I discovered how wrong I was.

"The Yankees did not win," the Phner said to him.

Standing on the edge of the seawall at the foot of the monastery path, Ira looked down at him. "You're the Phner I met in the bar," he said.

The Phner nodded slowly. "That is the person that is me."

Ira looked back out to sea. They spoke Lingua, which

handled both the Phneri time-sense—or lack of such—and Ira's sense of time equally well. "We lead by one game, then. What is your name?"

"Ksak-k-ksos," whistled the Phner.

"Ira Bloom." He solemnly reached down and they shook hands.

"I do not understand baseball," confided Ksak-k-ksos. "I wish to understand humans. I am a physician. If we are to live here, I must be a doctor to them as well as ourselves. And we must live here. We have no choice. Is this baseball important?"

"Very much. To me, at least."

"Then it must be another thing which I must learn." The Phner indicated resignation with a motion. "Explain it to me, please."

"It's about time."

"You are unclear."

"It's something a Phner would find hard to understand. To you, nothing except memory is unique because everything is recreatable. But a baseball game is timeless and by its nature unpredictable. No ballgame can be duplicated."

Ksak-k-ksos seemed nonplussed by this. "The game is a process, not an object."

"True."

"Could it not be reenacted?"

"It could."

"It could be recreated, then," said the Phner triumphantly.

"No," said Ira, shaking his head. "It could not."

"If all of the players were recreated, and the same playing field were completely recovered, as were all of the equipment and the weather, could it then be recreated?"

Ira pronounced his words solemnly. "It would be a different ball game."

"Is it holy?" asked Ksak-k-ksos slowly.

"Holy?"

"That which is truly unique cannot be understood. This indicates the presence of divinity." Ksak-k-ksos shivered.

Ira stared into the water. "Some think so. It might be uniquely human and holy in that way. I don't know."

"Humans never take divinity seriously," the Phner said bitterly.

"I disagree," said Ira. "We take baseball very seriously indeed."

Ksak-k-ksos did not speak for several minutes. "This is a more interesting place than I had thought."

"Do you know anything about the Bishop?" Ira sat down on the bench and watched the shadow of Boston gradually lengthen across the water.

"Some," Ksak-k-ksos said and sat beside him. "We are judged sentient by the Centaurs."

"Did the Bishop test you?"

"No, it was another," said the Phner. "It was long ago. Before the Sh'k came and destroyed us by bringing us here."

"What was the test?"

"I don't know. It was unique. We don't remember it."

"You remember everything."

"We do *not* remember it." Ksak-k-ksos sniffed him quickly. "You go to see him tonight."

"You are very intuitive. You will be a great doctor."

"What do you want from him?"

"I seek his blessing."

My Harvard dorm was just as spare now as it must have been a hundred years ago. My roommate had never liked this—had in fact attempted to install some Targive modified lichen as wallpaper. Either it had mutated or was a Targive idea of a joke, but it had covered the wall with scintillating designs for about a week. Then it had gradually faded back into exactly the same yellow paint that had been on the wall before. I could see, if I looked carefully, the pattern of the veins and overlapping threads of the lichen, but to the casual observer (and Rick had never been more than a casual observer) the room was the same as before. He had stayed a few weeks after that but had moved out. I think he was scared of the stuff, though he wouldn't admit it.

I found the reemergence of the old room comforting, a kind of biological *pentimento.*

I was watching the news: a new ship had contacted IPOB. It hadn't come through the Loophole and so it wasn't clear whether it came under the Venture Capital charter. It had not been released who was in the ship, or where it had come from, but this didn't stop the reporter from speculating.

A call came in from Gray.

"I bring you news of your family," he said immediately.

"Aunt Sara's all right, isn't she?" I'd heard from her last week. She was on a construction project in Quito.

"She is fine, I am sure. This does not concern her."

"She and you are the only family I have."

"Not so—at least, not so any longer."

It took me a moment. "The new ship—that's great!"

"It is the new ship. A few escaped." Gray stopped.

By that I knew something was wrong. "You're not acting like this is terrific news."

"The Bishop has said that allowing us to land would be a Loophole violation—and he will dissolve Venture Capital if permission is granted. In effect, he will not let us land."

I was stunned. "He can't do that—by any definition he can't. I've read the charter."

"He is doing it."

"Fight him in court—even the Bishop can be sued."

"It is being done, Ira. I had hopes when I found out he had never deposited eggs—even to this day—that we could meet here as neutrals. I was wrong."

"It wasn't just for me. There was more to it."

Gray nodded. "I needed to know for two reasons. We

will wait for judgment but it will likely go against us. Then we'll wait just a little longer."

I felt cold. "To do what?"

"To leave—go somewhere else in the system. We need someplace to live. We haven't decided where yet. And when we do, we will likely wait for a good position."

I shook my head. Everything felt vague to me. "What will you do, Gray?"

"Go with them, of course. They need me."

The Bishop's Venture Capital offices were in the IPOB tower. But those offices and the tower itself were where the Bishop dealt with humans and were, therefore, under Boston jurisdiction. When he dealt with others, he used an office in Miller's Hall, where Ira had the appointment.

He waved to the guard as he entered. The guard, a small Phner, whistled a greeting and waved back. Ira had been known here for a long time.

Ira passed through the main lounge to the lifts, waving to his friends and acquaintances. At the lift entrance, he was approached by a human.

The man was short and dark, with an even darker mottling to his skin that Ira recognized as a sign of extensive Targive modification. "Mister Bloom, I am Avram Smith." His voice was well modulated and controlled, but one of the mottlings covering his ear quivered and pointed, as nervous as a rabbit.

"I'm sorry, Mister Smith," said Ira, stepping into the lift. "I have an appointment."

"It's with the Bishop, isn't it?" Avram blocked the lift doors. "It's probably about the Spatien ship. Right? My clients would like to know what your opinion on the ship is. They would pay—"

"Sorry." Ira smiled at him and pushed him out of the lift. "Have to go now."

"Mister Bloom, this is your family we're talking about—"

The lift cut him off.

"Exactly," Ira said softly.

The Bishop's office was on the top floor. A small alien with large blue eyes sat at a desk in the room. He looked up when Ira entered.

"I know you," he said.

Ira nodded. "Gnoza, isn't it? I saw you here years ago. Were you working for him, then?"

"I've been working for him most of my life." Gnoza leaned back in his chair. "What brings you up here?"

"I think the Sox can make the series this year. Thought I'd come up and see if the Bishop would take a bet on it."

Gnoza snorted. "Nobody's that stupid."

Ira shrugged. "You have to have faith."

"Funny," said Gnoza. "You know the Mayor actually asked the Bishop to toss out the opening ball this year? How do you figure?"

"Anything's possible. Even the Sox taking the series is possible. Like I said, you have to have faith."

"Yeah." Gnoza snorted again. "Go on in. He's waiting for you."

Inside, the light was dim. The Bishop sat at his desk, waiting for him. He stood as Ira entered, but he was not as large as he once seemed. Now he looked thinner, deadlier: the difference between a broadsword and a rapier. He gestured toward Ira and the motion was the same: feigned slowness. The Bishop was always waiting for the world to catch up.

"You are Ira Bloom. Do I know you?" He spoke English.

Ira replied in Lingua. "Not recently, sir. I was with Old-one-of-many-names several years ago when he came here. You spoke with him then. He asked you about your off-spring."

The Bishop stiffened. "I have none. Neither adolescent

passed the test. I remember Old-one-of-many-names. Should I remember you?"

"I am adopted into his clan." Ira swallowed hard. His throat was dry.

The Bishop cocked his head one way, then the other. "I remember a missed meal. What are you now?"

"An adolescent, sir." For all the world, Ira thought the Bishop knew everything there was to know about him. This was a charade.

"Do you desire instruction, then? Or are you here for him? Or his clan? We are enemies, you know. He prepares to make war on me because I will not let them land. Did you know this?"

"He will leave and die on another world."

"Both possibilities are no doubt being discussed. You are naive."

"So I've been told, sir. In this, your motivations escape me."

"There could be many reasons. Perhaps I don't want my see here contaminated by old, broken allegiances. Perhaps I don't think a hundred Spatiens on Earth is a good idea. Perhaps I wanted to flush you out to me. Did you consider that?"

"No, sir."

"Good. I wouldn't want you to think you were too important. You came to me for something. What is it?"

Ira could not speak immediately. It's a difficult thing to lay your life down for another. "I desire a sentience test."

It was the Bishop's turn to pause. "You cannot make this request. This planet is under my jurisdiction and therefore you cannot yet be tested—you are inedible by reason of incompetence."

"Miller's Hall is not part of your jurisdiction. Here you are not the Bishop of Earth, but a representative of your order and the Centaurs."

"I know my role here, child." He stared at Ira, the slits in his eyes open and dark.

Ira stared back. "I know also. And now you know that as well." He straightened. "I am an adolescent and I wish to grow."

"Kneel."

Ira did so and the tip of the Bishop's mandible rested on his head. Ira tried not to flinch.

"Why here? Why now?" the Bishop asked quietly.

"Because Gray is my family and they must have a home. You will not speak with them, but perhaps, if I come to you an adult, you will speak with me." Ira felt sweat roll down his back. All the rehearsal and thinking he'd done about this moment seemed very distant. He felt small, ineffectual.

"That is a great risk for a small probability."

The tip of the mandible was cold and hard. The next moment it would fall and he would die. From the complex to the simple, he thought. His fear left him and he grew calm.

"What else could I do, Holy One?" he said. "Gray's family prepares for war or death. You won't speak. Who else is there? My duty was clear."

"How shall I test you?"

"I choose the test?"

"How could I make that choice for you? As you say, who else is there? How shall I test you?"

The other tip of the mandible touched his throat delicately. For a moment he had a wild hope. It faded: he was dealing with players old to the game. They were better at it than he was. This was not a contest over how well the game was played, but as to his worthiness to play. How do you measure a man? He did not know.

"I don't know, Holy One," Ira said. "I only know I must be tested. I leave it to you."

Ira waited in the dimness, doubt like a vine curled around his thoughts. He could have done things differently, but it was too late now.

The tips of the mandibles were removed from his neck and the Bishop moved away from him.

Ira looked up, rubbing his neck. The Bishop was standing at the window looking out on the Boston evening.

"You are not ready for a sentience test," the Bishop said. "You will be so tested when the rest of your people are tested."

"But I asked for it!"

"It is my prerogative to decline."

Ira clenched his hands, so angry tears leaked from the corners of his eyes. "Then why did you act as if I were?"

"You were tested. It was not a sentience test."

The Bishop turned back to Ira. "I have a job for you, Ira Bloom. Gnoza is leaving me and I need someone to fill his place. Would you do it?"

"I—"

"The first task you would have to perform is to negotiate a settlement between the Spatiens and myself."

Ira closed his mouth. When he could speak again, he said: "I accept."

"Good." The Bishop nodded. "For the next few years, this position should not interfere with either your Olympic aspirations or college career. The position of secretary to me is not an easy one and it will take some time to train you."

Ira felt stunned. "Thank you."

"Not at all."

"But why?"

"Because there is no one else. At this stage of my work I need a human, and you are the only one acceptable to me."

"Why me?"

"I tested you."

"Tested me for what? I don't understand."

"There is no reason that you should."

"Did you plan this?" he cried. "Was this all a plan to bring me here?"

The Bishop's head swiveled around and looked at him

over the Bishop's back. "Do you think you are so important?"

"I couldn't possibly."

"I will not answer you. How will you live with such a mystery?"

It came to him that this was an act of faith. All of his actions bringing him here were expressions of that faith: faith that good can come from the unexpected, that one's small effort can accomplish lasting things, that something can be accomplished if only one acts with conviction but without guarantee. It was not religious; it was a belief in possibility in the face of an unpredictable world. The Abbot was wrong: faith could not move mountains. Faith enabled one to act so that the mountains could move on their own.

He looked outside at the shining sun, stared back at the Bishop staring at him.

"Bishop," Ira said at last, speaking Lingua as one did to an equal. "Would you like to go to a ball game?"

THE PLACE OF NO SHADOWS
ALEXANDER JABLOKOV

THE POURED-CONCRETE BUILDING had once been the head-quarters of a software company of some sort, part of the office developments that had replaced the decaying warehouses in Kendall Square, Cambridge. The glass in the windows was long gone. The gray acrylic carpets had been rolled up, exposing the concrete slab of the floor, and the shattered plastic office furniture had been dumped in the parking lot. Owls roosted above the acoustic paneling.

Two men in students' long robes sat in the large windowless third-floor room which had once housed the high-speed Cyber computer, cooked stew over an alcohol burner and studied scenes of Procyon IV on a holographic wall screen.

The stew was of fish, clams, and mussels, flavored with a fennel bulb. Lester Kronenbourg, a heavyset man with drooping jowls, dipped his spoon in and tasted the stew. He licked his spoon clean and stared off into Procyon IV, where two moons were rising over a sinuous sand dune. A spidery vehicle with five balloon tires sped over the dune and vanished from sight.

Chris Tolliver ran a long-fingered hand over his high bald head and raised his eyebrows.

"What do you think?" he said.

"I think five wheels is an ridiculous number for a dune buggy." Kronenbourg got up and walked over to the data reader, a leathery device that pulsed slightly, with the obscene look typical of Targive technology. He had rigged a link to the storage codes of the octahedral Procyon dataform which he had bought that morning at Copley Mall. Manipulation of the soft projections on the data reader changed the scene, now following the five-wheeled dune buggy as it sped past a field of what looked like photovoltaic panels. Its driver, of a species of alien as yet unseen in Boston, and hence on Earth, was squat and muscular, with a head like a washtub. "Look at the complexity of the suspension," Kronenbourg complained. "Absurd."

"Never mind the suspension. The stew. What do you think about the stew?"

Kronenbourg shrugged. "What about it? I've been in Boston for ten years. My blood is clam juice. My sweat smells like kelp. Fish stew is fish stew. I eat it. Don't expect me to discuss it."

Tolliver lived in the building, in a somewhat better-appointed room on a lower floor, with plastic sheets across the windows. Kronenbourg lived off in Charlestown. They met in this room to perform their research and argue. The arguing took up most of the time.

The bank of lights in the ceiling, connected by a data feed to the reader, had changed its spectral characteristics to match Procyon's. Somewhere outside, it was a December Boston day, cold and overcast, but the blank-walled room was filled with harsh, too-white sunlight.

These abandoned buildings, near the large concentration of alien schools and academies in Cambridgeport, were filled with students. Too poor to live elsewhere, they lived communally in the old offices, fought, argued, made love, and studied the deviant philosophies of several dozen worlds. Tolliver found the presence of students stimulating.

Kronenbourg tried to recruit them for the Institute, his great cultural engineering project.

Tolliver stood up and stretched. His thin neck and wrists stuck out of his billowing, colorful robe, and he looked like some festival scarecrow. Students of alien cultures affected such robes, because they made the bodies underneath them anonymous.

He peered into the wall screen, where the dune buggy rider was now speeding along a beach, Procyon hanging low over the water beyond.

"Look at the way the skull sits on the spine," he said. "Interesting. Looks like a torsion arrangement. It could use that huge head as a battering ram, like a goat."

Kronenbourg fiddled with the data reader, which sucked unpleasantly at his fingers. To create it, the Targives had modified some hive insect until the queen had a mass of hypercircuitry in her abdomen. The Targives never liked leaving anything the way they found it. As he changed the settings, scenes of mountains, cities, machinery cross-sections, chemical structures, and elaborate taxonomic diagrams of leafy plants flashed on the wall.

"Can you pull anatomy and physiology on the sentients?" Tolliver said. He was trying to formulate a general theory of sentient physiology across all planets of origin, a grand synthesis.

"Out of this mass of useless knowledge?" Kronenbourg grumbled. "Bah. I shouldn't waste my time."

"It's not a waste of time, Lester. The more we know—"

"The stupider we become. Just so." As Kronenbourg bent over the reader, a thickset oriental woman burst through the door. She was gasping for breath. She had no eyebrows and her head was shaved.

"There's a dead alien in the quadrangle at EDS," she managed to get out, and sat down on the floor.

"At the Div School?" Tolliver asked. "What is it doing there? What species?"

"I don't know," Ang said. She sprawled out on the floor. She wore a green suit covered with metallic scales. As she moved, colored ruffs erected on her back and her arms. These were part of her outfit, controlled by myoelectric connections to her muscles. "It's no accident," she moaned. "It can't be. It isn't just dead."

"Murder, then." Kronenbourg said. He shut the reader off. It shuddered and Procyon IV vanished. "Or suicide? Witchcraft? What are you saying?"

She glared up at Kronenbourg and her back ruff erected in anger. "Good for you either way. You like them dead. You can study them, and they don't threaten you. This one taught modes of perception and had thoughts like crystal. You knew who he was. Did you kill him, Lester?"

Kronenbourg flinched. "I did not. You know that."

She laughed, a liquid, burbling sound. "Yes. But you know who did—don't you, Lester? How does that fit into your search for truth?"

Kronenbourg looked at her bleakly. "Truth? Where does that lie? With Braak-Kha, your cosmic swamp philosopher from Rigel? There is no truth there, not for a human being. All you have done, Ang, is sink into that swamp which to a Rigellian is the universal ooze, but to a human is just smelly mud."

She breathed heavily. The room had become suffused with an odor of sulfur and damp. She lay on the floor, resting her weight on her forearms, and for a moment, despite simply being an overweight woman wearing an odd suit, she did not look a bit human. "You wouldn't understand," she said. "None of you understand! It's a place of quiet and peace that they have found, and none of you can even come close to that center."

"Ang, please—"

"Stop it! I know what you want, and what she wants, and you can all of you go to hell!" She hunched herself on the floor, as if trying to get to her feet. She got partway up, then slumped down. She crawled out the door, muttering to herself, and gasping.

Tolliver stared levelly at Kronenbourg. "What do you know about this?"

For a moment, Kronenbourg did not meet his gaze. Then he raised his eyes. "I'm not going to make any accusations. Go to the Episcopal Divinity School and take a look. Think about it. And you'll know."

"What are you hiding? Why are you being so mysterious?"

"Because you damn well refuse to see what's in front of your eyes!" Kronenbourg said, suddenly fierce. "I've been arguing with you on behalf of the human race for, what, five years now? It's not just an intellectual game, Chris. I don't think you understand that. You can study the races of the universe, put them into your clever taxonomies and cross-reference them. Where does that leave us? Is the human soul just a spot on your charts?"

Tolliver turned away and started to pull his equipment together, putting it into a large canvas bag. "You're being ridiculous. We have an agreement, don't we?"

"We do. Free exchange of information and free decision. I thought you would have agreed with me long ago." He quirked his lips. "So much for free decision. But I still won't prejudice you. Examine the corpse of that teacher of perception and think about everyone you know. If you still can't figure it out, come to me."

"Damn it, Lester—" Tolliver took a deep breath. "You can be an annoying bastard." He stepped toward the door.

"The road to truth is long, and lined the entire way with annoying bastards. Aren't you going to eat your soup?"

"No time. The Koltsoi have a lot of influence at IPOB now, and they're an officious bunch. If they seal off the area, I'll get nothing."

Kronenbourg knelt by the pot and pulled his spoon out.

"Well, it certainly won't keep. I'll take care of it for you. We can talk later."

The alien corpse rested against a puddingstone wall in the quadrangle of the Episcopal Divinity School on Brattle Street. Rock-hard, the body looked like a giant translucent blue glass paperweight, a suitable public sculpture for an academic institution. Snow had settled over it, obscuring its features.

Dr. Maureen Lionel, Professor of Patristics and Dean of EDS, hovered nervously over Tolliver as he unpacked his equipment. Events had caught her on her way to Chapel, and she wore a long cassock with a stole over it. The Cambridge cops had cordoned off the corpse, and a curious crowd of divinity students, human and alien, had gathered just outside. A police officer leaned indifferently against a wall and smoked a cigarette, looking at nothing in particular. Dr. Lionel shooed the students away with quick gestures, as if driving crows from a cornfield. Tolliver watched the heavy, pachydermish form of a Tulgut lumber away, a *Book of Common Prayer* under one of its four arms, and wondered why someone would come light-years to become an Episcopalian.

Dr. Lionel excused herself. Tolliver brushed snow off the alien and attached his instruments. There were hints of form within it, but no more than hints. The corpse gave him a frightening feeling of familiarity, though he knew he had never seen anything like it. He tried to turn his mind to the purely technical aspects of his instruments but was distracted by the echoes of Kronenbourg's eternal arguments. They had been going over the same problems for so long that Tolliver sometimes felt that it was no longer necessary to have Kronenbourg around in order to argue with him.

"The only point of the knowledge I help you gather," Kronenbourg had said, "is for us to become more human. Not less. But you mistake me if you think I'm one of these

Little Earthers, dressing up in historical costume, being self-consciously Terran. I don't even know what the hell that means. But the alternative is even worse. You know that, Chris, because your own students show it to you."

Tolliver looked toward where the cassocked Dean had vanished. The narrow spire of St. John's Chapel, a nineteenth-century Bostonian imitation of a fourteenth-century English parish church, thrust toward the overcast sky. The heavy puddingstone and sandstone buildings around the quadrangle, built just after the Civil War in imitation of a Flemish village, certainly looked self-consciously Terran, as did the sober, self-confident eighteenth- and nineteenth-century houses that lined the rest of Brattle Street.

Tolliver resented the fact that Kronenbourg's best argument did indeed come in the form of one of Tolliver's own graduate students, perhaps the most brilliant one of all. He wondered what Gavin Mercour would make of the body in front of him. Tolliver could have used his help here. Far from figuring out how the alien had died, Tolliver was having trouble understanding how it could have ever been alive. As far as he could tell, what had happened to it was that it had crystallized. If that made any sense at all. Crystals . . .

He remembered how Mercour had looked the last time they met, wild-eyed, his shock of blond hair forever on end, seeking truth. Or rather, Truth. "It's amazing what they know," Mercour said. "They know that everything is transient, that to start something is to conceive of its end. It's incredible!"

"So now it's the Phneri who have the secret?" Tolliver said wearily. He rubbed his bald head. The Phneri looked like bedraggled sea otters. They were great builders, and great destroyers, whose perception of the inner natures of objects was nothing short of supernatural, but whose perception usually included that object's destruction. Whether one found them profound or ridiculous was a matter of personal preference.

"No . . . I don't know." Mercour turned away to look out a window. They stood among the old walnut-and-glass cases of the mineral collection of the Harvard Peabody Museum. It was late on a pleasant Sunday afternoon, and the museum was virtually deserted. Mercour, for some reason, had thought this a good place to meet. "They drive me a little crazy, sometimes, you know? All of them. As if they had the secret, but wouldn't tell me. Because I'm a human, and wouldn't understand."

"Gavin," Tolliver said gently. "You should stop a little and think. They all have secrets. Each of these alien truths is like a light to you, held up in the darkness. Each of them shows something. But each of them casts shadows all around it. You'll never see anything this way."

"Would you rather I was like the rest of your idiot students?" Mercour said. "Spending my time studying neurotransmitter binding sites and joint motion in species that have ways of seeing the universe that we could never dream of? That's stupid. Never mind your shadows. If we on Earth light everything at once, then we can truly see. But to do that we have to learn." He gestured at the amethyst crystals in a nearby case, which glittered in the sunlight coming through the window, and chuckled, a derisory sound. "Imagine intelligent crystals, beings that are the end result of a billion years of evolution from viruses, rather than eucaryotic cells, as happened on Earth. Think of what we could learn from them, of the different way they would see."

"Please try to be sensible," Tolliver said, with futile patience. "You're supposed to be a graduate student in Systematic Physiology. Instead you chase after every alien guru who appears in Boston. They can't all be right. I want you to concentrate on your work, that's all. We're supposed to be working on the biochemistry of Spatien energy transfer, remember? Your work has been superb. You may think it's stupid—"

"Not stupid, Professor. Irrelevant." Mercour walked into the light refracting off the corner of one of the cases and a rainbow played across his face. "I have someone who is teaching me modes of perception. He thinks I'll be able to see everything clearly. You'd like taking a look at him, Chris. He has a real weirdie of a physiology. I'm not even sure what keeps him alive."

Tolliver felt like sighing with exasperation. When he argued with Kronenbourg, at least, he had the feeling that he was dealing with a comprehending intelligence. Arguing with Mercour was like shouting at the wind. "So you think this one has the truth, and sees everything clearly lit? No shadows?"

Mercour's face tightened. "He does. He sees everything. I'm sure of it. He says that I don't want to see things that way. He doesn't understand. Why don't any of you understand?"

What would Mercour have made of this crystallized being? Tolliver was beginning to suspect that he already knew. He heard a hiss and looked up from the dead alien. A gleaming vehicle floated off the street and into the quadrangle of EDS. Snow blew around it in a blizzard. It settled down on its ground-effect skirt, its curving black carapace still dripping water from the Charles River. Hatches opened, puffing vapor into the cold December air. INTERSTELLAR PORT OF BOSTON was written on the side in red script.

Two willowy figures leaped out of the vehicle. The Koltsoi landed lightly and stepped forward, their motion improbably liquid. Their feet barely seemed to touch the ground, and even after they stopped and gazed watchfully at Tolliver their torsos moved, arching back and stretching forward, as if their muscles could not bear a moment without flowing motion. A third figure followed them, more slowly. She was a human-Koltsoi translator. Tolliver glanced at her face and looked away, feeling ill.

One of the two Koltsoi twittered in several simultaneous voices, sounding like an aviary. Its arms floated up as if they were so light that it did not take muscle to move them, and it gestured, turning its hands in a set of curving gestures like a Balinese dancer. Despite himself, Tolliver watched in fascination, forgetting to judge the anatomy that made such grace possible.

Its movement held such a promise of indefinite extension in space that it was possible to forget the face. A Koltsoi face was occupied by six eyes of different sizes, two heat-sensing pits, a scent organ that resembled a drooping goldenrod. Its flat slash of a mouth opened slightly to release two needle-pointed fangs.

"Move away, Tolliver," the human-Koltsoi translator commanded. "You are in violation. Move away."

"Don't be so touchy, Sudb," Tolliver said, addressing himself not to the translator, but to the Koltsoi that had spoken. "You haven't lost anything by my looking at this one. Do *you* know what happened to it?" The Koltsoi were an officious bunch, and sought to control not only IPOB but Miller's Hall, the main arena of contact between humans and aliens. If possible, Tolliver suspected, they would have tried to rule Earth, but this of course was not permitted.

The translator twittered at the Koltsoi, which twittered back.

"That is irrelevant. Move away!" the woman shrieked. Her implanted fangs had left creases in her lower lip, and she had to close her mouth with close concentration, to avoid wounding herself. "Your curiosity is inappropriate."

Looking at her made Tolliver sick, but he forced himself to examine the surgical technique. A human had probably done it, someone with a good hand and a bad soul, like Teagarden at Brigham and Women's, but he had gotten the technique from the Targives. Things like turning humans into Koltsoi seemed to charm the Targives.

Her eyes had been removed and replaced by the bulging green hemispheres of Koltsoi primary eyes, which stared relentlessly since her eyelids had also been removed. Secondary eyes had been inset into her temples and chin, feeding into auxiliary image processing centers linked into the occipital lobe of the brain—or at least that was how Tolliver would have done it. Two heat-sensing pits had replaced her cheeks, and the very bones of her face had been bent and modified, as if they had been hard wax exposed to the heat of a furnace. Her nose was still human.

Bone insets in her arms, legs, and spine made her eight feet tall, and she stood only with difficulty, the stretched long muscles weakened by the modifications. The operation had given her a turnout that would have been the envy of any ballerina, and she stood in fifth position, heel of one foot to the toe of the other. There were traces of her humanity left, but no more than that.

Tolliver imagined her as a young woman, gawky and rawboned, perhaps studying dance and longing for transcendent grace. What was more graceful than a Koltsoi? So she had tried to become one and as a result could barely walk. She still moved her arms in *port de bras* like a ballet student at the barre, but compared to the Koltsoi she jerked like a mechanical insect.

And Ang had come to him the previous week, pleading for webbing, for gills, for a protective shell of implanted scales, so she could live with her Master in the aromatic mud of Rigel, safe from the world in a cocoon of earth. What horrors were humans incapable of?

"Curiosity is always appropriate," Tolliver said. "Aren't you curious? Don't you want to know what I've found out?" He knew that the Koltsoi weren't at all interested. For once it didn't bother him that his understanding was considered to be irrelevant. He had too much to think about. A dead alien, Kronenbourg, and Mercour . . .

"We should arrest you," the translator said.

Tolliver sighed in exasperation. "Be serious, Sudb," he said. "I have violated no human laws." He raised his eyebrows at the Cambridge policeman, who shrugged elaborately and lit another cigarette.

Both Koltsoi now twittered, faster than the translator could handle their angry speech, but there was nothing they could do except bluff. Dealing with Koltsoi was like being in grade school and dealing with the sort of kid who became hall monitor. Tolliver suspected that they knew nothing of this alien either, or where it had come from. They probably didn't care. All they wanted was for things to operate smoothly.

Eventually, they loaded the corpse and all climbed into the IPOB vehicle and sped away. As soon as they left, the policeman began to take down the cordon. He had not said one word the entire time.

Their meetings were always planned, but her arrival was always unexpected. Kronenbourg sat by his window, listening to the lap of the running tide. It was growing toward evening and the lights of downtown Boston were coming on across the water. Out in the harbor, where once the dark silhouettes of the Harbor islands would have been visible against the star-filled sky, piles and nuclei of colored lights now climbed their way toward the no-longer-anonymous stars. These were the headquarters, trade emporia, and palaces of a variety of races. A single narrow tower out in the water stretched upward into the night like a glowing string held taut by an invisible hand. The Boston skyline of Kronenbourg's school days had vanished beneath new construction. Just visible against the chaos of the Boston shore was the sharp spire of Old North Church, preserved as a historical monument.

"One if by land, two if by sea," Kronenbourg muttered to himself. "One billion if from space. Where was Paul Revere when we really needed him?"

He heard the wash of her vessel and walked down to the water entrance that he had chopped out of the brick wall of what had once been the kitchen of the first floor. His building had once been a warehouse near the Charlestown Navy Yard, down at the base of Bunker Hill. After a brief flowering as condominiums it was now abandoned and sinking into the water along with the rest of Boston.

Her boat was a Boston whaler with an elaborate dragon prow. She cut the engine, swung the tiller over, and drifted in expertly, allowing the backwash against the once-white kitchen cabinets to slow the boat enough that it just bumped against the tire Kronenbourg had tied to the microwave oven. He reached out and helped her step out onto the large cutting board that served him as a dock.

Mi Nyo was a middle-aged woman, hair graying. Her round face, however, was virtually unlined, with a small, flat nose. She was a Shan, a hill tribe from eastern Burma, and Kronenbourg's recognition of the distinction between her and the rest of the "Cambodians" that had emigrated to Boston had been an early element in their association. Mi Nyo wore a gray wool skirt, bulky sweater, several large lacquer bracelets, sensible leather shoes, and a string of pearls around her neck. She had never been pretty.

"Well?" Kronenbourg said.

"We have more support," she said, sipping the tea he had made her. Kronenbourg had exactly two unbroken Spode china cups left from his family inheritance, which he brought out only when Mi Nyo visited. "Serebrikov of Karnaval and the Subramanyan brothers of Fogg Ltd. have agreed to provide you with funding 'for the preservation of human culture.' "

"For the preservation of their profits, you mean."

"As long as we get support for the Institute—"

"I know, I know," Kronenbourg said, irritably. "It shouldn't matter that they support me simply because human culture is the market where they sell their goods, but it still does."

"We will get help however we can," she said, eyes glittering. Beneath the elegantly dowdy Boston matron Kronenbourg could see the pirate and looter she had once been, when she and her lover had run a speedboat armed with a .55-caliber chain gun out of Hull, before its destruction. Her crimes had been the foundation of the wealth of her interstellar trading company, but twenty years had passed, and her past had vanished into oblivion along with Hull. Now she looked as if she'd spent those years at Vassar. Her hobby was orchids, which she grew in a hothouse and displayed at the Boston Horticultural Society.

"Yes," he agreed. "However we can."

"And do whatever we need to remain human." She nibbled on a stale water biscuit. He was too poor to offer her any other food. He'd had dinner at her apartment once, high above the water, where the endless stream of boats on the wide reaches of the flooded Charles had looked like water bugs. She had made cod cakes and Boston baked beans. The cod cakes had had peanuts in them, and the baked beans had been flavored with *phuoc nam*. The salty Southeast Asian fish sauce had made the beans, for some reason, taste even more Bostonian.

She was a fanatic, he knew. All those who supported him were. For that matter, so were all those who opposed him. Didn't anyone do things simply because they made sense? Thirty years before, aliens had dropped through the Loophole and made contact with Earth. Boston, more by chance than anything else, had been established as the regulated contact zone. Since then, aliens from the entire galaxy had been pouring through the staid old town, and the tensions caused by their arrival had been increasing geometrically. Kronenbourg was beginning to suspect that they were becoming too strong for most of the human race to handle.

"Have you seen her?" Mi No said, her voice suddenly low and sad. "How is she?"

Kronenbourg had been afraid of that question. He thought about lying. She would catch him. She'd been a businesswoman, of one sort or another, for over twenty years. She would know. "Yes. I saw her. I saw her this morning."

"And is she—"

"She's the same. The same, dammit! What do you expect to hear? Your daughter thinks she's a Rigellian swamp lizard. She's covered with scales and lives in the mud. She's not just going to get over it and come to her senses. Why do you torture yourself?"

She took in a quick breath but didn't cry. For one terrifying second he thought he had pushed her too far and she would. He had no idea of what he could do then. He needed her. She provided him with sense, with stability. Without her harsh understanding he would slide across the surface of things as if on hard ice. The Institute would remain a fever dream. He saw himself years in the future, a doddering old academic, still squabbling with Tolliver.

She straightened up in her chair. "You are right. She is an example of what must not happen to the rest of us. But— she does well?" She looked sharply at him, worried that he would tell some comforting lie.

"Extremely well. An excellent businesswoman, to all accounts. Braak-Kha's school is booming, his philosophy is most influential. It's comforting, nurturing, promising return to primal oneness. The student bars near Fort Washington all smell like wet sulfur."

She sighed. "Poor Ang. What a waste. She was so clever as a child. Why does she flee from the world in such a way?"

Kronenbourg thought of a childhood lived on a speed-

238 ■ ALEXANDER JABLOKOV

boat, listening to the chatter of a machine gun and the screams of her parents' victims, followed by the flaming destruction of home and father, when the Metropolitan District Commission aircraft had destroyed Hull. "She has reason enough, I suspect," he said.

As Mi Nyo sat quietly, remembering her daughter, Kronenbourg could just hear the rats scurrying under the floorboards. Rats, and others, pests from a dozen alien vessels, some chittering and insectoidal, some silent and lizardlike, all living on floating garbage in the interstellar amity of scavengers. Had rat culture been affected? Did some rats wonder if they were any longer truly rats? Kronenbourg killed them all alike, rat and giant pill bug, but their noises still kept him awake at night.

"What about Tolliver?" Mi Nyo asked. "Do you still seek to recruit him?"

"Yes," Kronenbourg said. He remembered that morning's argument. Tolliver had found the body of a murdered alien in the quadrangle at EDS. Had he drawn the correct conclusions? That body was a clearer argument than any Kronenbourg had ever come up with himself. It was also incredibly brutal. If he'd had the choice, Kronenbourg would never have used such an argument. Fortunately, he hadn't been offered a choice.

"Why do you want that academic?" Mi Nyo said. "He studies the aliens, does he not? How can he help us?"

Kronenbourg sighed. The discussion was getting old. "I'm tired of fanatics." He could say that, because Mi Nyo would never recognize the description as applying to her. "I don't want futile revolts against the alien presence. All that will do is spill a lot of blood. I need a man who can *think*. I need a man who can help us define ourselves in this new universe."

Mi Nyo shook her head in admiration. "You are so impractical, Lester. If you worked for me, I would fire you."

"Yes. I suppose I'm lucky that, instead, you work for me."

"With you, Lester. I work with you."

Kronenbourg smiled. "We all work together."

Tolliver passed through the great vaulting structure of the Copley Mall. The sun shown in through the high roof, gleaming off the supports and reflecting at odd angles. There were hundreds of shops here, selling things from a hundred planets. It was here that the open retail trade with the stars was conducted, the most visible part of commerce and, Tolliver knew from Kronenbourg's lectures, by far the least important. The various trading combines handled the real high-value exchanges, somewhere high up in the new towers that changed the Boston skyline almost daily.

The squat tower of Trinity Church, with its peaked red-tile roof, refracted through the glass planes ahead of him, appearing and reappearing as he walked. He went down the stairs and out onto Copley Square, moving quickly through the cold wind. The Romanesque bulk of Trinity still reassured Bostonians that some things remained unchanged, though the tilting, twisted tower of the John Hancock Building next door was a definite opposing viewpoint.

Mercour had insisted on a clandestine meeting. Tolliver walked into the church, counted up the proper number of pews, and sat down. He looked up into the great cubic volume which hovered overhead. The La Farge murals of biblical scenes painted there fascinated him, largely because they were so difficult to see. A body at the Episcopal Divinity School, a meeting at Trinity . . . was Mercour's madness tending toward Episcopalianism? To be driven by the multiplicity of truths inhabiting the universe into genteel Anglo-Catholicism was a quintessentially Bostonian spiritual trajectory.

"Professor Tolliver," Mercour said behind him. "Please don't turn around." Tolliver felt the cold sharpness of a knife at his neck. "I'm glad you could meet with me outside of your regular office hours."

"Where have you been?" Tolliver said. "Everyone in the department has been worried about you."

Mercour chuckled. "Working on some extracurricular projects."

"Like murdering aliens and dumping their bodies in the quadrangle at EDS?"

Mercour took a breath. "Ah, so you figured it out. But why should you be mad at me? It was the perfect problem in alien physiology. How do you kill a crystalline being? 'Precipitate' might be a better word. Relax some of the bonds and the whole thing falls into another conformation, a more stable one."

"Death is more stable than life, Gavin, and life inevitably collapses into it. That's not news. He was your teacher, wasn't he? They one you told me about that afternoon at the Peabody. Why did you do it?"

"I hate them," Mercour said. "I *hate* them. All of them. This one dropped through our Rabbit Hole on his own, from God only knows where. Landed in the Contact Area like a good little boy. In Newton, though. Lucky the gangs didn't get him. Then he ate his spaceship. Just sat down and ate it, drive core and all. Without salt. Then moved down to Cambridgeport and opened his own school. It probably took him three months to get there from Newton, walking along the bottom of the Charles."

"Stop it, Gavin, please," Tolliver said. "Quit cluttering things up. I want information. Why did you kill that being? Was it for knowledge?" He felt a deep frustration. Mercour's mind had been so bright and sharp once, like a jewel. How had this happened to him?

"I tried so hard to see the universe clearly," Mercour said. "He was a telepath. I begged and pleaded with him. I was his only student, you know. He was discouraged by the fact that no one seemed interested in what he had to teach.

Finally, he let me see the universe through his senses." Mercour choked. "It was madness! He saw the insides of things, and their ends, and their beginnings, and so much more, and still none of it made sense. *None of it made any sense at all.*"

His voice was so anguished that Tolliver wanted to turn around and comfort him, remembering the eager boy Mercour had once been. The knife at his neck stopped him.

"You can't see the universe clearly until you know who you are, Gavin," Tolliver said. Annoying as he was, Kronenbourg was right about that. "Who are you?"

Mercour's breath hissed out, and Tolliver felt the knife edge press against his neck. Mercour, who was familiar with the anatomies of a dozen species, certainly knew where the jugular vein and carotid artery were in the human body.

Three Boston police officers suddenly came through the door behind the baptismal font. They stopped and peered into the darkness of the church but did not move further.

"Oh, God," Mercour said. "How did they find me? You led them here!" Mercour shouted. "You bastard!" The knife edge pressed harder, but then the pressure vanished. Mercour leaped over the pew and ran for the doors. The police watched impassively as the graceful figures of the Koltsoi appeared at the doors, dark shadows against the light streaming in. They moved with slow curves, swaying like water plants, their once-human translator in front.

"Halt," she said. "Halt, or—"

With his shoulder, Mercour hit her hard in the side. He must have gauged his blow precisely. She shrieked and crumpled to the floor, bent double in the wrong direction. Bones protruded through the skin of her chest. She continued to scream, a high-pitched sound like a teakettle on full boil. Blood spattered on the floor. Mercour dodged toward the doors but the Koltsoi, strong despite their slenderness, gathered around him.

Pulling a can out of his student robe, Mercour sprayed them with a dark mist. They clutched at their eyes and stumbled away, twitching as if electrocuted.

"Remember this trick, Professor!" Mercour yelled over his shoulder. "Koltsoi are allergic to WD-40. Hah!" And he was out of the doors and gone.

Tolliver started to get up, and felt a hand on his shoulder. It was one of the three officers. He had at first taken the hand as a gesture of comfort, but it tightened painfully.

"Professor Tolliver," the officer said. "Will you please come with us? We have some questions."

"Don't we all, Officer. Don't we all."

Tolliver stopped at the edge of highest pool of water. Its outflow poured down into a series of pools below, and then into the ocean. They were surrounded by snow and rime ice. "Damn it, Kronenbourg, what are you doing? Why have you brought me to this godforsaken place?" In the week since Mercour's disappearance, his face had become gaunt and tight. He had kept to himself and stayed away from his department.

Kronenbourg had somehow arranged for the charges of accessory to murder to be dropped, and gotten him released from jail. Tolliver was bewildered by this unexpected display of power. "You said there would be no quid pro quo."

Kronenbourg slumped after him, his face mournful. His heavy coat flapped around his knees. "That's what I said, and that's what I meant. You're under no obligation to me. I didn't spring you from jail to get something from you. But our argument isn't over, Chris. Mercour has something to add."

Tolliver turned to him. "Do you know where he is?"

Kronenbourg nodded heavily. "I do. That's why I brought you here. Come on. I think you'll find his argument quite convincing."

The ruins of what had once been South Boston could be

seen beneath the ocean surface. Out of the water rose Telegraph Hill, the only place surviving. It had once been the site of a high school, but now supported the elaborate black structures of the Targive citadel. They looked like tents, or folded bat wings. Kronenbourg thought that they actually were the wings of some beast modified beyond recognition, bones forming the supports, skin the fabric. No one knew for sure, of course, because the Targives kept themselves secret. Conduits carried streams of water from the citadel and out to here.

Steam rose from the Targive outflow, filled with exotic metallic salts which formed poisonous blue-green and orange crystals on the ruined building foundations. Nothing grew here, on either land or water. This part of town had once been inhabited by conservative Irish, deeply prejudiced against the influx of blacks and hispanics. Now they were gone, and an alien citadel spread its wings above their abandoned community.

"How did you know that Mercour had killed that alien?" Tolliver said. He had kept away from Kronenbourg all week, but the questions had been eating at him.

"Do you still think I had something to do with it?" Kronenbourg said. "Don't be ridiculous. I pay close attention to the madness that goes on in the schools in Cambridgeport. I can draw obvious conclusions. It's time that *you* started to pay attention, Chris."

Scavengers lived near the water in huts built of old vinyl siding and asphalt cut from the twisted and useless roads. A variety of objects found their way into the Targive outflow, no one knew whether by accident or on purpose. Some were useful devices, others deadly traps. The scavengers stayed near the toxic water, sickening and dying, but bringing forth treasures. One treasure they had found was the body of Gavin Mercour.

Hollow-eyed men and women examined the interlopers from the doors of their shacks, motionless save for their steaming breath. Several of them greeted Kronenbourg familiarly. They directed the two men to their discovery.

Mercour lay on the edge of one of the pools, face up, eyes open. His eyes were refractive transparent spheres, like rock crystal or leaded glass, and the rest of his body was of dark, translucent blue stone. He looked like the victim of an unusually artistic Medusa.

"Nothing of him that doth fade, but doth suffer a seachange into something rich and strange," Kronenbourg recited.

Tolliver knelt by the pool. The physical structure of Mercour's body was identical to that of the alien he had killed in Cambridge.

"How did they do that?" he wondered aloud. "They must have replaced his body bit by bit, like making petrified wood."

"Except that they kept him alive while they did it," Kronenbourg said. "That's the Targive way. They never deal with anything that isn't alive. They probably gave him the structure of the living alien, then crystallized him the same way he murdered his victim. Poetic justice, with a vengeance."

Tolliver looked into the deep transparent eyes. "He was hoping to find a place with no shadows, where he could see. I suppose that's why he finally tried to get to the Targives. Do you suppose that he saw the truth before he died?"

"I doubt it. Human beings don't have much aptitude for being crystals." Kronenbourg sat down on a pile of old bricks that was slightly higher than the surrounding tidal marshes, and started to dig small flat stones out of the soil nearby. "They don't have much aptitude for being swamp lizards or Koltsoi, either, but that doesn't stop them."

Tolliver sighed. "I suppose not. Where there is light, there are shadows. If only they didn't tempt us the way they do! Sometimes I think that all aliens are just personifications of our neuroses, physical manifestations of what we fear or desire. But they are actually, demonstrably real. That's what's so terrifying about them."

"They *are* real," Kronenbourg said, irritated. "Have no doubt. Just ask poor Mercour. We can't blame the aliens for luring us and causing us to doubt our own humanity. The fault is our own." He had dug out quite a pile of stones. He handed some to Tolliver, who looked confused. "Look at their shape. You can see what they're good for."

Kronenbourg stood up and pitched his first flat stone at the poisonous water. It skipped twice. Tolliver smiled and whipped his arm in a lazy arc. His stone skipped seven times, clear to the far side. It had been years since he'd done anything like that.

"So now I'm to help you in your great enterprise?" Tolliver said. "The Institute of Human Culture. Or whatever."

"You think I take your acquiescence for granted? I don't. But I also don't see any other choice for you. You know whose eyes you look through."

Tolliver paused, idly tossing his stone in his hand. "Do I?" At least Kronenbourg wasn't gloating over the wreck of his ideals. Kronenbourg was more of a politician than he himself realized.

"You do. You'll join me, you'll subvert my goals and ideas, you'll reinterpret, redefine. My original intentions will get lost in the footnotes. I won't mind. There are more ways of being human than any of the billions of us on this planet have managed to figure out. Comparing ourselves to these bugs, lizards, and crystals from other planets may just help us get better at being humans."

"Okay," Tolliver said, feeling an obscure sense of surrender. "Let's see who can first figure out what a human is."

Kronenbourg grunted. "Someday, the Institute will be a large building with marble columns. My statue, and yours, will stand in the Great Hall, looking nobly off into the future. The custodians will believe that human culture is preserved in the Institute's glass cases. They will be wrong, but their error is inevitable." His next stone sank straight into the water.

Tolliver's stone skimmed across the water and almost wanted to fly. "What do you mean?" The long-strained muscles of his face relaxed.

Kronenbourg smiled at him. "I'm glad you're with me, finally. We'll spend the rest of our lives dealing with morons, but we'll survive. And who knows? We may actually get some to use their human minds against the universe properly. The same way that you use the flatness of the stone to skip it across the water." His next try was perfect— nine, at least. He looked pleased with himself.

They stood there, skipping their stones and talking, until it got too dark to see.

BOSTON IN 2050

A built-up causeway now connects Boston with the mainland at the Washington Street Gate (1). The Back Bay remains partially submerged, but the Phneri have begun to wall and reclaim it.

A submerged artery connects Boston to the Interstellar Port of Boston headquarters (2).

Above the City Ring, the Cube extends 130 stories into the air, a vertical conglomerate of four centuries of architecture. Buildings are built inside buildings, on top of buildings, encasing buildings. Like the water-soaked land surrounding it, Boston changes its contours daily. In keeping with Boston tradition, major traffic routes are twisting, obscure, and unmarked.

Heat and waste disposal are enormous problems. The Charles cools Boston, flowing under it at the Charles gates, near the Washington Street Gate, and boiling out at the Clivus (3).

THE *LADY OF PORT MORESBY* INCIDENT
ALEXANDER JABLOKOV

UNITED NATIONS HEARING TESTIMONY
2054

SELECTIONS FROM TESTIMONY AT UN HEARINGS:
INVESTIGATION INTO THE DESTRUCTION OF THE SPACESHIP
LADY OF PORT MORESBY, MARCH 2054

TESTIMONY OF ALVIN FALKENBERG, PILOT AND SOLE PROPRIETOR
OF THE *KARAGANDA*, AT THE TIME OF THE INCIDENT OPERATING
UNDER CONTRACT TO THE INTERSOL TRADING CORPORATION,
HEADQUARTERED IN KUALA LUMPUR, MALAYSIA.

Falkenberg: The *Lady of Port Moresby* started to close with the Sh'k vessel immediately as it exited the Loophole. A nice job of maneuvering, I must say. There isn't any predictability about how ships emerge from the singularity. I'd been on station there for the past two years, trying to make trade contact, but all those aliens did was sweep past me. The captain of the *Lady* did some fancy jumping around. Not that it did much good.

Q: Did you witness the actual destruction of the *Lady of Port Moresby*?

Falkenberg: One minute she was there, closing in on the Sh'k ship, the next she was just some debris. I'm not sure what I witnessed. And you know what? That Sh'k could've been just running excess Phneri refugees in to Earth to dump them in the ocean. I doubt she had anything worth contacting aboard.

Q: What do you think they were after?

Falkenberg: After? What we all are after, Councillor.
            Wealth. Power. An honest deal. Those
            bastards from Boston suck up everything
            that comes through that Loophole.
            Knowledge from the entire Galaxy. We just
            wanted to contact those ships, to make some
            fair trading. Nothing unusual. And they
            blew up the *Lady of Port Moresby*. What is it
            they say now? "Removal of flotsam and
            jetsam is the responsibility of the receiver."
            We should blow those Boston bastards clear
            off the map.

Q: Mr. Falkenberg, I am afraid that is out of the
            purview of this committee.

THREE BOSTON ARTISTS
SARAH SMITH

OIL PAINT SHOULD never feel the damp. Drop by drop water works into canvas. Manets and Picassos sprout fungi. Brown rings spread like Phneri nests in the waterlogged Back Bay. Under the hard surface, layer splits from layer. Then it is time for Ernest, the restorer. Then it is too late.

In the great marble hall of Boston's Museum of Human Culture, in the forty-third year of the aliens, the restorer Ernest Pole met the old woman and the Phner under the greatest painting in the world, Rembrandt's *Juno*.

Juno dominated the exhibition hall, immortal, serene, and ruined. Cracked varnish bloomed across her dress. Oily smoke stains had obliterated all but the shadow of her hands, and a long rip struck across the canvas from her right shoulder down into her bosom. Her magnificent eyes held all time in them, endless and full of blessing.

"Jennifer Fenner, Boston Demolition and Rehabilitation." The woman sat on one of the velvet banquettes, boots half open, hands in her pockets. Her overalls still stank of Back Bay mud and her dirty hair had a permanent hard-hat dent. Ernest could have collaged her from the Frans Hals postcards in the museum shop. For a moment his hands itched to try it. Ernest was a secret collager. Late at night in his room he tore and pasted paper scraps from the streets: fugitive materials, the secret vice of the restorer.

The alien was chunky, beaver-shaped. Its claws clicked once on the marble pavement and it only stirred, half-twitched round, then settled back down to look at the painting. It smelled doggy, like wet fur, overpowering the Museum's own smell of lemon oil and flowers.

"That's the painting?" the old woman said. "It's in bad shape."

Restoration didn't use words like "bad shape." Ernest had been in restoration five years. Five years to fall in love with a painting too beautiful to lose and too fragile to restore.

"*Juno* was in the Los Angeles earthquake," Ernest said. "There's extensive water damage, burns in the canvas, and the rip and smoke damage that you **see**. She's *got* to be restored."

"It would help if you could see what's happened to her," Dr. Fender said, half to herself, half to him. "The structure of the painting."

She stood up, legs spread apart, hands on her hips, head thrown back and to one side, her lower lip thrust out, looking at *Juno*. Definitely Frans Hals.

"It's not our usual work. We *esfn* mostly buildings. It'd be a challenge." She meant: it'd cost. More than you want to pay an alien, here at the Museum of Human Culture.

Ernest stole a wary look at the Phner. From closer up the Phner looked like an otter, animals Ernest had sometimes seen gliding through the drowned alleys of the Back Bay. Under the mud his fur was tabbied gold, the color of Juno's crown. He didn't look dangerous, any more than the woman looked like what the law said she was, a keeper of dangerous animals.

"Anyone can tell you—nobody sees structures better than a Phner. Phneri can look at a brick house and find the

252 ■ SARAH SMITH

stress cracks humans wouldn't see, whistle at a concrete pil-
ing and know where it'll break. They *esfn* how things are
built." She shrugged. "We've never *esfn*ed a painting. But
structure is structure. Let me ask him."

The alien sat back on his hind legs and chirped at her,
bird-music rising into a squeak. She picked up the translator box and began to play its keychord with one hand; soft
trills echoed in the chilly room. The little alien banged his
tail on the floor, trilling back.

"*He* wants to do it." The old woman looked down at the
alien with a crooked, affectionate smile. Her eyes snapped
back up to Ernest. "Of course, he's just an animal."

Up close she had the pale-eyed, fanatic look of any Bostonian who'd worked too long with aliens. She was probably a lot crazier than she looked. Ernest had come from
Chicago and Bostonians frightened him. Boston had made
him take up collage: torn edges, uneasy juxtapositions.

"You realize—" he pointed at the alien— "he'd have to
work under guard."

The old woman let bitterness show in her face.

"I'm sorry," Ernest said.

"Mr. Pole." She sighed. "I've been with the Phneri for
forty years. The Phneri are neither dangerous nor destruc-
tive. The Phneri are political exiles."

"I don't know about politics," Ernest said. "And I
wasn't even born when the Phneri came. I just want to save
Juno." Ernest looked into the painting's majestic eyes and
his heart lifted a little. "*Juno*'s my job," he said.

"The Phneri are my job. I employ most of the Phneri in
Boston. Who are probably all the Phneri there are, anywhere. I don't care about human culture. I do care that each
and every living Phner in my custody needs between five
and six pounds of fish a day. A ton of fish a day, Mr. Pole,
and your Museum wants to pay me half what I get in architectural work."

He was not a rough man, but he took the old woman by
the shoulders and turned her to face the painting. She

looked up and for a long moment kept looking. For a moment Ernest saw in the old woman's face some reflection of
the young one Rembrandt had seen.

"Be *human*," he pleaded.

Forty-three years ago, he wanted to tell her, the aliens
landed in Boston. Six lost tourists at first, now—how many?
More aliens than humans, Director Kronenbourg had said.
A collage of the unknown. Humans were just another species now, unless they remembered who they were.

She wriggled out of his hands.

"When one of my Phneri eats a fish, he understands the
structure of the fish. He worships the fish while he eats. He
esfns the fish. They have art too. They have poetry." The old
woman looked at him. "Your *Juno*'s a good painting. But
Rembrandt's dead; he doesn't eat. My artists eat."

"What do you want?" Ernest asked.

"Enough fish, Mr. Pole. I want the Miller's Hall Court to
reclassify the Phneri. Their culture's twenty thousand years
old; I want them to have the same status as the Spatiens and
the Targives. I want teachers for the Phneri, I want them to
learn English—they can do it, some of them speak like they
were born to it. I want money for teachers. I want to get the
Phneri out of those raft slums on the South Boston Shoals. I
want them to be out of my custody, I want them to be able
to apply for work permits on their own, to get into the Cube
on their own, because that's where the money is, Mr. Pole, I
want them to be able to *live* in the Cube if they want."

"The Museum can't do anything to influence Miller's
Hall," Ernest said quickly. "We don't talk to anyone there.
You'd have to talk to the Bishop."

She picked up her translator box to leave.

For *Juno* he would do anything. He held her arm. "I'll
look at their art," he offered.

"What?"

He blushed. "I mean—if they make art, if they don't
just—eat things—" His hand dropped. "I mean—it isn't
much—I'm not a critic, just a restorer. It wouldn't do you

any good with the Bishop." He added after a moment, "It wouldn't really do any good at all."

The woman stared at him. After a moment she smiled, recovering herself again, she crossed her arms: jeering smile, arms akimbo.

"Mr. Pole, has anyone ever told you you're dangerous?"

"No."

"You're honest. You'll tell me what you think. The same way you'll do anything to help your precious painting. It won't get you anywhere," she said. "People know you care too much. They think you're dangerous."

It had never occurred to him not to be honest in criticism. What was it for otherwise?

"All right," she sighed. "If you can criticize art for *dangerous animals*, we can work for Museum wages."

"You'll *esfn Juno*," he breathed.

The alien was sitting up, trilling at the old woman. She shot one sharp whistle at him. "I shouldn't bring him when I'm bargaining," she said dryly. "Yes, we'll do it. Not for *Juno*, though. Not for anything human."

The old woman took his elbow and steered him out of the marble room. Outside the doorway, French windows threw on the parquet a square of wavery sun. "Look out there." They stepped out the windows onto an enclosed balcony, ribbons of steel vibrating with the wind. She pointed toward the South Boston Shoals. A guard looked up at them from the terrace below, another one materialized efficiently inside the doorway. The Museum took its treasures seriously.

From this distance the domed raft-slums looked like fantasies from a Buckminster Fuller drawing.

"And I'm going to give you more than you think, Mr. Honest Man. I'm going to show you the real Boston artists."

The hand was dead black, workmanlike, stubby, a big palm spanning short wide fingers. An old man's hand. It hung attentively at the end of a glittering technology of glass in the restoration room, facing *Juno*. The north light shone over her. Dr. Fenner explained that *esfn* didn't need light. "It's closer to sonar. He generates waves." The alien, who had eaten his fish in the basement, clicked around the oak floor, whistling softly. "He likes your floor's history," Dr. Fenner explained. "The trees it was made of . . . He sees the seasons."

The small alien sat up and looked over its shoulder toward Ernest, an unreadable beaver.

For the *esfnai* they had taken the protective glass off *Juno*. Ernest looked at the helpless paint, thinking of pollution, flaking. "He *esfn*s the structure. He records his *esfnai* on this computer," Dr. Fenner patted a small green box. "He checks the *esfnai* as he works by using the waldo-hand to copy the painting. You get a runtime license for the translation software we use," she said, "and the copy of the painting. You can make more copies." She grinned. "Sell them in the museum shop. We get a two-percent royalty."

"We only want to restore her."

Esfn. The Phner ability to see structure, see it gesture by gesture as it had been built. Ernest looked across at *Juno*'s young, serene face, the steady eyes under their grime and smoke. Immortal beauty made of white lead paint, made of old canvas, burnt and stained and cracked. The white lead was oxidizing; the canvas would never hold paint well again. Ernest had spent five years convincing himself *Juno* was not too hopeless to restore.

What would she look like new?

"You'll end up hanging the copy," Dr. Fenner predicted.

"No."

"Why not? The artistic process is what's important. Not what it produces. The Phneri would let her rot. If you want a record of what she looked like during part of her lifetime," the old woman shrugged, "well, that's only process, isn't it?"

"We think like humans here," Ernest said a little stiffly.

"What's wrong with thinking like a Phner?"

Ernest moved over to the window. Outside, the terrace overlooked the Wall. The ragged rafts bumped each other down at the Shoals slums where the Phneri lived in the little bustling tides.

"I don't want a Museum answer, Honest Man," Dr. Fenner said. "I don't want to hear 'because it's not human.'"

The old woman took a bite out of her lunchroll. Jennifer Fenner had bought lunch at the Raanda kiosk just outside the Museum. Her roll was bright yellow and smelled of fish and hot linen. Ernest had brought human food in a brown bag from home. The alien clicked over and sat up, begging bites.

"Dr. Fenner," he said, "do you remember back before there were aliens?"

"There were always aliens. They just weren't here," she said sharply, then laughed. "Ernest, I'm old enough to remember Fenway Park being dry."

"Before they came—" Ernest put his sandwich down and tried to figure out what he was saying. "All the food was human food. Everything that everybody ever ate was human. It had been grown, or invented, or something, right here on Earth. Everything that people said was human. People used Boston whalers instead of waterwalkers. They didn't have to worry about what human was, because that's all there was. But when I was born, the aliens were already here."

She shook her head. "Are you that young?"

She fed the last of her lunchroll to the alien. "Human or not, my food has more vitamins. Come on, guy, time to work." The waldo cap, a gold net, was already fitted over his head. She plugged the leads in, patted the alien, and set him down in front of the painting.

"There's a thing about isolated cultures—" he began. "Do you know anything about cultural anthropology?"

"No," she said dryly. "I have a degree in it."

"Oh. Well." He still needed to say what he meant. He

found what would help in the cabinets at the back of the restoration room. He slid it carefully into a small holding box and carried the box back to her, one hand cupped over it. "Look at this." The fragment was so small, light enough so that, when she leaned over to look at it, it stirred with her breath.

"This came out of a Polynesian culture. A very isolated culture, on one or two islands. It's a miniature grass-weaving. The Polynesians made beautiful things, grass mats and pots." A perfect thing. For years, guiltily, he had wanted to steal it and center a collage around it.

She stirred the inch-square mesh with her finger. "It has *esfn.*"

"We were isolated and we didn't know it. We made Boston whalers and ate baked beans. Or we painted Rembrandts," he said, looking up at *Juno*'s serene face. "Rembrandt was a human, and Shakespeare, and Beethoven. Matisse and Henry Moore. And we thought we were all alone."

"And then the ships come," she prompted. "And they introduce the Polynesians to top hats and brass buttons. And they all go off to New Bedford and the Polynesians learn to kill whales."

"Do you know what happened to the grass mats and pots, Dr. Fenner? They're in museums because they are beautiful. But the Polynesians today can't tell you what those pots and mats are for. And they can't make them."

"But there are still Polynesians," she said.

"Are there?"

He put the box and the weaving down carefully on a table. He moved over to the window, by her, and looked out through the wavery glass. The mylar-covered rafts bobbed in the winter sunlight. Down by half-drowned Back Bay, waldos moved over old brown houses, shoring up and tearing down. A dot of bright red walked slowly over the waves toward the harbor. "Nobody knows what those pots and mats are *about* anymore. I never knew what human culture was like when it was all human. This is an alien city. There are at least twenty-four intelligent species in Boston. We're getting to be like all of them. We're changing. Someday we're all going to be eating krill crackers and operating fish-divers for the Hnarfil; we'll be imitation Manam or Raanda, or Bishop-worshipers. Maybe then we'll know what we're doing. But we won't know what we were." Ernest grinned uneasily. "I think I need to know *Juno*, to know as much as I can, to love her. I need to be a restorer."

"Don't worry about it, Ernest," she said.

In the corner of Ernest's eye, movement caught. The alien was whistling softly at the painting. The waldo was holding a brush and had begun to pick at the canvas, delicately as a dragonfly.

The painting blossomed on the canvas like a dream. Ernest spent every hour that he could spare watching the intoxicating calligraphy of the brush: creams and ivories of skin, translucent shadows, sculptural gold.

The art trip was put off until the day the painting would be finished. The whole Phneri community was excited, Dr. Fenner told him. They would make a piece of art just for him.

"Something like kites, they said." She smiled. "I met my first Phner because of a kite. I'll tell you someday."

On the day the picture would be finished, they went down to the rafts in the South Boston Shoals. They would come back in the evening and see the finish of *Juno*.

"They live in a slum," Dr. Fenner had warned. Ernest picked his way across the bobbing floats, following her through the crowd of humans and aliens. He had not expected to see so many humans. They stood huddled around the fires built in the center of the rafts, scarecrows in layers of dirty clothes, gaping at the Phneri as they would have at a street fight or a hopter show.

The float lurched under a heavy wave. Water slopped over Ernest's shoes, fish-smelling and brown.

The waves here rolled unremittingly, every few seconds, not regular. Ernest felt it as a gravity tug in his stomach, then a sudden light-headedness. Across the water, through the late afternoon sea mist, the City Wall rose up as solid as a planet, the Boston Cube behind it. The sun came through the clouds and turned everything to vapor. Turner, he thought. The sunlight strengthened until their shadow across the waves was a choppy nettle green.

A small tawny-gold paw pressed something into Ernest's hand. He looked at it, not recognizing it. "A flare-gun," Dr. Fenner said. "That's for later. You don't have to use it." He turned it around in his hand, puzzled, then put it in his pocket.

He saw the artists' float tethered at the end of the long strip of slum. Small tawny creatures crowded around the constructions on the raft.

The constructions themselves—Ernest caught his breath and held it, held it till it hurt.

Kites, Dr. Fenner had said. They soared. In the whipping wind, banners and windsails raced skyward, whirling. Gray-green with honey orange, gold skirled with a no-color that tugged at the eyes: fragile towers, bumping, colliding. One shot up into the sky, propelled by some air-engine, and tumbled upward like a vast acrobat. The sky bobbed with rippling shapes. Sails flew glorious and urgent; Cisos and dragons breathed fire into the clouds. Ernest's heart shot upward on that rippling as if it had been on a string.

"Oh," Ernest said. The longing in his voice startled him. Dr. Fenner's face was wet with tears.

"Look! Animals?" she said triumphantly.

Ernest watched, rapt out of himself.

Some of the constructions stood on the raft, not meant to be borne on air. They were towers, so gossamer that the walls themselves caught the light and passed it through in dazzle. They ignored gravity, careening castles in a fantastic landscape, balanced on their own secret center.

He watched, lifted out of time.

The light changed, and shadows stretched across the water. The sun was sinking red. Ernest was startled. It seemed as though he had been looking only a few minutes.

"I don't want the sun to go down," he said like a child. "This—this is magnificent. I want it to go on . . ."

Dr. Fenner laughed. "You'll remember."

It was only dusk. He could clearly see what happened next.

On the raft, the tawny bodies began to tug at a tower. The arms of a windmill flailed, fell. A silken wall tore across and jerked like an animal with a broken back.

"What are they doing? They can't—" One of the largest sails was buckling now. But you can't, they're too beautiful, Ernest said silently like a man just killed, watching the towers fall like blood out of his heart. The sail swayed back and forth in front of the setting sun and the sun flashed red, shadow, red.

In the sky the great dragons floated, untouched as yet.

The sun touched the ocean and died. From the raft slums, someone, human or Phner, began setting off flareguns. A vicious light stabbed through one sail. Sparks from the flareguns jabbed at cloth. Sparks cut through lines, crawled purposefully up lines. A burning kite blundered into another and light exploded across the sky so that Ernest could see the crooked Hancock Tower with light blossoming in its glass. What the kites had been made of, gauze or silk, hung painted in flame, then fell charring. Smudges stung Ernest's face and hissed into the harbor.

And the Phneri sang.

It was a trilling vibration in the rafts, so huge a chorus that the humans' bones shook and their teeth chattered. The dark water pulsed with it in little waves. And in the sky the kites caught and blazed and died until the last of them was only a flaming in the sky.

In the dark the raft closed its shield over them and turned up its heat. "Lights," Dr. Fenner said. "No," Ernest said, and he sat bent over in the dark, aching all over.

"Was it beautiful?" Dr. Fenner said.

"Beautiful?" he said.

Below them, in the dirty water, the last of the destroyers' songs faded away in groans.

She lived in one of the cheap hives above Kendall Square. Her room was cold, smelling of the river, of Phneri fur. She ordered coffee from the hive kitchen; it arrived in a heat-retaining cup—technology of the Abelnelna, which had replaced Japanese covered cups, plastic heat-baffling cups, everything that had been part of human culture before the aliens came.

"I'm sorry you felt hurt," she said.

He saw the memory of kites floating in the afternoon sky. Somebody had spooned out his soul, bit by bit.

"Beautiful," he said dully. "I thought of Los Angeles. All those paintings in the earthquake, burning."

She raised her eyebrows. "It must be nice to be cultured. All right, I guess I was hurt too, the first time I saw an *esfnai*. I didn't think of Los Angeles. It was before Los Angeles. I was nine."

She put her elbows on the table. "I had just moved up from Houston and my family was breaking up. They left me pretty much alone. So one afternoon I went out and got lost and I saw a Phner. My first alien. He was little, for a Phner. Malnourished, I know now. Nobody else saw him. I didn't know what he was. We watched Cody kites together. Those big boxy kites. I took him home. He made me the most wonderful thing I had ever seen, a very little Cody kite out of silver foil." She held her two hands apart. "Then he destroyed it, just before—I saw him smash it. It was years before I found out why that was love."

"Love?" he said.

"And culture. And art. They destroyed the kites for you.

So you could see every moment of them. So you could live their whole life."

He stared at her, trying to reconcile anything rational with what he felt. He swirled the coffee again. The dark liquid swirled in front of his eyes. Gold-orange and gray-green and the lifting sails.

"Structure's beautiful when it changes," she said.

She whispered commands to the computer. The printer hissed out a page, still warm. The words meant nothing.

> *(to finish/begin*
> *all-structures*
> *(unit=not-here-previous-duration)*
> *(unit=not-here-duration-to-come)*
> *(esfn to contemplate*
> *(all-structures)/is=existence . . .*

"It's some of their poetry. It means something like

> *Finish and begin. Everything is*
> *and there is not-presence; in* esfnai *it is.*
> *Volcanoes exploding in air*
> *volcanoes in water*
> *Finish and begin—*

"They don't have a word for individual existence, or for not existing. Only for duration." She tried again.

> *Visible, not visible,*
> *here, not here,*
> *fires in air*
> *in water*
> *All seen is seen forever.*

"They must remember for a very long time," Ernest said dully. He would never forget.

"They don't think about time."

THREE BOSTON ARTISTS ■ 263

"But humans—" Ernest started. He couldn't say any more. Dr. Fenner had said he was an honest man. He wasn't honest, he realized, he was just human.

"The Museum is wrong," Jennifer Fenner said. "The Museum has a lot of influence in this town—the Museum, the Institute, Humanity First, all you people—but it all goes to preserving human culture 'uncorrupted.' No such thing. Ernest, the aliens are here. This isn't a world of humans anymore, not humans alone. We pretend it is. We classify intelligent beings like my Phneri as animals. We stagnate, like your Museum, that can't even bear a new taste in its mouth. And all the time, there's so much we could know."

"Like the Polynesians?" Ernest said bitterly.

"Phneri aren't destroyers. They could make those kites again; there were three hundred Phneri at that *esfnai* and they all *esfn*ed the kites before they burned them. But they'd only do that for humans; those kites were made for this day, that mist and wind and blowing sunlight. And to remember."

It was ignoble of him, clearly, to be happy that he could see those kites again. He looked up at her. She was smiling at him mockingly. "And will they ever be again the way they were today, Ernest? And will you ever forget them?"

He threw down the cup; it closed before it hit the ground. "Humans keep art! That's how we remember!"

She shook her head. "Finish and begin."

"Not *Juno*!"

He had meant it as bluster, and then he realized what he could have known all along.

"Finish *Juno*," Ernest said. "The Phner's going to *finish* her tonight." For all the time of the *esfnai* of *Juno*, he had watched, as happy with the process as the Phner must have been. He had gone off today to the art show as if he knew what it meant. The art show and *Juno* were one work. But he had been blind, been human.

"Don't worry, I told him not to finish her—"

But Ernest knew better. "That doesn't matter!" he shouted. "He's an artist."

From the Kendall Square hives to the Museum, late at night with only the robocabs running, it was so long, so long. The robo jounced them over the night-sleeping river. Jennifer passed him her translator box so he could call ahead to the Museum. But the comm-address of the restoration rooms didn't answer, which should have told them something. In front of the Museum, swarming police lights flashed red and blue and the policemen tried to stop them at the doors.

In the brightly lit restoration room, blood spattered across the floor. For such a little animal, the Phner had made a lot of blood in dying. The vidcameras hovered around him like flies. The policeman who had shot the alien was being interviewed by three reporters. "That animal just started to tear the painting apart!" the policeman was saying. "Tear it right up!" Blood was splattered across *Juno* too. The Phner had ripped the center of the canvas away. Juno had lost most of her hair, her neck, and both her magnificent eyes. Jennifer Fenner knelt down and cradled the Phner's body in her arms. The Phner's head lolled down over the crook of her elbow. Ernest touched its fur for the first time; oily and smooth, with a soft undercoat, and still warm.

The waldo-hand was still painting. It was almost done. On the canvas *Juno* bloomed, young, bright, perfect. It was the most beautiful thing Ernest had ever seen. Untouched by time. Untouchable.

And not painted by a human anymore.

Quite suddenly Ernest sat down on the floor and began to cry.

The City Wall is a place where young lovers meet, friends stroll on the seawall top, gawkers look out over the Shoals. Ernest and Dr. Jennifer Fenner met there one day much later, in spring. The winter winds were over and the first sailboats were cutting their white notches in the river. The granite bulk of the Museum was at their backs.

"They fired me, you know," Ernest said. "From the Museum."

"Well," Jennifer said. "I've been 'retired.'"

Neither said anything for a while. He looked up at the Museum. He thought he could pick out the glass balcony where he and she had stood the day they had first met. There were no mylar rafts to look at now; the Phneri and the humans who had shared their slum had been moved away.

"I wonder who has custody of the Phneri now," she said.

"They aren't yours," he said bitterly.

She shook her head. "They never were."

Someone had got a copy of the *Juno* data the Phner had produced, and the waldo street artists had passed copies from hand to hand. So now, on one of the windbreaks at the top of the Wall, on a faded poster, a waldo artist had used up a few idle minutes and copied *Juno*. Her magnificent eyes smiled over drowned Boston. Her pigments were already fading.

"We weren't important," Ernest said. "He was making a collage and we were pieces of paper he needed." He put out his hand and touched the fading face. "She was the big piece in the middle. But she wasn't important either."

He looked out over the river. When he had come to Boston, he had thought he could go away from it and begin understanding things again. "I'll never leave here," he said.

"Ernest," she said. "I'm sorry."

He picked up a piece of paper that had got stuck in a crevice of the Wall, looked at it without quite seeing it, and stuck it in his pocket. It had the look of something human.

"You still make collages?" She dug in her pocket and half held out her hand. "I wanted you to have this. For a collage. If you want."

It rested on cotton in an old-fashioned cardboard box marked FILENE'S: a crushed bauble with the sheen of tarnished silver, coin-flat and lighter than tissue. He could see in it the shape that it must once have had. A Cody kite like the kites a nine-year-old girl had watched with her first alien. It was small in his hand: made for a girl's hand long ago, a girl not full-grown, needing to wonder at something much smaller than she.

"You said something once," she said. "Humans keep art." She shrugged and turned away, turned back. "Come show your collage to me when you're done," she said. Then she was gone.

Ernest stood looking out over the river beyond the wall. Humans keep art. Humans have a past, have memory. In the sky the kites were still flying in his head. Memory burns, memory cracks and falls away, memory dies under alien claws. Art hurts and will not stop. What could art be about in a city of aliens?

He reached out and touched the paper with Juno's face, but left it on the wall. In his room were all the things he picked up in his wandering. At night, in his room, he pasted together old Coke squeeze bottles, feathers of birds of Earth. He drew on them, eyes, clouds, gestures, hands, urgent shapes on feathers and paper. Collages. Undeniable things thrown up by the city, the fragments of hard answers.

Humans keep art. And somewhere in the human city waited the Phneri and all the somber aliens. He wished that he had dared to steal the Polynesian weaving.

He turned the little ruined silver thing between thumb and forefinger. She had kept it, and kept with it her nine-year-old self, an afternoon on the Common watching the kites fly. Is art only the stories we tell about ourselves? The sunlight shimmered across the metal. "I could put it into something," he thought, more or less, or merely felt about it what he felt about almost everything, all the time now, the focus of some question. He dropped it back inside the box and put the box in his pocket and wandered on, down the path, toward Boston.

FOCAL PLANE
ALEXANDER JABLOKOV

Mrs. Powel: Well Doctor, what have we got, a Republic, or a Monarchy?

Benjamin Franklin: A Republic, if you can keep it.

[September 18, 1787]

THE JANUARY WIND blows a fine spray off the ocean, coating everything with a salty rime. I hang from the icy seawall watching the waves crash beneath me. I flex my left arm to crack the ice off. The morning sun is still invisible. Nothing has happened for hours. I hear my boss, Zenaïda Speck: "You knew the job was boring when you took it, Baka." Right, Zen. Boredom and danger, the reporter's friends.

Above me looms what's left of Dorchester High School, all mock-Norman turrets and arches. Half of it's fallen into the ocean, to join the ruins of the rest of Dorchester. Good visuals. For destruction, ice is great and will certainly suffice.

In search of secrecy, the Greater Boston Chamber of Commerce has decided to have its meeting here, under the guise of some high school women's regional swimming finals. A ridiculous touch, which helps. It's going to be hard to make a Chamber-of-Commerce-sponsored revolution interesting.

Dark figures appear on the wall above me and peer down into the uneasy water. I make like one more irregular piece of the crumbling seawall. The part of me that's human flesh is covered by a nonreflective insuit, so I should be un-detectable. I can't tell if the guards are human, Koltsoi, Ad-jawi, or some other alien species. Humanoid, at least. The wealthy don't use the weirder insectoid, crystalloid, or pasta-saladoid aliens in private service capacities.

A violet flicker of laser and the lump of ice next to me cracks and vaporizes. The security guards look down for a few more minutes, then duck back in. A little lax, maybe, but it's freezy-ass cold. I can sympathize.

Zenaïda gave me crap about spending the day covering a high school girls' swim meet. Hapnet needed my imaging capabilities for a dozen different things, she said. Boston was buzzing, on the verge of chaos. She tried to attract me to a local-interest story on the tangle of environmental sup-port systems near the Columbia Gate: yesterday someone accidentally hooked a chlor/fluor Rigel VII atmosphere pipe into an oxy/nitro one leading to a beauty parlor, dis-solving several cubic meters of elaborately curled hair. In-teresting, but not interesting enough. I said so.

"Interesting?" she said. "A swim meet when the entire city of Boston is sinking into the ocean? That's interesting?"

"You're going to have to trust me, Zen. It's a bigger story than it looks. You'll see." Being Hapnet's most popular imager and its most sophisticated piece of imaging equip-ment simultaneously gives me some advantages in an argu-ment.

She dropped her eyelids over her protruding blue eyes: suspicion. Zenaïda's facial expressions are as stylized as a Kabuki actor's or a Koltsoi hierodancer's. "Are you trying to provoke something?"

She knew me too well. She no doubt had some fantasy of my calling in the nightstalkers with an anonymous report that an alien spacecraft violating U.S. Customs was landing on the running track at Dorchester High. I could see it: Cus-toms stalkers bursting in, guns blazing. Innocent teenage girls dead in the water. Vortices of scarlet as a swimmer is pushed out of the water by some maintenance Phneri, their fur wet and matted from living under the diving board. No. It's fun to create that kind of farcical tragedy, and Zen knew how I enjoyed flirting with the nightstalkers, but not this time.

I shifted in the weird seat Zen had made for me, the only one that fit my only half-human butt. I swiveled my right eye, changed the focus, and examined the fine gold hairs on her upper lip. It started to quiver and she turned away. "Stop it, Barney." She didn't call me that much anymore.

"All right?" I said, cheery. "I've got images to catch. A city on the move, the swinging Hub of the Universe, a businessbeing's paradise. Can Boston buy enough United States senators to continue its vital work of making money from the rest of the Galaxy? Will we instead be forced into an unpleasant civil war? Let *Baka* show you the score!"

"Are you all right, Baka?"

"I'm fine, Zen. Just a touch of *mal de terre*, a Boston affliction."

She didn't smile. "Barney. *Baka.*" She turned to her event board. Several nightstalker raids on illegally landing alien spacecraft in the past week. Customs has been busy. An anti-Phner riot in Charlestown. I've never figured out why people hate those little hairballs so much. Seems like a waste of mental energy. Six indictments in various Federal courts against Boston trading magnates. A strongly anti-Boston speech by President Masterson, accusing us of sucking wealth from the United States. The burning of a Boston Chamber of Commerce office in Milan. A typical pee-on-Boston week, in other words.

"The nightstalkers hit a Tulgut ship in the middle of Spot Pond last night," she finally said. "It's frozen into the ice. Customs is getting better informers."

"They're still not as good as mine, sweetheart." I imagined the elephantlike Tulguts sliding around the ice in a panic. They'd come hundreds of light-years from somewhere out in Corvus, only to have their cargo impounded by human Customs officers. Breaks of the game.

"How good are yours, Baka? Do they ever tell you the whole story?"

"Stop it, Zen." That really pissed me off. "My sources are my own." So sometimes they screw up—and leave me with half a body. Who's perfect?

"I'm just—" She turned away. "Go cover your damn swim meet. I'll take care of the environmental system story."

She was trying to make me feel sorry for her again. I leaned over and kissed her ear. My lips, at least, are all mine, and I know how to use them. She nodded without turning around. "See you later, Baka."

"Later, Zen." Sometimes I think she loves me. Wouldn't that be nice?

Now Dorchester High School leans over me. It's encased in not-quite-quiescent plastic, and the rime cracks off as it flows, flexing molecular long-chain muscles. The donation of some nostalgic alumnus, no doubt. Boston trading magnates are rich and strange. Spending millions to save an obsolete high school is the sort of thing they enjoy.

I catch the early pearly of morning on the twitchingly shiny school. Archival stuff. History. How Boston Made a Revolution. From the private museum of Barney M'funu Kanezane. Baka, my netname. Baka means "stupid" in Japanese. A useful nickname, if you're not too sensitive. Believe me, I've earned it.

Time. I unhook my right eye and fling it out toward the water. The space-folded Targive optics give me a flash of aquatic microflora: phytoplankton, diatoms, blue-green algae. Amazing, how much useless stuff the thing shows me. Then the Eye is up, whizzing through the icy mist. It hasn't snowed much this year, and I can see the great stretches of shining ice that now cover what were once the low neighborhoods on the seaward side of Dorchester Heights.

A procession of vehicles snakes toward me across ice and water on enhanced surface tension, magnetic fields, ground effects. The Greater Boston Chamber of Commerce on its way to cheer on the girls competing in the big swim meet—as clandestine as a Fourth of July parade on Comm Ave. Boston trading magnates are convinced that they're invisible unless they want to be seen. And then no one can ignore them.

The vehicles pull up in a semicircle in front of the school. Accompanying them are hovering school buses, filled with schoolgirls and their coaches. The magnates get out, pushing their way through the crowd of gym-bag-toting swimmers.

They're all here: the Subramanyan brothers, Mudande, Segné, the bastard Kastor Basilides who caused so much trouble, Lissa Trant, and . . . there she is, the old biddy herself. Mi Nyo. All here to watch teenage girls swim.

Feeble though the subterfuge is, it worked. Baka's the only nethead here. None of my so-called colleagues seems to understand how the real story always grows in the dark like a germinating seed.

They mill around: no idea of how to behave for posterity. Just another meeting, after all. This is a revolution which, instead of stirring manifestos, will leave nothing but memos behind it. I don't envy future generations of schoolchildren.

Time to give them some help. I pull myself up with one of my manipulator arms. The Targives gave me two when they repaired me, for no good reason save that my brain's motor control section could handle that many. A doctor examining me later muttered something about a vestigial tail-control nexus that had been modified. Great. So I wiggle my nonexistent primate tail, grab on to the rusting iron bars of the high school's foundations and swing through ice-covered trees over a freezing ocean. Isn't evolution wonderful?

As I clamber up through the ruins of what used to be the library, I try to think of a good tie-in: "Mao Zedong proclaimed that a revolution is not a dinner party. True enough. But neither is it a Southeast Regional Swimming competition . . ." Ah, screw it. Historical references are a waste of time.

I never skulk. It implies inferiority. Ridiculous! Without us netheads nothing really exists. We are the witnesses that give reality its substance. Read Bishop Berkeley. Kick a stone to refute him, if you want, the way Dr. Johnson did. Would that have happened if my predecessor Boswell hadn't been there to record it? "No one wants an arrogant nethead," Zen tells me. "Just watch what happens. Save your opinions."

I climb out of the ruined library, pulling rotting pieces of obsolete books out of my hair, and swagger toward the assembled dignitaries: that is, as well as I can with a right leg that bifurcates into two hooves. Sometimes at night they clack together, waking me up. I'm always afraid I'll see a water rat dead between them, but it's never anything. Just a sleep jerk, useless brain signals.

The richest and most powerful people in the world all stare at me. My Eye sits behind them on a tree. Its socket in my head, about three times as large as that required by a regular ocular, isn't as bad to look at as you might think. The Targives lined it with smooth enamel, so it looks like a light blue egg cup. Still nothing I show women to warm them up, understand, but acceptable in social situations. I watch myself as I strut unevenly: the nethead as historic actor. The sun's behind me and a little image processing could give me a nimbus. I resist.

I hold up my press card, an antique issued by the powerless City Hall. Even in the age of information-based reality, a physical gesture carries power. Particularly when made by a right arm that looks like a pair of intertwined pythons.

Mi Nyo ignores my Eye and stares right at me.

"To what do we owe the honor of coverage from Barney Kanezane himself?" she says. She's a wrinkled old woman, face like a monkey. And behind those sagging almond eyes: power. The home viewers see only a bent old lady who acts a little self-important. I've known her for years. She still scares the shit out of me.

I examine her, front and back, looking for signs of nervousness. My unexpected presence raises the stakes. My Eye is the future staring at her.

"A little human-interest story," I say breezily. "I wanted to cover this swim meet. Girls showing off the human body. With so many deviant anatomies strolling around Boston these days, I think people have forgotten what human beings look like. Times are tough. I want to show that something's going on besides nightstalker raids."

I bring up the thing that ties us together. It's always there, no matter how I try to get away from it. She doesn't react. I don't think she's ever felt sorry about what happened to me: it just offended her sense of neatness.

The morning sun, winter-cold, has managed to rise high enough to force itself through the sea mist. The magnates' shadows suddenly stretch across the frost-covered grass. Each is arrogantly individual, from the flamboyant colors of the unrepentant Kastor Basilides to the dark, fur-lined kimono of the ever-unspeaking Lissa Trant. Standing together, hunched slightly against the cold, the sun illuminating half of each face, they wear a common mask of power, like figures in a frieze. Once inside the walls of Dorchester High, they'll squabble, accusing each other of trying to seize personal advantage. Here they provide me with an image of calm sovereignty.

I flip my Eye back into my head and confront Mi Nyo binocularly. If I were an ordinary nethead, there would be a dozen other cameras floating around the school, climbing the towers on tiny prehensile legs, installed in the sandwiches to be served at lunch, surgically implanted in a guard's belly. But I'm Baka, and I only have one Eye. That's my image, and in image there is strength.

"Mr. Kanezane." She never uses my netname, just the one I was born with. It's rudeness masquerading as politeness. "I'm glad you are present. Our young ladies are here to participate in an honest and open competition, unaffected by acts of Congress or Presidential pronouncements. *And* without the payment of shipment taxes at the end of each lap." Deadpan inflection, not the hint of a wink. I can always count on her for a few sharp words.

She smiles slightly, for all the world as if she's glad I'm there. Sometimes, at night, when I feel the uneven rustling of my alien body parts under the sheets, I hate her for what she did. Hate her enough to choke on it. But I have no weapon against her, no way to reach her. Except my Eye.

She turns under its scrutiny. My sources in her private household tell me she came here today to seek compromise. Mi Nyo Enterprises is in too deep with the Feds; too much money is invested in bribes and clandestine agreements. All that would be lost with a break. Enough of her colleagues are fat from the same system for a compromise agreement to be a possibility.

My Eye hates compromise. It hates concord. These things are dull. It wants color and action. It wants revolution. I'm going to make sure it gets it.

My Eye glitters at Mi Nyo, sucking in her image. Every one of her gestures is becoming history. Will she appear as a vacillating compromiser?

Her face is suddenly stern, resolved. "Let us go," Mi Nyo says, her voice ringing decisively. I follow, not daring to smile. Because of her, I have my Eye.

The irregular geometrics of the quarry's rock walls overhung the water. Silent as flotsam, I paddled a kayak through the stillness, the cool November air brushing across my face. The receding ocean beyond sucked the water slowly from the abandoned quarry like soda through a straw, and my return path would be through shallows. The kayak had been designed, as far as I could interpret the polyoctave spiel from the rhododendron-on-roller-skates who sold it to me, for use on semifluid mud flows on its home planet of Canopus II. Incredibly unstable, it kept trying to dump me into the scummy water.

I used a set of electronic cameras then, like a normal person, with absorptive field lenses, the blackest things on Earth. The technology had originated somewhere around Alpha Crucis, and spread everywhere reachable by a loophole. An efficient technology is like the flu: like it or not, sooner or later you end up with it. The cameras sucked up photons like vacuum cleaners and had quantum-effect photomultiplier circuits operating at absolute zero. Sexy stuff for an image journalist.

One of the cameras scanned the cubistic granite to my left where a variety of garish dwellings clung to the rock, hexagonal windows glowing. A number of illegal manufactories hung up there, making semi-intelligent jewelry, impact-resistant clothing, nasal inhalers, that sort of thing.

Zen had learned that a ship from an obscure world called Nieqcptse was due to drop down with optical resonators and quantum inertia suppressors. A big-money smuggling deal, in other words. She wanted me to image the biggest story of 2057. If I pulled it off. She knew I loved these guys. There was no one more fun to watch in all of Boston.

It's fast-whip work, smuggling into Boston. Ships follow curving lines, Einsteinian geodesics skitter-jumping through the linked singularities of loopholes: skipping stones on the galactic pond. Down the long arch of the Sagittarius-Carina Arm to the bright bead of Sol, then in to the roiled dot of Boston where the lines knit together into a knot. A megaparsec of clear space, cosmic dust, translight demons, then you have to deal with the locals: gleaming, raven black assault vehicles, come to collect the tariff. Customs nightstalkers. Welcome to Boston and the U.S. of A.

I shipped my paddle and floated slowly through the dark, lifeless water. Boston monuments had once been flensed from these hills. Man tried to gain significance by such connection to the rock, but the rock had taken its revenge, sinking incontinently beneath the water like a child frightening a parent in the bathtub by sliding under the bubbles. Zen warns me about literary images. They don't come across the net at all. So I keep them for myself. And for history.

"Ah, Baka," a voice said from the darkness. "I recognize you. We are quite ready to begin." I looked up. Standing over me on a shattered rock slab was a plump Asian man in a purple silk shirt. Though everything around was dark, he had supplied himself with a baby spot which lit him up and picked out the silver threads in the weave.

Sitigar Malik was not as ugly as the later version of him that now hangs in Mi Nyo's office. He did have blunt features and a square head topped by thick, short hair, like a divot of sod pulled up by a post-hole digger. It was a face you could pound on all day and get nowhere, tenacious and stoic. Not to say desperate. This Nieqcptse shipment was his last chance. Zen had slipped me his financial records.

He stood above me, arms akimbo, Smuggler-As-Culture-Hero, and grinned at me, one blue enamel tooth winking.

"Come on, Baka," he said. "Let me show you how a real trader operates."

It's always amazing. Smugglers are accomplished diddlers of parameters, sliders through interstices, light as shadows, evaporative as ether, smooth as helium II. They could be sleeping next to you for years and you'd never know that they spent their time in Boston's black economy, two steps ahead of the nightstalkers, but never more than one ahead of their competition. Most of them even get off on the contrast: well-behaved hive drone by day, edge-diving galactic entrepreneur by night.

Then Baka shows up and they're kids showing off on the high diving board: "Hey, lookit! Lookit me! Watch this one!" Always precedes a truly spectacular belly flop. I've seen it a thousand times. Malik looked like he was heading for a glowing pink belly.

He leapt off the rock and onto the front hull of my Canopan kayak, landing with bare feet. The kayak stayed rock-steady. Counting coup, showing the nethead what a real man could do. I just kept imaging. Without me to see it, his bravado was irrelevant. He might as well be sitting home watching someone else do it on the net. He raised a hand and twiddled his fingers. His fingernails were long, of some refractive crystal, and I could just see the flicker of interrogation lasers as they hit the fingernails and received the proper responses.

The kayak slid onto a tiny beach at the base of the wall. It was made of shattered glass, not exactly a place to lie around and get a tan. It glittered in the light from the cliff dwellings like a child's nightmare of summer camp swimming.

Malik, tough guy, stepped off onto the beach with his bare feet and grinned back at me. I wondered what the soles of his feet were coated with. I picked up my camera equipment and draped it, feeling it wrap itself around me, eyes pointing every which way. I stepped onto the beach, wondering how long my boots would last on it.

"How did you get the Nieqcptse to ship direct?" I asked. "Don't they usually transfer goods in Sh'k or Adjawi vessels for the run to Earth?"

"When they come here. Which is rarely. But how?" He shrugged his shoulders eloquently. "It seemed mutually beneficial. What else is the point of business?"

"You are a romantic, Mr. Malik."

He grinned again. That damn blue tooth made him look like a crook, which was why he'd put it in. We Bostonians don't respect honest-but-dull working stiffs, and Malik's sod-divot head made him otherwise the image of rectitude, like a dumb bank president. Not good for a smuggler. The tooth was raffish.

"Perhaps the time for such romance is not past, Baka," he said. "A few more arrangements like this one . . . there are those who would like to see it happen. Free trade. Free Boston."

He wasn't only a romantic, he was crazy. The Bar Harbor Gang would squish him like a bug. He looked at me and winked. Did he believe these things even when I wasn't there to see him do it?

"I'm going to show those bastards," he said. "Starting with that head bitch, Mi Nyo."

We climbed up a set of stone stairs to where the rest of Malik's team waited. Rising behind them, the symbol of their aspirations, was the magnificently arbitrary structure of Boston, luxuriating under the golden shower from the stars. An intentional double entendre that would never get past Zen: "If you want to say something obscene, Baka, for God's sake just say it. People don't like to figure things like that out. It's too much work."

Malik's colleagues were dark silent men and women, just the way they were supposed to be, nothing like their flamboyant boss. Private businessmen just trying to make a living, their own businesses destroyed or stunted by the trade restrictions that surrounded the city, they were taking an even bigger chance than just smuggling in defiance of the Feds. They were bucking the Bar Harbor Gang. Now *that* was crazy, surfing a breaking wave of razor blades. I tried to catch their desperate insanity from the way they hunched their shoulders, twitched, exchanged quick glances.

Back in 2031, the gang met at Bar Harbor, on Mount Desert Island, setting up the largest conspiracy in restraint of trade in human history. The big magnates divvied up the stars into a cartel. An efficient marketing system, I understand. It's run Boston for a generation.

Shut out, Malik had decided to move on his own. A desperate move. He had a quivering energy that I could feel just by standing next to him. It made me wish I wasn't standing quite so close.

The dark-clad figures distributed themselves over the half-carved chunks of rock like crows on fenceposts contemplating eternity. They produced spidery contraptions with points that vanished into some other space, rotating out of our universe.

"They were toys," Malik said in my ear. "Somewhere in toward the Galactic Core. Infants used them to understand 7-space."

It's hard to get a coherent image of something that refuses to stay in the three-dimensional world which our eyes can see, so I concentrated on the tensely hunched postures of the summoners. The complex distortion of gravitationally bound space-time would serve as a beacon to the arriving craft. I thought I could feel my liver being flexed through hyperdimensional geometries, then reeled back in. Sometimes I wonder if Boston's sinking is itself some sort of beacon for arriving spaceships, a blaze on a trail like a bent branch on a tree.

I looked up past the quarry walls. No one I know spends much time looking at the stars. Those glowing points are millions of years old, not at all the places that our visitors come from. The stars above are obsolete, images of a more leisured time, when the skies were scanned by lovers and seekers after knowledge. Now they serve solely as a backdrop to serious business. The granite walls bulked against the stars, hemming them in. There is no escape, for any of us.

The spaceship made a noise like a warbling bird as it floated over the cliff dwellings, swelling orange. Its swirling spiral pattern compelled attention. Since the most obvious point of attention is not the place to be looking, I tore my eyes from the wanting center.

Malik's troops were standing on their rocks and waving, some of them jumping up and down. They were ridiculous cargo cultists, praying for wealth that they didn't have to work for. Their magic had fetched a spaceship from the skies, full of goodies. Near Boston, magic worked. An alien ship could come down and make someone a wealthy man in an evening.

The Nieqcptse craft extended glowing pseudopodia, grabbing rock to steady itself. The water roiled underneath it, reflecting the flame of the craft and giving the image back to the sky. Malik ran down to the water's edge, barefoot on glass shards, and gestured imperiously at the spacecraft. It tilted toward him, obedient to his contractual authority.

At his gesture, a goods-laden raft drifted across the water to float, bobbing slightly, directly underneath the spaceship. The Nieqcptse lowered glowing orange spheres which were exact duplicates of the spaceship. They bounced and rolled across the water, seemingly reluctant to be scooped up by Malik's men.

I saw it first. Everyone was mesmerized by the wealth right in front of their eyes, even those who were supposedly lookouts. That was Malik's flaw. His desire focused so sharply that he failed to see the shadows that rose up around it.

Glancing across the cliff dwellings, I saw a black figure, silhouetted for an instant against one of the hexagonal windows. A flicker, and gone. I turned toward Malik, but it was too late.

It all happened at once. Three black nightstalker skiffs whipped across the mirror-smooth water at us, searchlights glaring like novas. Other lights flared on top of the quarry walls, revealing United States Customs troops as they rappelled down the steep sides.

"No," Malik moaned, standing barefoot in the dirty water. "No, this can't be it."

A typical Boston *posse ex machina* ending. I'd hoped for something more interesting. Everyone's tired of watching textbook arrests on the net. I was pissed. It'd be just a lot of procedural gunk from this point on.

"God damn it!" Malik shouted from the depths of his soul. He reached up, grabbed the back of his collar, and pulled. The silver wires came free of his shirt and coalesced into the symmetrical antenna of a neutral particle-beam weapon: what the well-dressed smuggler is wearing this year. And he opened fire on the approaching Customs agents.

The insuited figures paused for an instant, then dropped, bringing their own weapons to bear. In that instant, however, three of them died. One, obligingly flinging his arms up in a perfect photojournalistic pose, toppled off a rock into water.

"Wait!" one of Malik's colleagues shouted. "This isn't—"

A stream of vapor bullets ripped him apart, spattering him across the granite.

The air was full of crisscrossing laser beams, wailing plasma spheres, bullets. Nightstalkers use whatever they've confiscated. They all made beautiful music together, as terrifying a sound as I've ever heard.

"Surrender!" an amplified voice bellowed. "Put down your weapons and surrender."

"We surrender!" some of Malik's people yelled.

"My ass, we surrender!" Malik shouted. He did look magnificent, standing in the water, firing his tangled weapon. "Surrender, my friends, is lousy business practice. Boston will be free!" And he reopened fire, to cries of "You stupid son of a bitch!" from his erstwhile business associates.

An IR laser, invisible save for its results, finally nailed him. His head flared brightly, his sodlike hair burning for an instant before he fell into the all-consuming water with a stinking hiss.

Cries requesting surrender started up again, but now the nightstalkers had lost control. Not used to this sort of armed resistance, they continued to blast away even after the source of the resistance was dead. I suddenly understood that they would keep it up until all of us were dead, and most likely for a good time after that.

So I did something I had always promised Zen I never would do: I linked live into the net and preempted the signal, cutting through whatever show was on. I'd been carrying the interface arborizers and signal maskers for years, updated regularly under Zen's authority. She let me carry them on the condition that I never use them. Sensible, right? That's my Zen.

"This is Baka, live!" A view of Malik's body bobbing facedown in the polluted water appeared on every screen in Boston. "I am undergoing a violent assault by nightstalkers." I gave them the visuals: leapfrogging troops, flaring weapons, whizzing assault skiffs.

"If help does not reach us, we will be dead within minutes." I've always been proud of that one. No plea, just a simple statement of situation and consequences. Let them figure it out.

Evil-smelling bonfires marked where several of the smugglers had been. A skull freed itself from one of them and rolled, bumping, down the rock. Things were setting themselves up for me as if I had choreographed them. I pushed myself up a little to get a better view.

I had thought Malik was dumb, but this move proved I could give him some serious competition. A plasma sphere tore through my shoulder, searing agony. I screamed, echoing in households all across Boston. Instead of hugging for cover, I stood up.

"What are you doing?" I said. "I'm Baka! Baka!"

"Baka?" someone replied quietly. "Bye-bye, Baka."

A laser swept out of the darkness and cut my right side right off my body. I toppled, not even screaming. Screaming was irrelevant. I rolled down the rock toward the water, the world strobing around me. It took an infinite length of time before I found darkness.

Even my Eye can't do everything.

The meetings are so boring they seem planned as an aid to meditation. The business path to enlightenment. All I get with my Eye is shit. Kaka. They know I'm watching, but they don't seem to care.

I hang on the wall above the proceedings, half man, half surveillance device, three-armed, bifurcate-legged. My appearance does help me get seats in restaurants. Everyone in Boston knows who I am.

The scene *would* be improved by a few nightstalkers. I've gotten addicted to those bastards since they wasted me. Seeing themselves, black symbols of essential justice, prancing around on the viewscreens of Boston has only increased their violence. Anything would be better than this convention of jawing businessmen.

A rescue copter from Hapnet pulled me out of the water before I died. Zen says the pilot spent quite some time looking for the rest of me before deciding that it no longer existed. They slapped amoebic quick-seal over the edges, plopped me into the hospital, stuck me on life-support . . . and didn't know what to do next. As Zen put it to me once: "We couldn't decide whether we'd found the right half." Thanks, Zen. I always like a boss who sticks by you.

Mi Nyo passes beneath where I dangle. She's deep in discussion with Lissa Trant, though Trant, as usual, says nothing, simply agreeing or disagreeing with sharp movements of some alien gesture syllabary. My image computer does not recognize the configuration. Lissa Trant retains her mystery.

So does Mi Nyo. Hanging in her office, directly behind her desk, is a large painting of Sitigar Malik, based on one instant of my images from that night. He wears that ridiculous purple shirt with the silver threads, and is looking off nobly over the viewer's shoulder, searching for an approaching alien spacecraft. No blue tooth, though. A bit of editing. The legend under it says, in austere block capitals, FREE TRADE. He is a martyr to the cause of Boston independence. Quite an effective image. You'd never know that she was the one responsible for his death.

One night, four years ago, to save my life, I linked directly into the net. If my doing so hadn't made me a hero, I would have been prosecuted. Now, to give some meaning to that night, I do it again, though more subtly. No need to appear in everyone's living room. I probe through the interfaces of the net, a feeling much the way sex used to be, before the Targives had a hand in my anatomy. Back at the office, Zen must be going crazy.

A monitor screen near Mi Nyo suddenly spills a collage of images. Nightstalkers hit a house in suburban Waltham and prisoners are hauled out through the flames. A rally in Chicago, under banners like Bloodsuckers and Give Back Our Wealth demands the reduction of Boston by Federal troops. The pathetic figure of Larry Metzes, a businessman ruined by Federal confiscations, dangles from the end of his rope. Hungry children beg. She and Trant stand silhouetted, motionless, ineffectual, and above them can be heard from afar magnates' voices prophesying new tax abatements.

She looks at herself and her fellow magnates. Looming above, at the top of the screen, is the face of Sitigar Malik, his blue tooth glinting. It's even brighter than it should be: I've augmented it.

My footage of the Quincy raid is considered a propaganda classic. They even show it in cinema classes. Of course the entire thing was a setup from beginning to end. A staged news event, with real corpses. Malik had been horning in on Mi Nyo's biodevice business, and no one competes with a member of the Bar Harbor Gang. Certainly not anymore. Malik was the last independent to try anything so foolhardy.

"Ms. Nyo," I say, from my perch, "Any words for us?"

She glares up at me. After Malik turned that night's simple arrest into a high-profile massacre, her role had changed from that of a sharp businesswoman to that of a betrayer. Zen had fastened on and, in exchange for my silence, compelled Mi Nyo to have the Targives repair me on their island off Southie.

She can see what she looks like in my Eye: a pettifogging businesswoman, ready to fatten herself on Boston's misfortune. We've tolerated their cartel for a generation. Now is the time for revolution. But we can't make a revolution without her.

Mi Nyo walks slowly to the front of the room. She's not as crabbed and tired as she appears, but it gives a good image. An archetype. The wise crone. The room falls silent. They all look at her.

"Ladies and gentlemen," she says, a smile creasing her face. "Let's face it. We've got to have a revolution before we all go broke."

You can feel the relief like a cool breeze. They babble to each other. They don't have to worry about deciding anymore. Mi Nyo has thrown the snowball that starts the avalanche. It's suddenly out of their hands, and they no longer have to worry.

So there it is. A historic remark. Not quite "Give me liberty or give me death."

"Ms. Nyo!" I shout, and clearly focus my Eye on her.

She knows what I want. She takes a deep breath, thinking. And she gives it to me.

"Shortly before his tragic death," Mi Nyo says, looking straight at me, "Sitigar Malik said something I'll always remember. He said: 'We all take our chances to be free. The odds may be bad, the game fixed. But what else can we do? To refuse the gamble is to die.' That is where we stand today, ladies and gentlemen. We must stake ourselves and risk everything. And pay a very old price. Our lives. Our fortunes." She stares directly at me. "And our sacred honor. What is your choice?"

They cheer wildly. A few moments ago, they were compromise-seeking businessmen. Now they are revolutionaries. Right before my Eye. I get it all, knowing, the whole time, that she has made the whole thing up. Malik, who never mentioned Mi Nyo's name without spitting, is now an icon to bless a revolution that will cement in power the very woman that he hated. And I will help do it.

"It's your job, Baka," I hear Zen say in my head. "What else can you do?" The woman loves me, but sometimes, I wish she'd say something different in person than I imagine her saying in my head. It would make her seem real.

When it's over, Mi Nyo strides past me, on her way to other business. Now that she has decided on revolution, she will make it work.

"What have you given us?" I ask.

She glances at me, sardonic. All debts, her look says, are paid.

"A revolution," she says. "If you can afford it."

YE CITIZENS OF BOSTON
SARAH SMITH

THE CITY OF Boston rises out of the Charles River and the harbor like a dark ragged pillar. Around it stand the smaller alien monuments: the web-shaped walkway that leads to the IPOB Tower out in the harbor, the Targive-modified black tents that ring its drowned hills. The shadow of Boston stretches for miles.

Ten million people live in the City, in a space a little smaller than the Puritans' Boston. Approximately 275,000 people are born there every year. Less than a thousand leave by choice. Approximately 100,000 die.

Boston's citizens daily use 180 million gallons of water, eat 625 tons of meat and 5,000 tons of bread, throw away over 2,000 tons of garbage, and generate over a trillion net calories of heat.

To cool Boston takes multiple interlinking systems of recyclers, heat sinks, water tanks, vents, and sweat pipes. To cool the city, multiple hearts constantly circulate liquid through the skins of the internal and external buildings of Boston. Boston drinks the Charles River and pisses it out again. All these processes are less figurative than the citizens of Boston would care to know. The Targives are excellent bioengineers.

If you look closely, you can see the City shimmer like a mirage in its own heat, frail as a flag.

Outside the City itself, outside the City Wall that keeps back the water, are the neighborhoods of Cambridge, Brookline, Somerville, and the Back Bay: dwarfish remnants of the city of fifty years ago, before the aliens came. One of their allegiances is to the fading United States of America, one to the unimaginable future inside those strange walls—a future in common with Targives, Phneri, Spatiens, Bishop 24, and who knows, the Cisos and the big Clivus slugs in the Boston sewers.

IPOB. The Interstellar Port of Boston.

The summer of 2061 is hot. Very hot . . .

July 2, 2061: Assassination of Janet Nyo

"Bill Barnhardt the Customs Secretary he will soon have screw you up enough yet?" the Phner squeaked hopefully. "Do you already go to war?"

Halfway through opening the front of Cap'n Snow's Boston Tours, Lem Snow paused to work out the convoluted sentence. *War* stuck in his mind. The Phneri were good at saying things no one was ready to hear. "Yeah, Customs wants to improve my business, Sammy. Travel to Boston, see the—" *war.*

Oh yes.

Already you could feel it in the air, you could taste it, like the endless faint tang of strange biologicals and machine oil in this artificial city. Lem tasted the word on his tongue as his shop sign unfolded flag-shaped wings and chose its colors and slogans for the day. Tourists usually wanted twenty minutes' sightseeing, two hours in the gift shop. (Baked Beans! Lobster! Authentic Replicas Crafted While You Wait!) But for the past weeks, the sign had relegated the usual tourist come-ons to tiny sidebars and kept one headline rolling sternly overhead: Authentic Revolutionary Battlegrounds.

Authentic Revolution.

Signs weren't bright, but they knew marketing.

"What do you think, Sammy?" Len asked. "Is Boston going to war with Customs?"

Squinting up at Lem's sign, Lem's supplier of Authentic Replicas shrugged furry shoulders. The human gesture seemed very much like an Authentic Replica. Lem liked Sammy himself well enough, but he'd never got used to the Phneri's mimicking human gestures; a big intelligent water rat is still a rat. "It will already be better to fight," Sammy squeaked. "Boston will be free." Sammy waddled over toward the fountain in the middle of the Mall and clambered awkwardly over the edge.

"Yeah." There was always a market in Phner stuff. But with the tourists gone, Lem's business was dying. Lem shook out his tour-guide costume, stood his Revolutionary flintlock against the side of the booth, and cocked his tricorne hat over one eye, taking on Yankee-accented Captain Lem'l Snow's persona. "Can't stand f'r it no more, can we, brother American? No taxation without representation."

The Revolution, the *American* Revolution, Lem thought, had been about ordinary people putting their lives on the line. Not "No taxation without representation." All men are created equal. Principles that thousands of ordinary men and women had chosen freely to die for. Lem's ancestors had been slaves then—"but we were equal to Washington and Jefferson themselves, the moment those words were written down," Lem's grandfather had said in his rich preacher's voice, which had made history sound like the very workings of God. "It took those white men almost a century more to see it; but with words like that, a man builds his life. Equality was inevitable."

Mayor Biko, the Nyos, the Endicotts, the Mudandes . . . they wanted money. No taxation without representation;

no taxation at all. They were sitting on the golden egg of alien culture and they wanted it to hatch more golden eggs. This revolution was a sandlot baseball game out of control, with a handful of kids yelling about the ball—"Mine, mine!" Any one of them would betray it for enough money, and the only reason that Boston would fight was that no American had enough to bribe a Bostonian.

A revolution made by bankers. Authentic replica.

Lem sighted along his flintlock at Sammy, who blinked back unconcerned. "There will be death?" the alien squeaked.

"Be some kind of a fight, don't you think?" The Mayor's Council had retaliated for Srinagar Malik by dumping alien cargoes—Mayor Biko might as well *be* Mi Nyo—and three weeks ago Barnhardt had retaliated by freezing all Boston-owned or -controlled assets worldwide. Boston's economy looked like a Phner funeral.

"Lem, would you have such a thing as a box?" Toby Fitzpatrick had framed in the authentic Revolutionary timbers on Lem's stand, over the objections of the Phner who had wanted to make them much more authentic. Lem looked at the pile of foodpacks Fitzpatrick was carrying. His backpack was stuffed and he'd taken off his jacket to carry more, but foodpacks were falling out his sleeves.

"Hoardin', Toby?"

"Ah, don't you get at me. The family won't leave, the grocery clerk gave me a lecture about taking too much for myself, and you wouldn't believe the prices—" Toby grinned to show it wasn't personal. "Half the city's crazy to get out of here and the other half's filling their bathtubs with water. You going to be in the front lines with your flintlock?"

Lem shook his head. "Hope it don't come to that. Janet Nyo's headin' the negotiations, and she's more sensible than her aunt. I read enough about when the British embargoed the Americans, boxed them into Boston, winter of

1773, I don't want to see it. Sammy, what are the Phneri going to do if it's war?"

The Phner shrugged, sloshing the water in his improvised cool-tub. The water was low in the fountain, and Lem wondered how serious Toby was about people filling their bathtubs. "Everything changes. We will make an appreciation."

An *esfnai*, he meant. A combination of an esthetic experience and a Phneri ceremonial funeral.

Somebody screamed, and Dolly Charinsky ran out of Scollay Square Sweets, her face ashen. Two hot red dots marked her cheekbones. "Janet Nyo—"

Big Jake Wilson followed her, punched the public video screen's On button. "CitiNET. Run Janet Nyo."

The manic chipmunk face of orange-haired Dave Daly, the CitiNET announcer, filled the little video. "This is Daaave *Daly*, the Voice of Boston! Here at City Hall Plaza, a major demonstration is pitting the Mayor's Council against the Municipal Laborers' Union. Speaking for the Boston workers, Srinavasa O'Connell-Reeves is demanding that the Mayor's Council make peace with the Federal Government. I'm talking with Janet Nyo, negotiator for the Mayor's Council. Janet, what does the Council intend to do for the Boston worker?"

"Dave, we're all suffering together." Mi Nyo's lawyer cousin nodded gravely at Daly. Her eyes were hollow; she looked like she hadn't slept in a couple of days. Conservatively, Lem figured, the gold-and-diamond bioengineered brooch crawling over her lapel would have paid a year's rent on his store. "We're all hurting."

"Janet, isn't it true that, like yourself, most of the Mayor's Council belong to one of the Families? And, so far, all decisions made by the Council have supported Family policy?"

"The Council represents a very broad spectrum of opinion in Boston," Janet Nyo said firmly, "and—"

A second pin, a huge red one, bloomed at the base of Janet Nyo's neck. She put her hand up to her neck, uncertain, as if she'd forgotten what Mi Nyo had told her to say, and fell out of the frame. Someone screamed in the crowd. Dave Daly began shouting. The picture froze. Dolly Charinsky was crying, hot tears of anger.

"Oh the bastards, to kill *Janet*—" Dolly's voice shook.

"Who did it?"

"Who else? Some Customs bastard. Some *American.*" Dolly's broad face was tense with hatred.

Lem wanted to shake her. Some American . . . didn't Dolly realize what she was giving away? The Constitution. The Bill of Rights. Giving them away to rich criminals who'd sell Dolly and everyone like her for exclusive access to a bunch of alien artifacts. The Indians sold their country for top hats and trading beads. My ancestors sold their own people. Dolly, we're doing it to ourselves.

She stared at the screen as if she could speak to the dead woman. "Janet, Janet Nyo, I promise you, *Boston will be free.* Lem, what are you going to do for Boston? Whose side will you be on?"

"Dolly," Lem asked, "do you know anyone who's doing more than talk?"

She looked at him with a new respect, and raised her little soft chin. "I do, Lem Snow. And we've got better guns than your flintlock."

At their feet, the Phner was gazing at the screen with a barely restrained curiosity, like someone rubbernecking a funeral.

Lem reported to his cutout the next day while he bought a sandwich.

"The leader of the cell is a woman named Dolly Charinsky. There's a lawyer, Tommy Prescott, who's all for legal secession. A food deliveryman named Mark, he drives for King Stores. A secretary at Miller's Hall, Sean Powers.

Small stuff. Also my Phneri supplier at Copley says the Phneri are going to be neutral. That's all." The middle-aged Irish lady at the deli counter smiled as if he'd just told her that Mi Nyo was a secret Customs agent. Cute Lucy the Deli Lady had been Lem's cutout, his link with Customs, for the past ten years.

No one was within earshot. He leaned forward to speak to her, though, as if his message were as important to other ears as it was to his and hers. "I want a glass of water."

She smiled at him. "Stay cool."

"How much information does Barnhart need? Is he going to wait until these rebels are on the barricades? Janet Nyo wasn't enough to stop them. Lucy," he said, "I'm the only man who can go anywhere in this city with a loaded gun."

She sighed. "You want water that much?" she said quietly. "All right. I can give you some."

For ten years he had waited for that sign. Lucy filled him a glass of water only halfway up. "You know, we're going to be terrible short of water if there's war," she said in her old cheerful voice. "Do you know a woman named Iris Sherwood? She's Water Coordinator. I hope she knows her business."

When Lucy offers you a glass of water, Lem's boss had said, *but she fills it only halfway full, then listen for a name.* Iris Sherwood. Water Resources Coordinator. "Here's to Iris Sherwood," Lem said, touching the glass to his lips in a mockery of a toast. *I understand you.*

"Good luck," said Lucy under her breath.

The name she says, that's the one you kill.

July 4, 2061: The Last July Fourth in Boston

Sticky in her gray dress with a cameo at her throat, Iris Sherwood sweated in the reviewing stand in front of Boston City Hall. Under a bright blue holographic sky, holographic

Massachusetts and American flags whipped in a holographic breeze. The heat was real. In the Basement, as in any other basement of a large building, it was always a little damp in summer. And in the lowest ten floors of the enormous Boston pillar, buttressed with a six-foot-thick seawall, heat never escaped by itself. It needed to be moved out with pumps, sucked out by lowering the air pressure. In this hot summer of 2061, the Boston city air conditioners were strained to their limit. City Hall Plaza steamed with heat, damp Basement heat, human-smelling heat. And stout gray Iris Sherwood, whose job it was to keep clean water in the pipes and the temperature at an even sixty-eight degrees, sat in the reviewing stand and mentally ran over one water-resource scenario after another, trying to find the one that would get her a million gallons of cold water a day.

She had the gift of foresight, had always known what any situation would bring. As soon as war was declared, she knew, she'd lose Quabbin and the supplementary reservoirs. She could live with that, since most of the water that Boston used didn't come in from outside. It cycled endlessly through the city's enormous circulatory system: from holding tanks to faucets, fountains, gardens, to the thousands of antiquated toilets and showers that still existed in Boston. Some of it went into the air—she pushed her sensible graying hair up from her damp neck—but most went down the drain or into the sewer system, to be cleaned by Targive biologicals, stored in huge holding tanks within Boston, and used again. As simple and sensible as the circulation of blood—and, like it, needing a small but constant renewal.

A million gallons of cold water a day.

The sweat-pipes that veined the city's skin flowed into the Charles River, draining excess heat out of the lower part of the city. Through the enormous Charles gates, cold river water poured into Fridge Station #4 and into the holding tanks with the biologicals; from there it pumped through the city's skin like cold life. Superheated water bubbled into the river. Around the vents Boston Harbor geysered and boiled like a volcanic eruption. It reminded the Phneri of home.

And cold water from the Charles flowed back into the sweat-pipes of Boston.

The Charles gates were outside the city. As soon as war was declared, the Federals would block them. Water would flow out into the Charles, but it wouldn't flow in again.

When they lost the Charles, all that heat would stay in the city.

Behind her the bulk of City Hall loomed in the tense air. On the monitor, "Daaave *Daly*, the Voice of Boston," the CitiNET all-day talk personality, announced one more suburban marching band. A quarter of a million people had crowded into the plaza, restless, clapping. Too many of them had cheered the salute to the flag too loud; too many of them had hissed.

Police Chief Hank Carmody, next to Iris, murmured into his throat mike. "—And, Liz, make sure you strip-search every one of those bastards before you let 'em through the gate. No guns." Hank's lined Irish face was splotched dull yellow and red. Iris leaned over and touched his arm.

"And if the Americans drink any water inside, Hank, you make sure they go to the bathroom before they leave the Cube."

Hank grinned. Looking at his strained face, Iris didn't tell him she was serious.

Teddy Endicott, Iris's cousin and secretary, gazed down at the Mayor's Council in the front row, then across at the huge, mobbed plaza. "Iris, look at these people," he said, his blue eyes glowing. "In a few weeks they'll be citizens of independent Boston." She smiled back at him. He was the kind of smooth blond boy that at seventeen she had dreamed might ask her to dances. Well, she'd known how to foretell that situation too. At seventeen she had been stocky and already graying, with the manly carrying voice and big bones of her Boston forebears: not interesting to the men who interested her. Not destined for sex, she had decided. At forty-four she didn't need a lover. Boston was her passion; Boston's abstractions of anatomy fascinated her, its fevers, its multiple pounding hearts. It was as close as she would get to husband and child, and all she needed.

As for Teddy—The Net scandal channels gossiped that she hired handsome secretaries. Teddy merely pleased her eyes, and he had a Rigellian boyfriend. But she would never have hired him if he had been plain.

Down in the front row, Willie Biko, the Mayor, was just slipping into his seat next to Mi Nyo. Willie had somehow made it here too late for the salute to the flag. Back in South Africa, a hundred years ago, a relative of Willie's had stood up for the wrong thing at the wrong time. Willie had a genius to know when to be just a little late. Tall and stately in perfectly cut formal wear, the Mayor bent solicitously over Mi Nyo's small grim figure, a Brahmin matron dressed in mourning for her niece. Mi Nyo's stout figure was the merest whisper thicker than usual; under the dress she was probably wearing full Targive body armor. Mi Nyo also had the gift of foresight.

"Is he telling her we want a revolution?" Teddy smiled.

" 'We,' Teddy?" Teddy's tie was blue and gold, the unofficial colors of the city. Teddy saw her looking at it and grinned boyishly.

"It goes with your eyes," she said tartly. Teddy should have known better.

Down on the floor of City Hall Plaza, close to the reviewing stand, Iris saw one of Boston's well-known characters, the tour guide "Captain Lemuel Snow," in his full military uniform. She and Lem shared a passion for Boston history and she'd often stopped by his booth in Copley to talk with him. He turned, looking up into the stands, and saw her. His face broke out in a smile.

Suddenly, on the floor of City Hall Plaza, everything

grew quiet. The crowd had recognized the dun green uniforms of the next group. Iris looked up, startled. "The *Customs Service Band?*" Teddy muttered. In an absolute quiet,
the band marched into the plaza. The corridor they
marched through narrowed behind them, in front of them.
Hank muttered frantically into his mike. Looking neither to
right nor left, with no pretense of playing their instruments,
the Customs Service Band marched across the Plaza
through utter silence. Willie Biko was looking for his hat.
Policemen moved from the Washington Street exit to form a
blue protective tunnel around the bandsmen. Unobtrusive
guards moved into position around the reviewing stand,
and someone shoved poor harmless Lem Snow back.

The crowd muttered, talking again. The crowd wasn't
ready. Not quite ready. But— Iris let out her breath, realizing she had been holding it till it hurt.

How long?

Iris had the gift of foresight. She felt danger in the plaza;
the hairs along her arm stirred.

July 11, 2061:

Lem saw the real hostilities begin.

Going to the bathroom saved his life. At eleven forty-
seven P.M. Lem was sitting in the Level 14 jail, playing a
friendly game of Go with Tom Prescott, the one-man conservative wing of Dolly's Free Boston group. At eleven-fifty
he excused himself, and when he came back two minutes
later there was a hole in the side of the jail and Tommy lay
dead on the floor, a surprised look on his thin gray face.
Larry Nguyen, Tommy's ex-client, was screaming outside.

Prescott, that good man and lousy Go player, had urged
caution and legality. Lem knew the speech he would make
to Dolly and the others: Look where the law got him. I saw
Tom Prescott die, a martyr for Boston.

But just between us, Tommy, Lem said silently as he

looked down at the dead lawyer's drawn-down mouth, you died because you thought you could get rid of the government and keep the laws. That's martyr spelled f-o-o-l.

In the corridor the fighting was already general. Backed up against the wall of Police HQ, the Customs agents sent to guard Nguyen had been overwhelmed. They fired into the crowd but the crowd surged up over them and drowned them. Lem's lips tightened and he faded rearward while Customs Agent Nguyen was hoisted, kicking and gagging, to strangle slowly at the end of a rope.

The Boston bastards couldn't even hang a man decently.

Lem went home to his apartment, played channel roulette with the Net while he made his plans. The American channels were reporting tonight's violence as an attack by a Boston mob on Customs agents. Four men had died, just in time for the eleven P.M. news roundup. In retaliation, the Customs Secretary was ordering seizure of "relevant strong points" in Boston to provide for Boston's "peaceful reintegration into the political fabric of the United States."

Relevant strong points, Lem supposed, included lives.

He broke open and oiled his guns while he thought about Iris Sherwood. He hadn't managed to get close to her since the failure at City Hall Plaza.

July 13, 2061: Exchange Day.

"Look, we *own a place in the Cube*." Toby Fitzpatrick thumped his hand against the rough-procked wall of their new apartment. "I've been nine generations in Boston. I'm not Exchanging out. But you two women have got to go. I'm taking no discussion about this."

"I'm sixteen, Dad," Amy Fitzpatrick said flatly. "All my friends are staying and fighting."

"You're not doing any fighting," her stepmother said automatically. "I'm not going, Toby. I'm as Bostonian as you are, and this baby isn't due for two months."

"Ellie, this is no place for a pregnant woman."

Ellie threw open her new kitchen cupboards. "I got cans enough to last us two weeks, Toby, and freeze-dried enough for a long time beyond that." She touched the hard bulge of her stomach protectively, reassuringly, and looked up at her tall husband. "No chance our Little Fitz is going to be called an American, Toby. I won't go."

Amy nodded. "The Mayor's Council is meeting with the Bishop this morning. The aliens are with us, Dad. The Americans won't fight the aliens; nobody can."

"The aliens won't fight," Toby Fitzpatrick said roughly. "They'll leave that to us."

"There won't *be* any fighting." Ellie left the two of them to work it out and maneuvered herself awkwardly around the bubblecartons in the narrow hall. In the bathroom she drew herself a glass of water and leaned heavily for a moment against the sink. It was so hot here in the Cube, hotter than back in Watertown. It was better to be in Boston, they were meant to be here. But she wished the revolution hadn't come the summer she was as big as the Cube.

She was still thirsty. Seemed to her like she drank and drank and then carried all that water around, like a big fat fishbowl she had to carry in her belly. Every day it felt like the fishbowl was a gallon larger, and she still had two months to go. What use would this big belly be on the barricades?

But we'll march in the victory parade, Little Fitz, she told the baby. You and I, we'll march in that parade.

At the Washington Street gate, the exits were guarded on both sides. Regular Customs agents stood at the top of the escalators, grim in their dun green. At the bottom, Boston police mingled with the civilians of the Boston Citizens' Army. Some of the IPOB black-and-whites, theoretically neutral, had joined them. It looked like Friday afternoon rush hour—watertrains lining up like Cisos on the lower deck, commuters pouring down the flexitubes—but the commuters were carrying suitcases. The same announcement repeated monotonously through the hoverhorns: "After 1700 hours today travel may be restricted between Boston and any or all other points. Cube keys and work permits may not be valid for entry to Boston. Your property rights within Boston will not be affected . . ." A middle-aged woman guided her elderly blind husband through the barrier. She clutched a fur coat in the heat of summer and carried a jewelry case. "We'll be back soon, Elliot," she said soothingly. On her right hand an old-fashioned ring glowed red.

The few Exchanging in were mostly male. A skinny thirtyish man with, of all things, a huge roll of artist's canvas. A group of Cambridge dons who looked like they were out on a field trip. Standing by the escalator, with his new Boston Volunteers armband and his completely legal rifle, Lem watched them with professional disdain. Skinny intellectuals, toughing it out for a stupid cause. All these people were going to die.

So was he. Maybe. But he knew what he was doing.

Clustered on the edge of the Wall, the amphibious Phneri rats watched the exodus, whistling and murmuring like art critics.

July 14, 2061: Formation of the Joint Council

"Barnhardt screwed up," Teddy said wonderingly. Teddy was always surprised when politicians made mistakes. In the plush chambers where the City Council met, waiting for her cue, Iris Sherwood replayed on her Net feed the huge and unexpected mistake Barnhardt had just made: ripping up unread a resolution drafted by the Mayor's Council, announcing that he refused to deal with an "unelected advisory body."

Down on the City Council floor, the two Boston councils were busy electing themselves.

Mi Nyo had just proposed a resolution that Boston was "in crisis," whatever that meant. In one of her usual fiery speeches, Srinavasa O'Connell-Reeves was pledging the undying support of the Boston workers to the city government, "whatever it will be." In a corner, reps from the Mayor's Council and the City Council were scribbling at a mysterious document. Ragnhild Freyasdotter, one of the group, rose with papers in her hand and trotted forward to the podium, brushing her messy blond hair out of her eyes. Iris saw Dave Daly, the Voice of Boston, skittering into the back of the hall. Ragnhild was one of Mi Nyo's creatures, and, under her bird's-nest hair and rhinestone glasses, a powerful speaker.

Ragnhild settled her glasses on her nose. "Mr. Mayor, Ms. Chairman: Nearly three hundred years ago, fighting the British, Boston underwent a blockade . . ." Iris knew the history. Boston had been a neck of land then, more or less the same area that was now under the Cube. For all of one winter the British had bottled up the Bostonians into their mile-square piece of land, without food, without fuel for the fires in their homes. Half of the population of the city had got out; some had starved. The population of the city had been— what, in 1773? How many times larger was it now? Did Mi Nyo understand what she was doing? "We propose," Ragnhild said, "that our two bodies form themselves into a single Council, to meet for the duration of this crisis . . ."

Hank Carmody was named Crisis Coordinator, assisted by Lizbeth Faulkner. Iris Sherwood pleated the notes for her speech on water restrictions between her fingers. By unanimous vote the joint Councils elected a negotiating committee chaired by Mi Nyo.

On the Net feed, one of Dave Daly's rivals was interviewing the Bishop. As chairman of Venture Capital, the Bishop said, his rational interest was to preserve Boston as an economic entity. He would do what was required to preserve this interest, up to and including dissolving the board of Venture Capital and holding new elections.

CitiNET was running the story under the access line, "Bishop tells Barnhardt: IT'S WAR!" The American Channel was reporting, "Bishop will not act to help rebel Bostonians."

And a jubilant President Masterson held a news conference to announce the success of the blockade: "An iron ring surrounds Boston."

In the Basement in peacetime, twilight fell over the city slowly, an ever-changing glory of clouds and sweet sunset light programmed by one of Willie Biko's cousins. Tonight at eight, on Night One of the blockade, the holographic skies cut off suddenly, making black starless night in the Plaza. Leaving the joint session, drained, Iris Sherwood stared through antique glass windows into the dark. The only light came from the movers, streaking like comets under the rough-procked roof.

We'll have to restrict the movers too, Iris thought automatically. Boston will need that energy.

The big darkness hypnotized her. She was used to lit corridors twenty-four hours a day. It was years since she had seen darkness larger than her own bedroom.

"Look there," Lizbeth Faulkner pointed.

Down at Level 1, streaming into the plaza from its twelve entrances, rivers of tiny lights were forming and shaping. Liz touched the rim of her glasses to refocus them on the crowd below. "Bioglows, trouble lights, antique flashlights—look at that, a kerosene lamp. Everybody's got a light."

"They're celebrating." Iris lingered over the idea, wondering. The blockade meant water shortfalls, disabled movers, darkened corridors, shortages, people willing to kill for bread and water. Criminals who hadn't left in the Exchange. This big darkness. Inside, the conciliation wing was still bickering with Mi Nyo's forces, not willing to concede that Bill Barnhardt had cut them out of the game. These lights and energy were a waste; Boston would need everything. "No one here knows what it's going to be like."

Liz shook her head. "They're hanging together, like Ben Franklin said, you know? 'We must all hang together or we will all hang separately.' "

"They won't have to hang us. We'll die of the heat. If Mi Nyo lived in the Basement, there'd be no 'revolution.' "

"Don't you back out on us, Iris," Liz said sharply. "If this isn't revolution, you and I are dead."

Iris sighed. "I don't back out. Boston needs me." She looked down at the revelers. From three levels up— "They're so vulnerable." When she had been young, she had envied people who went to parties. It disturbed her that she was afraid for them now.

Lizbeth Faulkner shook her head. "Don't you be their mama, Iris. They're stronger than we think, and this is me the police speaking. Whatever Mi Nyo's doing behind the scenes, she's been at it for years and nothing like this happened. We've been doing our jobs, me on the police and you counting drops of water, Mi Nyo conquering the world, and all of a sudden *they* decided it was time, and there's a half-million folks out there on the plaza, shouting bad things at Barnhardt. And—"

Down on Level 1, someone turned on a spotlight.

"And look there," Liz said softly, "look there."

The spotlight was on one of the old City Hall flagpoles, unused for years. In the pitiless light the American flag jerked up the flagpole, halfway up, and then stopped. From the plaza, growing slowly, came a noise such as Iris had never heard before, an animal sound from thousands of throats together: massive, huge, a rage the size of a city. There was a struggle at the base of the flagpole, the details too far away for Iris to see—Liz focused her glasses on it and her lips tightened. Then someone loosed ropes, and the American flag fell down the flagpole, too fast for lowering, fell of its own weight with a death rattle of rope. What was hoisted in its place looked crude, unfinished: blue and gold on a green background, a lighted city on a hill, a woman representing Liberty, a harbor, a sky full of stars—and the fabric was wrong, thick, artist's canvas maybe, the flag just painted, someone's first thoughts. Looking at the unfinished flag, Iris saw bits and pieces, mistakes and revisions, one human moment piled on another: an organic thing, a thing to be tended, like a city. Through the open plaza rang a cry, a cheer, a roar, a cry like a woman giving birth, the voice of the city. Iris Sherwood raised her head; "Oh," she said, "yes," she said, her eyes fixed on her city's flag, finding her revolution.

Iris reached into her purse and touched the small barrel of her own trouble light. The same edge of her that had hired Teddy made her smile now. "Liz, come down there with me."

"No."

"I want to find out what the revolution is. I want to find out all about it."

Liz looked at her sadly. "Can't do it, Iris. I'm escorting you and Teddy up to 152. We can't afford to have you so close to the Basement. There are still Americans in the city."

"152? With the Nyos?"

"She'll keep you safe. Your office is being moved now." The policewoman touched her arm. "*Ms.* Sherwood? They're going to make the revolution. I'm going to have to control them while they do it, and—I can read water meters as well as anyone else—you're going to have to let some of them die. Until this is over, you're going to have to make some hard decisions. Don't look at their faces."

Down in the plaza the lights swirled and glittered like all the dances no one had ever asked her to. The voice of the city was speaking from a hundred thousand throats, a hundred thousand hands were holding the lights of the city. Above them, in the dark, Iris switched on her trouble light for a second and held it cupped in her competent, middle-aged hand. Iris knew the price of her responsibilities. She nodded and turned her light off, following Lizbeth Faulkner to the mover and up to her new office, where it was still day.

Across the plaza, in the shadow of an arcade pillar, Lem Snow swore and lowered his rifle. He moved through the crowd to the area below the flagpole. Some Bostonians were gathering up the torn rags of the American flag and throwing them into a fire. Lem saw one, a bit of red stripe gleaming like blood. He picked it up and palmed it as if he were throwing it into the fire.

We hold these truths to be self-evident, that all men are created equal . . . He looked up at the green abomination, which looked like a flag that had died and was stiffening before it rotted. America, I swear, I will see your sacred and legitimate flag flying from that flagpole before I die, and Boston blood on the ground.

When he looked down, he saw Big Jake Wilson, the manager of Scollay Square Sweets, staring at his hand.

"Show me what you got in your hand," Jake rumbled, speaking low.

Lem opened his hand easily. "Piece of trash." The lie left a taste in his mouth.

"Yup. Lot of it around." Jake stooped, grunting, and picked up a star from the plaza, still sewn to a rag of blue.

"Burn it, Jake?" Lem said casually.

"Don't think so," Jake said, still low-voiced.

"Burn it!" some kid told him. "Go on, get rid of it, burn it!"

Jake turned a big, friendly, scraggly-toothed smile on him. "I'm going to take mine home and piss on it." The kid went away, grinning. The two men looked at each other speculatively.

* * *

On Level 1 the Gathering of the Lamps went on all night. It was hot and everyone was out on the streets. People would remember this time as the happiest of the Revolution. Oil lamps, many of them ancient, were brought out to provide light. Rallies were lit by torches. Working at top speed in the Plaza, Ernest Pole produced the first of his Symbols of Boston series, an oil lamp burning on a dark globe. Many people were wearing Iron Rings, a crude metal ring resembling a large hex nut, on the middle finger of their right hand. Baka's videos of that night show people yelling "Fuck *you Barn*hardt" and waving the one-finger hello to President Masterson. One of Baka's shots shows blond Amy Fitzpatrick, in the Plaza until very late, singing with her friends. Eventually, inevitably, the whole Plaza was singing what would become the "Yankee Doodle" of this Revolution:

> *Oh ye citizens of Boston, don't you think it's a scandal*
> *How the people have to pay and pay?—*

July 17, 2061:

On CitiNET, Dave Daly made a hash of explaining the Bishop's position. Bishop 24 would participate in—in fact, insisted on—economic negotiations with Customs Secretary Barnhardt. At the end of these negotiations there would be a stable government in Boston, capable of ensuring the peaceful continuation of Venture Capital operations.

"And that's all," Iris said to Teddy. "He doesn't care who's in the government."

Teddy smiled tiredly, looking up from his computer. "I'm betting on Mi Nyo." Around his mouth unaccustomed bitterness cut little lines. Rigel had called all its citizens home and Teddy's boyfriend had told him that revolution was cheap sentiment. "I hope Mi Nyo wins fast. I want this to be over."

Iris glanced around the spring green brocaded walls of

Level 152. She wanted to put her arms around her pet butterfly and tell him to keep his mouth shut.

She cracked her knuckles—a habit she thought she'd got rid of in school—and, crossing her arms, stared thoughtfully at Teddy's simulation. On Teddy's burlwood desk towered a gray model of the Cube, with the water supply glowing in various colors: blue for cool drinkable water, red for hot, yellow for polluted. "Show me population concentrations versus drinkable water, Teddy." Exchange Day hadn't improved their situation enough. Yellow danger areas were scattered throughout the Cube. "Show me temperature rise over time. Move it up in ten-day increments."

She watched grimly as yellow and orange areas overwhelmed the blue. Black spread over Boston like the smoke from burning buildings. "Black means unacceptable loss of life," Teddy said unnecessarily. The pain lines around his mouth deepened. He smoothed his hair back, a once handsome gesture that was becoming a tic.

Iris thought of Liz's words. *You're going to have to let some of them die.*

"Put everyone on half-rations starting now." This time the black spread more slowly, but it spread. Teddy turned away from it, cutting the power. Boston faded.

Iris stared out her window. Outside she could see a sector of the Wall, the Cube rising within it, almost a part of it. Below them the Charles sparkled coldly, rising twenty-five feet above old Boston, held back by the Wall and by the closed Charles gates.

JULY 21, 2061:

"This is Daaave *Daly*. Our noon temperature in City Hall Plaza is 89.5 degrees Fahrenheit . . ."

"Sherwood's up on Level 152," Lucy the Irishwoman told Lem and Jake Wilson. "On the Upper Crust. They've moved the Mayor's Council and City Council up there too. It's crawling with Nyo police."

"She's still my assignment." He moved his hand on the counter in the sign for *I've got a plan.*

"It's too dangerous."

"Fuck dangerous." She blinked at him, then turned her eyes away, swabbing at her counter, barely wetting her cloth. "I don't want to get my pension from Mi Nyo."

July 27, 2061:

"This is Daaave *Daly* with the latest water conservation measures. As a safety measure, private kitchens and bathrooms will no longer receive water. Central water supply stations are being set up at each level. Each household is allowed three gallons of water a day per adult member, two gallons per child. Folks, that's enough to drink and bathe in, if you sponge-bathe, and enough to flush the toilet once a day. Our noon temperature in City Hall Plaza is 91.8 degrees Fahrenheit . . ."

Water sellers began to appear on the Common and in the Copley Mall. Questions about the source of the water were immediately asked in the Joint Council. Lizbeth Faulker was put in charge of regulating water sales. The average price of water was $2.50 a gallon.

July 29, 2061: Destruction of Refrigeration Station #4

"Salt."

The word echoed flatly through the black tunnels of Fridge Station #4. Lem Snow shone a dimming flashlight over the carcasses of the Clivus biologicals. The enormous Targive-modified slugs could digest almost anything, but a hundred pounds of salt had killed them. The smell poked a finger down Lem's throat and stung his eyes with methane. Under his boots, the crunch of coarse salt, slimy stickiness.

Good coup for the Federalists. Lem wished he'd done it himself. Jake and he were still figuring out how to get up-Cube.

"No wonder the water tastes like crap." Next to Lem, Toby Fitzpatrick coughed in the foul heat. "Holy Mary, with the slugs dead, we're drinking our own toilets."

Lem came up with what the loyal Bostonian was supposed to say. "It won't stop us."

"Wish it would," his neighbor said bitterly. "Ellie and Amy—"

The group leader shouted. "Fitzpatrick! Snow! We're going to—"

The men behind him had been unloading shovels from a cart. Illustrating what they were going to do, one of them bent to scrape up the salt, and sparks grated from the shovel's edge. *Methane?* Lem thought. He threw his arm over his eyes just in time. The fireball picked him up and carried him, a wall of hot air tumbling him over and over. He smashed against the curve of the corridor and crawled down it. The air moaned, pulling him back toward the fire; he staggered down the tunnel.

He knew Boston, but it was hours until he found a mover tunnel, disused now because half the movers were shut down. Climbing the fixit ladder to Level 1, he found himself in front of a vid of the tunnel fire. "Among the dead," Dave Daly was saying solemnly, "is the well-known Boston tour guide, Cap'n Lem Snow."

AUGUST 1, 2061: FIRST CITIZENS OF FREE BOSTON DECLARED

At his desk next to Iris's, in cool Level 152, Teddy watched Dave Daly's obituary column every day, keying in the latest deaths. He had begun sleeping next to his simulation and the vidscreen.

The roll of the dead for August 1 included Toby Fitzpatrick, 50, identified as having been burnt to death; Lester Kronenbourg, Director of the Museum of Human Culture, 61, of heat stroke; William "WalkMan" Higgins, 75, of heat stroke . . .

Heat stroke. Fires, from lack of water. Iris saw the faces pass on the screen; faces she had seen on the street. Lem Snow's death still hurt. She remembered the last time she had seen him, a tall man in his uniform, at the Fourth of July. A handsome man and a part of Boston. Less than a month ago; more than a lifetime.

"Free Boston," Teddy said, staring at the simulation. "That's what they call it." In the simulation, the fire had eaten its way up the mover shafts, leaving a permanent black stain. Unacceptable loss of life.

Iris turned her eyes away. There was no unacceptable loss of life, Iris thought, as long as Boston survived. She had foreseen all this. She knew.

In joint session, the Mayor's Council and City Council unanimously declared Toby Fitzpatrick, Lem Snow, and the other dead men "citizens of Free Boston." Amy Fitzpatrick was among those who attended the ceremony—which, short as it was, would be the most elaborate of what became an almost daily event. In Baka's videos, Amy had cut her long hair short and her face was scrawny and transparent. She looked as if she wasn't eating.

Ellie didn't go. She sat in her darkened, unfinished apartment where she had sat with her husband, and watched the ceremony over CitiNET. Ellie's only black blouse stretched over her bulging stomach and stuck, sweat-oiled, to her skin; she felt like she was carrying all Boston Harbor in a great hot fishbowl in her stomach, and somewhere in there too were all the tears she didn't dare to cry.

Next to her on the sofa they'd brought from the suburbs, Toby had sat so long he'd worn a low place in the cheap stuffing. Ellie sat next to it, trying still to feel his body next to hers.

Free Boston, she had discovered, didn't mean as much to her as Toby's death.

She was hungry. The Fitzpatrick women had run out of canned goods four days ago.

August 3, 2061:

"We have to get to her office," Lem told Jerry Leeford. "Sewer and Water's a multiply-redundant system; you have to take out the computer brain, which is located there, and the physical brain, which is Iris."

Jake Wilson's friend Jerry Leeford was a doorman at an Upper Crust hotel. He was a graying man of about forty, tall and handsome; under his uniform he was in better shape than Lem, who had always prided himself on his strength. Air-vent climbing was his hobby.

"It'd be a pretty significant climb," Jerry said. "The Nyo cops have security systems to keep climbers out, both in the mover shafts and the air-vents."

"How good?"

Jerry grinned. "It's a great climb, actually."

"How about it, fellow Americans?"

They'd need standard vent-climbing equipment, good boots, high-energy food. With money from the Federal underground, they would buy extra water.

"Can we get it together by tomorrow?"

Jake and Jerry nodded.

August 7, 2061:

"And this is Daaave *Daly*. Our noon temperature at City Hall Plaza is 98.1 degrees Fahrenheit, that's just under blood heat, folks, so you want to walk around slooow . . . take it easy!"

Working from Teddy's simulations, Iris Sherwood's office adjusted the water ration. For most this meant that water was cut in half. Lizbeth had her hands full with controlling the water sellers. The price of water averaged $10.90 a gallon.

Bathing, hair washing, and toilet flushing had virtually ceased in Boston. Trash collection had ceased on any but a local basis. All stocks of perfume had sold out, as had devices to control ants, cockroaches, and other more exotic pests. For the first time in her life Iris Sherwood wore perfume every day. "I want to go down to the Basement," she told Liz.

"You can't go."

She had started looking at CitiNET almost as obsessively as Teddy. "I want to see it."

Late the night of August 7, Lizbeth came for her, with three guards. They took a darkened express mover downward and stood, Iris and Liz and the three silent guards, on the same balcony where Iris had watched the lights. The same flag still flew from the same lighted pole, its weight now dragging it down into stiffened folds. The plaza was half deserted, but, for the first and last time, Iris smelled the revolution, the smell of the city during revolution: garbage left too long in the heat, cheap perfume, and the rank, sweet-acid, yeasty sweat of bodies beginning to starve.

"Are you done?" Lizabeth said sharply. "Let's go."

The smell of a body beginning to eat itself: the smell of death.

Amy Fitzpatrick paid twenty dollars for a jar of peanut butter. When she got it home, Ellie screamed at her.

"It's rancid!"

The smell from the jar turned Ellie's stomach but she dipped her finger into the peanut butter and licked it. The sour-sweet stickiness stuck to her mouth, more like a gag than food. By reflex Ellie turned the cold-water tap but not even a drop came out. Amy poured her a cup of water from the bottle in the kitchen. "Drink it slowly, Mom." Ellie's black blouse chafed her, stiff and tight. She hadn't left the apartment since Toby died. The heat was so bad, she leaned against the counter, her heart pounding and the ball of bad-tasting food halfway down her throat. She sat down on the floor, feeling dizzy. The baby gave a strong kick inside her and she swallowed and let out her breath, wanting to cry with relief, just wanting to cry. At least the baby was fine. She'd make it. She was an unsteady hot fishbowl, but her baby was a strong little fish inside her and as long as she felt those muscular flip-flops everything was okay. Little Fish-patrick, she muttered, half-laughing. For the baby, she took another bite of the terrible-tasting food.

After three days' climbing, Jake, Jerry, and Lem Snow had reached Level 93 of the vent shafts, climbing the fixit ladders. They made slow progress, having to dodge the vent shaft alarms and, once, an express mover, though the shaft was supposed to be closed down; they'd made barely thirty levels a day. The continual baking wind up the shafts bothered them all, and Wilson, the least in condition of the three, was suffering from muscle cramps.

August 9, 2061:

"This is Dave Daly at City Hall Plaza, where the noon temperature has reached a little over 101 degrees. The Office of Water Coordination has announced today that, for the duration of the crisis, water rations will be the same for children and adults, one gallon per day . . ."

The roll of the dead included: Boris Nancolm, supposed to have been one of the first men to see the aliens, 91, of heat stroke, and Chief of Police Hank Carmody, 58, of massive heart attack.

"That's Hank," Teddy said as one of the simulation neighborhoods darkened slightly. He looked up at Iris. Puzzled lines were etching themselves around his beautiful eyes.

"The thing is," he said, "they all have names. *Every one* of them has a name. Just like Hank."

"They're Boston, Teddy. We're losing people but Boston's surviving."

Lizbeth Faulkner was appointed acting Assistant Chief of Police. Mayor Willie Biko gave Carmody posthumous citizenship of Free Boston.

For about twenty levels above 100 there were no fixit ladders. Jake Wilson drank too much water at once. Rappelling up a vent, he retched suddenly, cramping again, and dropped the bag containing their food and water. They heard it bumping all the way down the shaft, then a rattle as it hit the grate over the big vanes.

Jerry climbed to Level 115 to reconnoiter for supplies. Lem stayed. Lem crouched on the ledge beside Jake. "I can keep up," the wheezing fat man pleaded. "I just got to get some rest." Sweat stood out on his forehead. Lem met his eyes.

"You know how it's got to be, Jake." The Bostonians would find the supplies. They had to find a body with it. A climber, a single climber, who had fallen.

"Shit," Jake muttered. "Dying because of stomach cramps." He rolled off the ledge, silent as he fell. Lem heard nothing, just the endless hot sour wind.

He climbed up to rejoin Jerry.

August 13, 2061: Federal Attempt to Destabilize Boston Currency

The siege had reached its first month's anniversary.

Ellie Fitzpatrick sent Amy out to buy extra water. Amy returned with the bottle a quarter full.

"There were people with all sorts of money. Some guy was offering a hundred dollars a gallon. I couldn't believe it. It's like money was coming out of the woodwork."

The Fitzpatrick women had flattened out their savings account long ago, in the prehistoric time before the revolution, for curtains and kitchen cabinets for the new apartment.

"I don't need any water," Amy said, adulthood sharpening her face. "You take it all."

"You can't live without water."

"I know where to get plenty," Amy said defensively. "Down on Level 1, near where Daddy died."

"Don't you ever do that!" Ellie lowered her voice. "They're storing bodies down there."

"It's okay. Really, I'm okay, Mom, don't *worry*." Amy, annoyed, left for a rally.

By 6 P.M. the price of water was over fifty dollars a gallon. That evening, riots destroyed two of the water distribution stations; Lizbeth's police had to fire into the crowds to disperse them. Ellie watched the CitiNET coverage late into the night, sitting alone in her dark apartment, waiting for Amy to come back.

August 15, 2061:

Lizbeth's eyes were bloodshot and haunted behind her glasses. "The money to buy water's coming from the Federalists," she told Iris. "The Phneri say so. They say it all came into Boston at once, in bubblepacks brought by divers through the Clivus."

Iris sat across the desk. Teddy raised his head from his simulation, looking at them. Beside her the Phner spokesman, a trundling, moplike animal, sorted money into "good" and "Federalist".

Willie Biko frowned. "How could divers get through the sewers?"

"Only with somebody's help," Iris said grimly. "The Phneri see on the money where it comes from. The pile over here was in Boston before this week."

"I show where your money comes-s from," the Phner offered, holding out his paw for Willie's money.

"I know where my money comes from," Willie said a little dryly.

AUGUST 16, 2061:

Dave Daly had stopped broadcasting the noon temperature. Iris knew it, 109.3 degrees Fahrenheit, and the average price of a gallon of water, $83.69. She had no time for mooning over CitiNET. Her boss had died unexpectedly of heat stroke, and Iris had been named Acting DPW Director and Acting Crisis Coordinator.

She had a bigger office with a window over the roofs of the Upper Crust. The roof greenhouses were growing tomatoes, cucumbers, late peas, green beans. The negotiators had turned vegetarian but they weren't starving. Every inch of roof that wasn't under cultivation was covered with ionizing water purifiers. Even transpiration from the leaves was caught in the greenhouse filters.

The VIPs couldn't starve. Who would negotiate? Who would manage? She ate the tomatoes herself and drank the water. So did Teddy, for all his obsessive counting of the dead.

She couldn't worry about all of them, just take care of them as best she could. She couldn't even worry about Teddy. She had responsibilities.

The temperature was rising by an average of 1.2 degrees a day.

August 18, 2061:

"This is Dave Daly, reporting from the Mayor's Office, where Mayor Biko has announced controls on water sellers . . ."

Ellie wasn't quite sure how long Amy had been gone. It used to get cooler at night but now it just seemed to get hotter and hotter. The clock said ten but the lights were always dim now, so was it ten in the morning or at night? She felt all fuzzy and her head ached bad. Once a day the city government gave out water somewhere close by. Amy always brought water bottles home in a plastic crate. She'd have to rouse herself and stand in line. But she didn't feel thirsty enough to bother, just sleepy, too tired to raise her head, even though the crate was right by her hand.

She was lying on the couch, listening to CitiNET, but nothing Dave Daly said made any sense.

The baby was kicking strong. There was still good water inside the fishbowl. Water for the baby. Holy Mary, it was hot.

Amy really should get back soon.

August 21, 2061:

"This is Dave Daly at City Hall Plaza, where a makeshift hospital is being set up for heat-stroke victims. I'm speaking with Dr. Rajiv Singh. Dr. Singh, it's rumored that polluted water from the Charles gates leaks is spreading typhus into the city . . ."

Teddy murmured instructions through his throat mike, but his eyes never left the CitiNET screen. There were no names among the victims now. Dave Daly read statistics.

"What can I do?" Iris asked. "Look at your numbers, Teddy. Do you know how much water a fever victim needs?"

"Tank D is still a quarter full."

"I won't waste water on the dying."

CitiNET blared in the background. Baka's camera was sweeping across the City Hall Plaza, covered with the bodies of typhoid victims, some already dead. Iris recognized one of them, a woman who had translated for the Phneri.

"Turn that off!" Iris snapped and blanked the screen.

AUGUST 22, 2061: PHNERI BECOME FIRST ALIEN CITIZENS OF BOSTON
UNIFORM RIGHTS ACT
DECLARATION OF THE BOSTON CONGRESS

"This is Dave Daly. Riots today over polluted water have resulted in the deaths of . . ."

Several Phneri volunteers stationed in public places, offering free water analysis, had been killed by Bostonians who had paid for undrinkable water. Lizbeth Faulkner had the perpetrators arrested for murder. When their lawyers objected, the Mayor's Council and City Council passed the Uniform Rights Declaration, affirming that all Citizens of Free Boston were equal under the law. (By a close vote, it escaped being called the Uniform Alien Rights Declaration.) By acclamation the Phneri were named Citizens of Free Boston.

Lem Snow and Jerry Leeford reached Level 136 in the vents, only to find it blocked. They would have to go through the mover shafts to the next level, a risky business: up here the movers were still operative. They decided to wait for evening, when it was cooler and traffic was low.

Level 136 was almost deserted; it had been an upper-level Federalist neighborhood. The two climbers sat in a luxuriously carpeted apartment, on a Targive-modified sofa, with their feet up on something neither of them could identify, and watched the Council sessions on CitiNET. They had found three cans of water-packed green beans and for the first time in days were not hungry or thirsty.

One of the lawyers, a woman named Thelma Adderley, objected that the Phneri were not United States citizens, that the Mayor's Council had no right to change United States law, and that in any case her client was not covered by the Declaration. Upon this, a little blond woman with rhinestone glasses proposed that the Joint Council rename itself the Boston City Congress and give itself legislative powers. She was seconded by Janet Nyo's brother Raymond. Willie Biko signed the hardcopy first, holding his pen up in a pose that looked like it was a rehearsal for a statue. "For Boston, freedom, and the future," Willie said to the cameras.

"Sign away your rights," Lem said. "Sign away your country. Your soul."

Waiting in line to sign the Declaration, a member of the new Congress asked seriously if Phneri could replicate drinkable water. A resolution was passed requesting that they try.

Unlike the Declaration of the Boston Congress, it passed unanimously.

In late afternoon Acting Crisis Coordinator Iris Sherwood, live on CitiNET, announced citizenship for the Phneri.

"Traitor Boston bitch," Jerry Leeford said broodingly. They had found some Boston middle manager's collection of antique Sam Adams beer. It was flat, hot, and barely drinkable.

Lem raised his bottle to the screen. "We hold these truths," he said slowly, "to be self-evident. That all men are created equal. That they are endowed by their Creator with certain inalienable rights. And that some bastards would rather be rich than take responsibility for those rights."

"America," Jerry held his bottle out for a toast.

"America. Amen."

August 23, 2061: Federal Forces Attack the Wall

"This is Baka, standing in for Dave Daly. In this terrible heat, City Hall Plaza has become a graveyard. The dying are brought to join the dead . . .

". . . latest news from the blast early this morning in the police residential area near the Washington Street Gate. Targive-modified earthworms, drilling into the base of the Wall and detonating themselves, have caused immense destruction in the area of the Police Ghetto . . ."

Lem Snow and Jerry Leeford jimmied open the door of a mover shaft just as the explosion, seventeen hundred feet below, ripped up the narrow shaft like the gases behind a bullet. Lem was thrown backward across the room. For a moment, eerily, it was a month ago in the tunnels of Fridge Station #4. There was a sound like a whip-crack and Jerry said "-ll—"; Lem rolled behind an ornamental mahogany bench, expecting to feel the fire blossoming out of the shaft, but all he heard was the round echoing silence after the noise. "Jerry?"

Lem dragged himself to the door of the mover shaft. Nothing was left of Jerry but a red smear on the procked wall. Lem couldn't support himself on his right leg, and a long red stain was spreading down his pants. No more shaft climbing or rappelling. The mover had been driven crookedly up the tight shaft like a bullet in a badly made gun. The broken mover cables dangled just out of reach. Lem looked at the setup and nodded.

Among those killed in the blast were Salene Faulkner, 60, past president of the Boston Roof Garden Club, and Capt. Jeremy Faulkner, 61, of IPOB, parents of Acting Assistant Chief of Police Lizbeth Faulkner. Lizbeth's only child, a fanatic baseball player, died with them.

* * *

The Boston Congress, speaking through Mi Nyo, re pro posed a meeting with Masterson. "We will stand forever. We will fight forever. And we will prevail," Willie Biko said.

August 24, 2061:

"Six degrees in two days," Iris said. She pushed her hair out of her face. On Teddy's burlwood desk the simulation of the City was a column of darkening grease-smoke, a nightmare from a Holocaust chimney. She cracked her knuckles, pressed her fingers against her upper arms in a sudden diffused hysteria.

Teddy hadn't shaved; his thin face was raw with stubble. He kept the video on all the time now. Dave Daly had died of typhus, but Teddy plugged in to Baka's transmissions while Baka roamed the Basement, playing his camera over face after face. In the Basement a moment of video was now the only roll call of the dead.

"Look," murmured Teddy, "that one's still alive." He flinched from the look she gave him.

She moved him aside from his computer display. The harbor surrounded the city and the Wall, ebbing and flowing with the tides. By the Police Ghetto and the Washington Street Gate, the weakened section of the Wall glowed red like an infected place. She poked her finger through it and the cold blue-green water flowed in. The temperature sensors Teddy had scattered around his simulation dropped abruptly.

"We could do that," she said brutally. "Flood the lower levels. Flood Boston."

She made him look at her. Teddy gave her a sad idealist's grin. "Iris, that's where the sick people are—"

"Most of them are dead. Not sick, dead." Throughout the lowest ten floors, the shadowed city had gone black. Unacceptable loss of life.

"I'll get everyone out who can walk," she told him. He stared at her wide-eyed as if the reassurance frightened him. She turned away. "Do you want the whole city to *die*?" she asked. "Do you think I have choices?"

"No, Iris," he said. "You're strong." She forgot herself then and put her arms around him to comfort him. He twisted away. "Stay away from me."

She heard the shot from Teddy's room a few minutes later. When she knelt by him he was already dead. He had worn his City tie, the blue-and-gold one that had suited him so. She closed his wide-staring eyes and picked up the gun he had used. Above the plain round hole in his chest, his face was beautiful again, free of weakness and the responsibility he had flinched from.

She stood up heavily. "I'm responsible, Teddy, I have to be." She stood looking down at him and then, without very much meaning to, she brought her foot back in its sensible shoe and kicked his dead body. She stared at her shoe. She breathed hard. Her fist around the gun tightly enough to hurt, she turned quickly back toward her office.

Judging by the pain, Lem's leg was broken. He sprayed it with Targive quickdry from the corridor's first-aid kit. But he hadn't straightened the bones right and the ends ground against each other every time he took a step.

Grabbing a Pain-No-More from the kit, he picked a vein and pressed the little spray against it. The scream in his bones fell silent. He thumped across the carpet on a suddenly wooden leg.

Arriving in Washington by special plane, Mi Nyo was finally shown into President Masterson's office. Customs Secretary Barnhardt was called into conference. Mi Nyo had brought samples of the newest Phner replicas: currency from many nations, in all denominations and states of wear.

* * *

Down in the Basement sirens were whooping. Baka was announcing over CitiNET, "Emergency. This is not a test. All persons please leave Levels One through Ten immediately. Proceed immediately to Level 11 or above. All movers are operative. Please proceed immediately to Level 11 or above."

On Level 10 Ellie's CitiNET screen blared the message too, but she hardly heard: half-dead Ellie Fitzpatrick was in labor.

On Level 1 the Phneri whistled around the weakened wall, fitting shape-charges in an arcane pattern.

Upstairs on 152 an alarm shrilled, set off by the opening of the drug cabinet.

"Unauthorized drug withdrawal we have here," Tommy Chen, a Nyo family cop, muttered. "Want a drug bust, Suzy?"

"Now? Lizbeth'll have our asses if we leave Sherwood."

"I'm taking a look."

Lem Snow shot Tommy Chen as he stepped out the mover, lowering his body to the floor. Even hampered by his leg, Lem slid into the mover without a sound. Tommy Chen's Cube key was still in the doorslot, showing its automatic return-to location in lighted letters.

Level 152.

Lem Snow smiled and pressed MOVER RETURN.

The Wall burst open like a madman's laugh, like a jet crash, a memory, a gong. Boston drowned.

Water ripped through brownstone streets and churned Boston Common into a fog of undersea mud. Bodies poured through the tunnels like water. The air crushed, thick as glue; Charles Bulfinch's State House dome imploded. The swan boats were crushed against the roof of Beacon Hill. All the windows in central Boston broke. Water rushed into City Hall Plaza and the dead and the dying were tossed together into City Hall, breaking the ancient windows, storming the old Council chamber and pounding on the Speaker's desk with tumbling, silent white hands.

Dimly Ellie Fitzpatrick heard a boom and the deep roar of water. Air screamed and exploded up through mover shafts, machinery whined and sparked, humans screamed—Ellie could hear words. And over everything else was the deep grinding roar, a voice like a crowd. Against her straining womb all the air suddenly clenched at once like Boston's belly contracting with hers. The fishbowl had cracked, oh yes, hot water was searing her, she screamed in surprise and fear, a child screamed with her. She felt the baby born all at once. It passed out of her, ripping her; something else came out of her, and then water kept pouring out, pouring and pouring, she gave birth to waves of agony like water. The lights were dimming, it was dark. She grabbed and found a tiny hand, a sticklike leg, pushed it into the old plastic crate that Amy used to bring water home in, ripped her blouse apart and shoved it over the baby as a blanket. She fell to her knees, Boston roared and screamed in her ears. Water! Toby—water—too much—there was too much water here! Ellie screamed silently through cracked lips. The water tugged at her. Half doubled over with the agony in her belly, she held the plastic crate over her head. The water rose; she stood up, screaming, screaming, holding the baby's crate above her head, while the water bubbled up around her mouth. She kept screaming at the water until she died.

Lem Snow shot the female cop as the mover door opened. He stood by the mover door, gun in hand, waiting for the noise to bring Iris out. No one came. It was cool up here. Windows were open. Very faintly, from far away, he heard strange noises, rumbles and explosions. He eased himself slowly around the edge of the room, soundless on his deadened leg.

The woman he had come to kill was sitting at a big wooden desk behind a feet-high blackened simulation of the black city. Even unwashed, she looked like she had on the video, prim and upper-class like a Harvard librarian. He shot through the simulation, forgetting that there might be hardware somewhere in it. His first shot ricocheted and only hit her arm and she raised her hand, like a librarian saying *Hush,* but she had a gun in it. As he fell he was still surprised that she had a gun.

Remember, he said. Remember America, you traitor. He wanted to tell her but belched blood instead. She shot him again and this time he died.

"I did what I had to," she told him in a conversational voice. She knew he was dead but she kept firing anyway. His body jerked on the carpet. Teddy had been wrong. It was easy, easy, easy to kill and keep on killing. For the moment it was just impossible to stop.

August 29, 2061:

At noon on City Hall Plaza the temperature was 68.2 degrees Fahrenheit, with a cooling breeze. The last of the Harbor water was being pumped out of the Basement. Most of the bodies had already been removed to Cemetery Hill in Waltham. Boston Demolition and Rehab, a corps of gleeful Phneri, was tearing down a water-damaged building on State Street before replicating it, and a popcorn alien was selling thumbtacks to a brick. Iris Sherwood, dogged by reporters, had finally reached Level 1 of City Hall Plaza.

A smiling Willie Biko, flanked by Mi Nyo and the new Customs Secretary, was announcing the provisions of the new Warren Amendment to the United States Constitution.

". . . Boston is exempted from all Federal taxation . . ." Cheers went up from the crowd in front of the Kennedy Building. ". . . Boston is granted the right to appoint the Cabinet position of Secretary of Alien Affairs and to advise and consent to the appointment of the Secretary of Customs . . . All Federal regulation of Boston is subject to the approval of the Secretary of Alien Affairs . . . Boston may establish its own internal currency . . . Boston may establish its own internal laws . . ."

Since early morning humans and aliens had been lining up in front of City Hall to apply for Boston citizenship, under the fluttering new Boston flag whose design still looked crude and unfinished. The Americans were calling the green flag the Dollar Bill.

". . . U.S. citizens may freely enter Boston but must have labor passes to work. Boston citizenship may be granted to any being or beings, human or alien, without respect of other citizenship and whether or not they are qualified for U.S. citizenship. . . ."

One of the English-speaking Phneri was translating this into excited supersonic whistles. The Phneri gave a very human-sounding cheer. One whistled, "Bos-s-ton is-s already free!"

In the Plaza, under Iris's feet, letters drifted, photographs, bits of clothing, locks of hair, piled up by the T-stop wall as relics of the Boston martyrs. Iris saw Lizbeth's parents' wedding picture next to a photo of Lizbeth's daughter.

A Phner waddled up to the photographs and began whistling appreciatively, then tearing them up.

A burned and bandaged man was helped to the head of the line. A moment later a cheer went up; Toby Fitzpatrick had been declared dead weeks ago, he was already a citizen of Boston.

Up by Center Plaza, under candy-striped tents, the children were waiting. The reporters already had a name for them, the Orphans of the Revolution. Children found next to dead mothers and fathers, starving in empty apartments, floating on tables in the flooded areas, among the unspeakable flotsam scoured out of Boston. Most were sick. Some were dying. Every one was spoken for sixty times over: Boston wanted to love its past griefs. Iris moved dry-eyed among these little ghosts.

Teddy, you were wrong.

She found herself counting the children as she passed them. Ten thousand of your mothers and fathers I killed, ten thousand of your sisters and your brothers, all gone to Cemetery Hill with a good and handsome man I knew, an American named Lem Snow, whom I killed on the floor of my office. And Boston lives. It was my job and I would do it again. Ten thousand people are not one person ten thousand times; they are one-tenth of one percent of the ten million citizens of Boston.

They are the price of the revolution.

I saved Boston. I was right.

Down at the end of one row, one of the babies began crying.

Iris strode to the baby and looked down at her. A newborn girl, the baby wailed in its crib: scrawny, red-faced, flailing tiny hands as small as chicken feet. At the foot of her crib was the clothing she had been found with, a ripped, filthy black blouse.

"She's the youngest," a nurse said. "Our first freeborn Citizen of Boston."

Iris picked her up in dutiful arms. The video cameras clustered around, seeing a photo opportunity. But the baby kept shrieking, wailing, her whole body stiffening with inconsolable cries.

"Let me take her," said the nurse. "She's hungry, or afraid of the cameras."

"No," Iris said. "I'll hold her for a minute." The tiny body bucked against Iris's shoulder, resistant. In the plaza everyone was happy except this child. The baby's hungry,

Iris thought. She's afraid of the cameras. I was right, she whispered to the baby. We won. Don't cry.

For a moment the reporters clustered around her (she looked for Dave Daly before she remembered) then, bored with the crying child, their attention drifted elsewhere until Iris did something interesting again. So much to do, so much to see, in this bright beginning of the world. The plaza was crowded with citizens of new Boston: Tulguts, a single big gray Spatien, thousands of bright human faces, people who had been dying of the heat five days ago. Holographic green flags whipped overhead, under the holographic sky designed by a cousin of the Mayor. The popcorn alien handed its head to a passerby, scattering dollar bills. No one noticed. It was the beginning of an inconceivable party, and everyone in Boston was going to be rich.

They had bought themselves a revolution. Boston would live. Six weeks ago, in another lifetime, she had looked down on this plaza at another party, at bioglows and flash-lights and trouble lights. She had heard the voice of the city then, roaring as the American flag fell and the new flag rose. So many had died since then so that this newborn child could cry in the city of Boston.

Iris would not regret.

She had always been right, and always knew what was going to happen. She would live under the green flag better than she had under the stars and stripes. Iris had nothing to regret.

But with her arms around her daughter, suddenly and roughly Iris began crying too.

BOSTON IN 2061

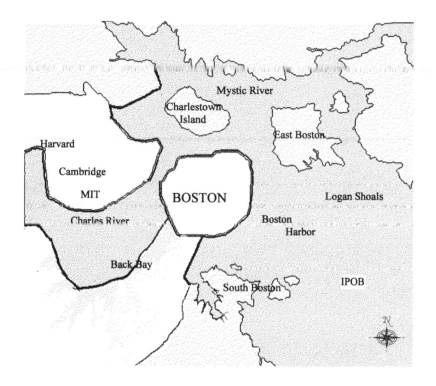

Just after the Revolution of 2061, the boundaries of the Free Port of Boston (white areas of map) comprise the Boston Cube itself, the IPOB headquarters in the harbor, Cambridge, parts of Somerville, and some portion of the Boston shore of the Charles, including the still-marshy Back Bay.

Numerous aquatic aliens, such as the cisos, live in Boston Harbor, which Boston also controls.

On all sides Boston is surrounded by the United States.

THE ADOPTION
ALEXANDER JABLOKOV

"DON'T YOU THINK this was a bit risky, Sussman?" asked
Salton Abt, a pudgy man in a padded blue jacket finely patterned with silver. "Yevgeni's gone too far this time, I'd
say."

Garner Sussman, a barrel-chested man with the large
nose and facial features of an Indian chief in an old movie,
pulled at his lower lip and stared back. Salton Abt was one
of Yevgeni Mudande's main business competitors. It had
been socially necessary to invite him to the adoption ceremony, but the bastard should have had the grace to claim
he was busy. Damn it, it wasn't Sussman's job to talk to the
idiot! "What do you mean?"

Abt glanced over his shoulder, sensing the passage of a
canape cart, and snagged several stuffed mushrooms.
"Well, I mean, really." He gestured Sussman to come
closer, as if wanting to impart a monstrous secret. "Adopt-
ing a *seaman* as an ancestor. I think your employer's losing
his touch." He swallowed the mushrooms.

Privately, Sussman agreed with him. Ever-deepening
water sucked at the foundations of the city, and decent people wanted to do all they could to forget it. Putting a sailor

in an ancestor chamber was like proudly displaying a child molesting uncle. "Not a just a seaman. Captain Standfast Endicott was a whaler. One of the mainstays of our city's wealth, in the old days."

Abt snorted, rejecting the distinction. "A water-rat. A sloshfoot."

This was close to serious insult. Sussman frowned and gestured with his huge hands. "I think you're forgetting what being a Bostonian means, Mr. Abt." He hated playing diplomat.

With a fine sense of his Alien Master's reluctance to defend a position he himself felt to be untenable, Yevgeni Mudande appeared at Abt's shoulder. He was a heavy and powerful man, with black skin and bushy pepper-and-salt hair. "Salton!" He pressed a large plate of steaming sausages into his rival's hands. "Fresh from the kitchen. Cumin and pepper, your favorite. I saved them for you."

Despite himself, Abt's many-chinned face lit up. He licked his lips. Mudande smiled at him, all genial host. "Come on, I want to show you some things. My venerable ancestor was quite an expert at scrimshaw, did you know that?"

"Scrimshaw?" Abt mumbled around a sausage.

"Engraving on the teeth of whales. I have some of his best work, I'm sure you'll be interested." Abt, torn between hunger and dismay, allowed himself to be led off.

Sussman looked around the party to make sure that there was no one else he needed to avoid. The house was full of a noisy crowd, for a Mundane invitation was something to be sought after, even for the adoption of a *sailor*. Iris Sherwood had come, with her sullen daughter Diana, friend of the Mudande brood's. Five species of extraterrestrial were in attendance, so Sussman, whose specialty was managing inter-species encounters, was on full alert.

A Tulgut stood by one wall like a multi-armed elephant. They were a calm race, easy to deal with, except that they tended to inadvertently step on and crush the furniture that was everywhere in the fussily overdecorated interiors of contemporary Boston.

Bishop 24, frighteningly, had put in an appearance. Mudande always invited him, and this time he had accepted. Mudande was pleased. High status came with having the only representative of the Centaurs on Earth at an adoption party. Still, the protocol problems of handling a six-foot-high armored praying mantis with inhumanly fast reflexes who liked challenging other beings to sentience duels— loser to be eaten—were something Sussman would have preferred not to deal with. He had made sure that the Bishop had an immense amount of high-protein food to support his high metabolism.

He could see the Centaur, whose body moved like a whip cracking, almost too fast to see, behind a potted palm, discussing something with an elegantly dressed Bostonian. Centaurs could be quite personable when they cared to. They could also eat you without ceasing to be personable. The Bishop had told Sussman that Earth humans were considered "inedible by reason of insanity." This meant that his threats to eat people were jokes. Sussman didn't like comedians.

Three Phneri, who resembled golden-haired sea otters, matted and bedraggled as if they had been poorly packed for shipping, examined an elaborate gadget that lay shattered on the marble floor at the base of a pedestal. They fluted and whistled to each other. Sussman breathed a sigh of relief. At least *that* had been taken care of.

"Garner," Tara Mudande's cold voice said. "How could you have let that happen? I told you to be careful with it. Now look at them. The present they brought us is broken. How can I face them?"

Sussman tried for a diplomatic expression and achieved something that looked like indigestion. "How many times do I have to explain—ah, never mind. Besides, Mastic did it.

You saw it yourself. He grabbed it and knocked it over onto the floor."

"I know it's your fault, Garner. It has to be." She glared at him with her green eyes and ran a finger through the elaborate coif of her red hair. "I don't care what you say about their racial ethic requiring the destruction of artworks. It's still not polite. I didn't even have time to clean it up."

Mastic, a large orange tom, sat on an overstuffed armchair, placidly chewing on the catnip mouse that Sussman had managed to shove inside the Phneri gift just before the party started. If they had arrived and found their gift preserved, like something dead, God only knows what would have happened. Mudande & Associates had important contracts with the Phneri that could have been imperiled by an act of such unthinking rudeness. But try to explain that to Tara Mudande. She knew what was polite and what wasn't.

Besides, she was still enraged that her husband had chosen a sailor as an ancestor. Mudande might not care, but it involved a lowering of status for her. She was not even mollified when the Phneri gathered around her, congratulating her on the clever way she had destroyed their gift.

As she tried to make small talk with them, Sussman escaped. Mastic lay on the sofa, eyes half shut, completely stoned. Sussman snagged the catnip mouse as the last piece of evidence and wandered toward the ancestor chambers. He peeked into the newest chamber. Mudande was still busily lecturing the unfortunate Abt on the finer points of scrimshaw. Abt stood glaze-eyed, his plate of sausages growing cold, as Mudande shoved a particularly large sperm-whale tooth in his face. Behind them, grim as death, stood the figure of Captain Standfast Endicott as he had appeared in 1790, with long, patriarchal beard and odd cylindrical hat. Made out of multicolored porcelain, he was a clever reconstruction from engravings. He held a massive iron-headed harpoon. The room was full of nautical artifacts and smelled of the sea. No one but Mudande and his victim had entered the room for the entire time of the party.

The next chamber was Amy Farnsworth's, an 1840s Abolitionist. She was almost as severe as her newest co-ancestor, hair pulled back, though with an inappropriate corkscrew curl dangling in front of each ear in deference to style, high forehead creased with care, eyebrows beetling like storm clouds. Probably the only time in her life she had ever smiled was when John Brown hit Harper's Ferry. The room smelled of tea and Bible leather.

The third ancestor chamber belonged to Chris O'Hanrahan, an Irish pol from the 1930s. He was a fat, genial, corrupt man, sloppily dressed. A map of South Boston as it had been before it sank hung on the wall behind him. This room smelled of tobacco and whiskey, and was Sussman's favorite. For someone whose father had been a Nuba tribesman from a hill village in central Sudan, Yevgeni Mudande had managed to acquire a distinguished Boston family.

"Garner!" Tara Mudande swept into the room. "Come here. That damn ecclesiastical insect—"

"The Centaur, Bishop 24. Be careful, Mrs. Mudande, he's one of the most influential aliens on Earth."

"I don't care! Mastic stole some of his food, and he wants to challenge the cat to a duel." Mastic was renowned in the household for his skill at hooking food.

"He wants that damn tomcat for dessert," Sussman said, cruelly. "I'm not so sure I shouldn't let him eat it." He thought for a moment. In fighting sentience duels, Centaurs were willing to accept their opponents' definitions of sentience: the equivalent of giving the challenged party choice of weapons. If he could convince the Bishop that the cat definition of sentience was the ability to catch mice . . . Mastic was damn good at catching mice. Sussman had watched him at it in one of Mudande's waterfront warehouses. What would the Centaur do if he lost a sentience duel to a domestic specimen of *Felis catus*? The thought was too charming.

The Bishop would be completely uninterested, the whole affair would turn out a total disaster, and Mudande would become enraged. Mudande had plans for Bishop 24.

"Stay out of the way," Sussman said. "*Well* out of the way."

Tara Mudande started to bridle, then nodded. "I'll wait here."

Sussman headed for the living room. Let no one say that he didn't earn his salary.

Only a small portion of the complex space that was the Mudande house, Garner Sussman's quarters were the only place he felt was his own: a small bedroom, an even smaller study, and a bathroom, now lit with the dim blue he preferred before bed. A humble monastic cell for the great scholar he had once wanted to be. He liked the feel of the smooth wood floor on his bare feet.

Sussman walked into the bedroom, undoing the sash of his velvet robe, and froze. Yevgeni Mudande stood at the bureau like some immense idol reminding a dilatory devotee that sacrifice had not yet been made.

Sussman yanked at his robe, outraged that his private domain had been invaded. "What are you doing here?"

Mudande glared at him, no longer the jovial host. "Sorry. Something's come up. *Business.* Let's go."

"But I want to sleep," Sussman said, looking with longing at the bed, its coverlet temptingly turned down to show the flannel sheets. "Can't it wait?"

"No."

"You're always doing this. You have no sense of moderation."

Mudande quirked his full lips. "Maybe that's why *you* work for *me*."

"Maybe that's why I can relax and you always have a bee up your ass." He paused. "It's important? Aliens involved?"

"Didn't I say that? First substantive contact with a new species. Just thought you'd be interested."

Sussman took a deep breath. "Let's go."

Mudande's office was three levels above the main part of the house. "House," in Boston in the 2080s, was a slippery term. Since the Inner Ring, that part of the city preserved from sinking into Boston Harbor, was virtually packed solid with living structure, individual buildings no longer existed. The Mudande house was a specified geometric airspace, closed in on three sides. The fourth side opened out on one of the deep light-canyons. It had copper cupolas and a fanlight over the door.

Mudande's office was an ancient subway car, its seats ripped out, welded into the structure of the residential tower. In contrast to the fuss of the rest of the house, it was almost undecorated. Light came from the original fixtures. The windows were quiescent now, pearly gray, though they could display data or holographic images on command. Sussman rubbed his eyes with the heels of his hands and sat down on one of the hard stools.

"I think I may have an interesting opening," Mudande said. "A species from out along the Perseus axis, called the Llonr. Know them?"

"As much as anyone does. Associated with the Targives, which means they probably have an improbable physiology and an incomprehensible psychology, though no one knows. They dropped through the Rabbit Hole about half a year ago and have been hiding out somewhere in Boston Harbor ever since. What do you have on them?"

"Not a lot." Mudande drummed his thick fingers on the desk. "An opening. I overheard a conversation two days ago during dinner at the Benedictine. That fool Abt and one of his pet sources at IPOB. Abt is just the kind of person who talks about things like that at the club. Crude. Abt thinks he can make money from the Llonr, because they have a problem, and someone in the Interstellar Port of Boston thinks they can profit from it as well. That fit with a few other things I had heard. Something's gone wrong. The Llonr need help. I put two and two together and got something between three and five."

The Benedictine was Mudande's club. NANA, as they said: No Aliens Need Apply. And very few humans had the qualifications either. Sussman had been in its Guest Lounge several times for a glass of Calvados, but that was as far as he was allowed to go. Beyond the heavy bronze doors that sealed the Guest Lounge off from the rest of the club, the real business of Boston went on. There the men and women who ran the most powerful economic machine in Earth's history exchanged gossip that caused gains and losses in amounts that required scientific notation for their expression.

"All right," Sussman said. "So, bright and early tomorrow morning I'll—"

"No. I need the information by tomorrow, sunset. That's when our appointment is. You should start now."

"What?" Sussman yelped. "That's outrageous."

"That's business." Mudande stood up. "Think you can do it?"

Sussman looked sulky. "Looks like I'll have to."

"That's the spirit I like to see! I'll meet you at the entrance of Miller's Hall, tomorrow sunset."

"You'll want translation?" Sussman said, slowly.

"Of course. We have an account with the Targives, don't we? It's part of the trading agreement. You can get Llonr language lessons from them easily enough."

"And turn my brain inside out."

"You think I don't pay you enough? Get to work. And change out of that ridiculous robe. You're not a student anymore."

The first thing Garner Sussman noticed when he stepped through the Pearl Street Watergate was the smell of the sea.

It smelled of salt and seaweed and floating garbage. It smelled of forgetfulness, for the mighty city that rose up out of the water had turned its back on it. Waves lapped somewhere below him. His eyes adjusted to that exterior night which never truly came inside the city, and he saw the moving lights of the barges, ferries, and launches that filled the moonlit harbor, physically supporting the city which ignored them. Boston grabbed for the stars, but its feet still stood in the water.

Sussman couldn't see the water itself, but he could sense it, wet and slimy, waiting for him. "Anyone there?" he called.

"Plenty of us," came the reply. "Who do you want?"

Sussman walked forward nervously on the floating dock, which rose and sank rhythmically in the waves. The walls of the Old City Ring kept the moonlight at bay, and he had neglected to bring a light of his own. Vessels crowded the dock, everything from hovercraft to augmented surface-tension waterwalkers. The summer night was surprisingly warm. Sussman couldn't remember the last time he had thought about what season of the year it was.

"Marco Tander," Sussman said. "Is he here?"

"I am," a voice answered reluctantly, as other voices laughed, or muttered remarks to each other. When city dwellers sought the water, it was for no good purpose.

"I need a water taxi." Sussman stepped forward. "It's important."

"Important, he says. What's so important about it?" Tander sat slumped against the mooring post of his boat, only the glow of the end of his cigarette visible.

"I'm buying transportation," Sussman said. "Are you selling? Or are you just hanging out here enjoying the breeze?"

The cigarette flared one last time, then arced off into the water. Tander coughed and stood up. "Why do you want me? My boat's a hull-down. Slow."

"Is everyone here as eager for business as you?"

"I don't know, why don't you ask them?"

"Francine Cherna recommended you," Sussman said. "She said you had guts. Frankie's smart, but she's been wrong before."

Tander paused. "All right, all right. Standard rates. Around the city and up the Charles? There are easier ways of getting to Harvard, God knows."

"We're not going to Harvard. We're going to South Boston."

"The hell we are, startit sucker."

Francine Cherna kept to the old life, the one Sussman had given up. She got dressed in the bedroom while her husband Ettore stood at the door, arms folded as if on guard duty, and stared coldly at the richly dressed stranger who had forced his way into their living room, a stranger who had turned out to be an old schoolmate, well forgotten

"I'm sorry about this, Ettore," Sussman said. "It's important."

"Of course it's important." Ettore was a big man with a thick neck. His bathrobe was tattered. "To someone else. Why else would you be here?"

"Stop it, Ettore," Frankie said from inside. She opened the door, dressed in jeans and a sweatshirt. "Go back to bed. Garner and I will talk. No, you'll just make trouble. Bed for you." With a final glower at his wife's former lover, Ettore vanished into the bedroom, pulling the door decisively shut behind him. The door was warped, and sprang back open. He pulled it closed slowly, in a silence more searing than any curses.

Cherna, big brown eyes and tousled hair, exactly as she had been as a student, tilted her head quizzically. "So, Garner, your businessman had insomnia, and you're awake."

"Something like that." He took a breath. "It's been a long time."

She stared at him solemnly for a long moment, so that he could remember how he had drawn away from her, from all of them, over the years. Then she smiled, her head tilted slightly the way she always did, as if she had just remembered something amusing that had nothing to do with the situation at hand. She timed it well enough that he understood that the smile was a gift, not something he deserved. "Yes, it has," she said. "What do you want, Garner?"

"What makes you think I want something?" He winced inwardly at the falseness in his tone.

"Come on." She quirked the side of her mouth. "Who makes social calls at three in the morning? You need my help. What is it?"

Frankie and Ettore's room was about the size of Sussman's own quarters in the Mudande house, but shabbier. In Boston even austerity cost money. The floor was painted gray and the walls were cracking and mildewed. A large blackboard hung on one wall, covered with molecular and anatomical diagrams. Two empty wine bottles lay against a pile of papers in a corner. Every available surface was covered with books, dataforms, and alien artifacts.

Cherna yawned widely. "Sorry. Lar, Ettore, Carol, and I were up late." She pointed at the blackboard. "Carol thinks she's got Spatien physiology figured out. She believes they were invented by the Targives. Hell, she thinks we were all invented by the Targives."

Sussman remembered what it was like to spend the night drinking wine and arguing with friends about things of importance instead of managing soirees for Yevgeni Mudande. "She might be right," he said. He moved some books off a chair and sat down. "What do you know about the Llonr?"

Cherna pirouetted slowly in the middle of the room, her eyes turned upward in thought. Sussman looked at her in wonder. Her hair its eternal mess, her eyes still sticky with sleep, was she really just as beautiful as she had been all those years ago? Age had seized her. There were crow's-feet around her eyes and her chin was less chiseled than it had been. But age had held her gently. The lines in her face were like the creases in fine fabric which grow more lustrous the more it is handled. And when she turned her dark eyes on him, looking at the hairy-eared, overweight tool of wealth he had become, he knew that he had never been as young as she was now.

She grinned at him. "Your boss is after some strange ones, isn't he? Let's see what I can show you." She dove into the clutter of books at one end of the room and unerringly pulled out a single dataform. The accuracy of her random-access filing system had always frustrated Sussman. But then, his old lover was a genius, which he never would be. "The Llonr are probably the most conservative race in the Galaxy, and with good reason. However they evolved, or whoever made them, they have a genetic memory component. They retain their ancestors' memories, back a thousand generations. There are probably Llonr who can still chip flint, or who remember being there when the first grain was sown. Even the smallest Llonr baby seems a hundred years old. It recalls having seen the sun rising over Eden, or the Llonr equivalent."

She fitted the dataform into a reader. A diagram of a Llonr gene locus exploded in the air between them and spun around, fragmenting and re-forming. Sussman walked forward into it and ran his hands up the curving stairway of a gene, feeling its smooth logic. He tasted the tang of sulfur-containing amino acids and the chalky sweetness of base sugars, and smelled the acrid manufacture of memory RNA. Endless rows of loci glittered around him like stained glass, back into time, their common genes rumbling in chorus like the leitmotifs of a Wagner opera.

He roamed through them, opening the genes up like a bear ripping through oozing honeycombs, examining the codings for organelle metabolism, the subtle pathways of nerves, the personality traits of shyness and love. Reduced iron atoms held the structure like linchpins, he noticed, catalyzing reactions. They vibrated lazily, buzzing at him like bees.

"The iron," he said. "It's very odd . . ."

Frankie looked impressed in spite of herself. "That's true. The Llonr home world circles an ancient Population II star and is short of heavy elements. Iron is the heaviest available, and even that is not abundant."

He looked through the genes at her. "Looks like the presence of iron is necessary for reproduction. Coming to Earth must be like an aphrodisiac to the Llonr."

She laughed, a trifle harshly. "The iron has to be entirely nonradioactive. Their genes have little defense against ionizing radiation. That means that it has to have been smelted before 1945, preferably before the 1800s, when coal burning started to release a lot of radioactive radon into the atmosphere. Not enough of that kind of iron around to stimulate them."

Sussman never failed to be impressed by her command of the minutiae as well as the essentials. Did he really now spend his time talking to the likes of Salton Abt and Tara Mudande? Why?

"How do they keep from scrambling the memories through recombination?" he asked, though he suspected he knew. He wanted to hear her voice say it.

"The Llonr rigidly retain gene lines, breeding in for pure memories. Each clan has its own shared memory store, and well as its shared tastes, neuroses, and obsessions. Some clans build the same building over and over, ever larger. Some have elaborate systems of music or philosophy that are incomprehensible to anyone else. The longer each clan remains distinct, the stranger it gets."

Sussman wandered out of the gene loci and stood in front of a pattern of curving lines, a simple drawing, the obsession of one Llonr clan. A sun rose in the cleft between two hills and a tree's long branches hung down over it. The pattern of two hills, a sun, a tree, remained unchanged for millennia. He saw it daubed in ocher on the wall of a cave, impressed with a stylus in a slab of wet river mud, carved deep into a massive granite slab, painted in fresco on the plaster wall of a villa, slapped in a thick impasto of oil paint on a stretched canvas, dyed on a garment with vivid aniline dyes, and finally flickering on a liquid crystal computer screen in two hundred fifty-six colors.

"Can I borrow that dataform?" Sussman asked.

She looked at him. "Why does your boss think he can profit from the Llonr?"

"Don't say 'profit' as if it were a dirty word," Sussman said, keeping his voice cool. It was their old, old argument.

"Why did you come back here, Garner?"

"I—because you're the best, Frankie. You always have been."

She nodded and with a quick movement tossed him the dataform. He caught it clumsily, almost dropping it. "You always were a practical man, Garner. You knew that I couldn't help but be interested in the Llonr, because no one else knows anything about them. We never change, do we? Where are you going now?"

Sussman sighed heavily. "Where else? Telegraph Island, to the Targives. I need translator training. We're meeting with the Llonr tomorrow evening."

For the first time he sensed she was jealous, which gave him some small measure of satisfaction. The Targives could provide knowledge, but the price was so high that only the great magnates could afford it. She stared at him. "And your boss expects you to rip your mind open so that he can talk deals with the Llonr."

He shrugged. "It's part of the job."

"So practical. Except about the things that matter." She turned away from him. Her body was still slender under the loose sweatshirt. Sussman almost reached out to her

344 ■ ALEXANDER JABLOKOV

then. But he didn't. Yevgeni Mudande and Ettore made that
distance too far for that. No, that wasn't fair. Garner Sussman had made that distance too far, without help from anyone. "How are you going to get there?" she asked
suddenly.

"Ah, boat. How else?"

She shook her head and smiled. "You never pay attention to anything, do you Garner? The water carriers are
barely traveling. They haven't been for a week."

"A strike?"

"No. A fear. Oh, don't ask me now. I know a man who
can take you where you want. I grew up with him. Marco
Tander. Ask for him. He'll do it." She looked back at him.
"You hate the water, don't you Garner?"

"You know I do."

He lay on his back in the boat, gasping for breath. Did the
mind-rooting really get worse every time? The Targive citadel at Telegraph Island lay behind them as Tander steered
their way home. Sussman gazed up at the sky as morning
drew itself across the stars and felt the crawling of Targive-
generated knowledge at the back of his head, like maggots
teeming in a decaying corpse. Who knew what neurons
now slithered through the interstices of his central nervous
system? In providing knowledge, the Targives sold not
only software but hardware, optimal neural processors that
mimicked the activities of alien brains. Some small part of
Sussman's brain would forever work like a Llonr cortex.
What had the Targives scooped out to make room for it?

Marco Tender glumly directed the boat back toward
Boston, ignoring the muttered convulsions of his passenger.
He looked as if he still regretted having been persuaded to
go, despite the obscene price Sussman had finally been
compelled to pay him. In the sunlight Tander turned out to
be a small man with a large handlebar moustache. Tander's
boat, an ancient Boston whaler called the *Queequeg*, was

much the worse for wear and, by daylight, did not look very seaworthy, at least to Sussman's landlubber eye.

Sussman sat up and looked at Tander. Tander ignored him, gazing off toward the horizon, where the swollen sun had just risen. Waves lapped at the boat. Water absorbed everything in the end—filth, bodies, and souls—sucked down into the wet darkness. Ahead of them loomed the glittering mass of Boston, less a city than a coral reef looming from the sea, growing ever higher even as it sank into the water. Sussman was anxious to feel dry stability beneath his feet again. Oddly enough, Tander, whose life was spent afloat, looked tense himself. His eyes constantly scanned the water.

"You and Frankie grew up together?" Sussman asked.

Pause. "Yeah. In Jamaica Plain." A poor neighborhood, not considered worth saving, now under the ocean. The engine thrummed. Tander minutely adjusted the tiller and looked out over the water again.

"What's out there, Marco? What are you afraid of?"

"Just shut up and enjoy the ride, black-hole licker."

Sussman snorted, amused in spite of himself. "Come on, Marco. It's a long way. Tell me."

"I don't expect you to believe it. You're a city person. You don't know anything about the water. There's a . . . sea monster in the harbor. Don't laugh. It lives down where the commercial wharves sank. You're lucky I took you. It's not every man that would have."

The meeting hall, long and wide with a low ribbed ceiling, was brightly lit and bare of furniture. The air system soughed gently, scented with spice. A vividly colored rug covered the floor, elaborately patterned with fractal geometries. Sussman and Mudande sank into it up to their ankles. They both wore short padded jackets in a minute diamond pattern—Sussman's black-and-white, Mudande's black-

and-red—with wide cuffed pants in contrasting lozenges, and narrow shoes.

"Where did this place come from?" Mudande asked. "I thought I knew all of Miller's Hall. The damn place keeps getting bigger." He looked down at his feet where the rug swirled in complex intertwined spirals in black, yellow and red. "Great rug. It would look good in the dining room, don't you think?"

"It's recent. The Targives added it for the convenience of some of their trading partners." Sussman shook his head, but the fuzziness caused by the Targive modifications remained.

Mudande stopped and glanced around, examining the hall more carefully. "All right, Garner. What are we in?"

Sussman grimaced. "A mouth, Yevgeni. A giant mouth. The original, I think, was a lizard that lives on Eta Carina IV. The Targives modified it, the way they like to do. Gives good environmental control and repairs itself." The edges of the rug, near the wall, curled up slightly and moved along in ripples. "The rug, of course—"

"The tongue." Mudande grimaced. "I get the picture. Has it ever swallowed anyone?"

"The digestive system is still the original size. Tiny. It's in one of the corners somewhere. It lives on the trash people drop, moved to it by the tongue. Still want it for the dining room?"

Mudande snorted. "Tara would kill me."

They stopped in the center of the room. Five Llonr came out to meet them. They moved slowly and ponderously, as if the accumulated centuries of memory had physical weight. They were bipeds, but had forelimbs so long that they rested their weight on them when they were not moving. Their bodies were invisible beneath elaborate clothing covered with colored straps and jingling bells. Their heads were sunk into their shoulders and they slumped forward, since their eyes were almost on top of their heads. These were members of one gene line. Sussman knew that other Llonr behaved and dressed quite differently.

One of them made a sound like ball bearings running over a corrugated iron roof, and Sussman sank into the words of the Llonr language. He listened for a while, then talked back, which hurt his throat. His new brain writhed in his head and he wanted to throw up.

Sussman finally turned to Mudande. "They have a question for you. The form of the answer is important. It's not just polite curiosity. They want to know if you are the descendant of Captain Standfast Endicott."

Sussman had known Mudande for almost ten years. This was the first time he could remember his looking surprised. The expression vanished quickly. "Tell them yes. I am honored to list Captain Endicott among my ancestors."

Sussman gargled at the Llonr, and listened to their reply. His head pulsed with each word. "That seems to have been the right answer, Yevgeni. I think this is the reason you managed to get this appointment. The Llonr have no concept of adoption. Now they want you to do them a favor. Say no." His voice was sharp.

"What? Why should I say no? Is that the polite formulation?"

"No, damn it!" To his surprise Sussman found himself shouting. "Saying yes will be a commitment. They have gene memories, remember. If you're descended from Endicott you must have the memories of a Boston whaling captain."

"Well, maybe I do, Garner." His voice was cold and angry. "You translate and give cultural advice, right? Don't screw with the business side. Salton Abt is hot on this contact too. If having a whaler as a ancestor is my advantage, good. Tell them yes. As my ancestor's descendant, I will do them a favor."

When Sussman turned back to him a moment later his face was white. "In that case, they would like you to recover for them something they have lost, their pet and companion, Miltor."

Mudande had been catching some of Sussman's tension. At this news he smiled in relief. "I remember once when Mastic got out and went wandering out along the canyons. I would have rewarded anyone for that damn cat's return. And I don't even like him. If that's—"

"Miltor is a sea-going creature weighing about fifty tons," Sussman said with dull solidity, slamming each word in like a blow. "He is their pet, and their god, and is something like half a million years old. He's somewhere out in Boston Harbor. They would be very grateful to have him back here by tomorrow." Sussman's mind was flickering. He felt the pain of the Llonr at the loss of their living idol. Miltor! His great bulk loomed over their world. None of them could remember a time when they did not have him.

A look of dismay flashed across Mudande's face and vanished. "Thank goodness the harbor isn't very deep," he said briskly. "Set up another engagement with them, will you Garner? Then we can go up to Standfast's chamber and talk with him about it."

"This is insane," Marco Tander said.

"Shut up," Mudande snapped. "I'm paying you enough, aren't I? A fortune for a slow and noisy boat."

"Making craziness profitable doesn't make it sanity."

Mudande snorted and ignored him, staring off at the horizon. The early morning shore breeze rippled the dark waters of the harbor. Boston loomed above them. Its shadows now fell out over the poorer neighborhoods north and west of the city and the sea was in full light. *Queequeg* growled along through the shallow waters of the old commercial dock areas. The water was too murky for the ruins of what was left of that part of Boston to be visible below. The only ship on the harbor was a rusty old fishing vessel with nets held up above its deck.

"Tell me what we're after, Garner," Mudande said.

"You've heard it a dozen times," Sussman said sullenly from his post at the center of the boat. The furry head of a Phneri popped out of the water to starboard. Sussman put an electronic talker to his lips and whistled at the Phner. The Phner replied with a fluting glissando and vanished again. The Phneri had been contracted to help locate Miltor, more as a favor to them than anything else. They took the whole thing as a lark.

"I want to hear it again."

"You're just trying to calm me down by taking my mind off the idea that we're all going to be killed."

"Tell me the story, dammit! Earn your goddamn salary." Mudande cradled the heavy wood and iron of Standfast Endicott's harpoon in his arms and rested his head against it.

"Miltor is a colonial organism, like a Portuguese man-of-war or a volvox, consisting of hundreds of lesser organisms who reproduce separately. It's been the pet, the focus, the obsession of this group of Llonr for hundreds of thousands of years, almost since they evolved enough to have consciousness. It's the last of its kind."

"As if a group of humans had a pet saber-toothed tiger or woolly mammoth."

Sussman nodded. "It remembers everything too, holographically, through all of its constituents. It's been escaping from them for all those years too, repeatedly."

Mudande scratched in his thick graying hair and snorted. "The things people will put up with to have a pet. Ridiculous."

A dozen Phneri heads suddenly popped out of the water at once and shrieked. Their duty finished, they dove under and swam like crazy.

"That's it then," Mudande said, the evenness of his words revealing his tension. He stood up and took off his shirt. His massive torso gleamed in the sun like polished ebony. He held the harpoon up over his head. "Here, Miltor," he crooned. "Here it is. Clean, nonradioactive iron. This harpoon was made in 1779. As clean as you'll find on this dirty planet. Three hundred years old. Come here, boy, and get your rocks off."

There was a moment of silence, as if, beneath the water, Milton were considering this offer. Then, sensing the iron, it came.

Tander yelped once and turned the boat hard to port. Torrents of water roared from bulk of Miltor as it emerged from the sea. *Queequeg* was cast into darkness as Miltor rose into the sun, featureless as a mass of volcanic rock. Mudande was thrown sideways by the unexpected swerve of the boat and cursed.

For a long moment Sussman was too terrified to do anything. Then the Llonr brain took over. Above them was Miltor, the creature that defined his gene line. Miltor was lost and terrified. Sussman wrestled the tiller away from Tander, elbowing him in the face, and turned the boat back toward Miltor.

"Excellent. Speed the boat, Garner!" They came closer. Mudande pulled his arm back slowly and, as gracefully as the *Queequeg*'s namesake could have, hurled the harpoon at Miltor. It flew smoothly, finally vanishing as a tiny sliver against Miltor's immense bulk. For a long moment everything remained motionless. Sussman had the sensation that Miltor had risen too far out of the water and was now toppling slowly toward them.

Then Miltor shrank and fell in on itself. It disappeared into fragments like a thick swarm of bees suddenly going their separate ways as the elemental iron was absorbed, serving as a powerful signal for reproduction. Miltor came apart into its elemental entities for this purpose. In five minutes nothing was left but the writhing fishlike shapes of Miltor's reproductive structures.

By this time Sussman had managed to remember how to

breathe. He dropped the tiller and collapsed, gasping. "We can recover any of these," he said, gesturing at the quick creatures beneath the boat, which made the water dense with silver. "Miltor's memory is holographic. Each is complete." Phneri leaped and chuckled among the fishlike fragments of the great creature, delighted with its dissolution.

"Each has the complete memory, but the focus will be hazy," Mudande said. "I am giving them Miltor, not a fuzzy reproduction of him. Thank God the Bishop has good business contacts."

"What?" Sussman looked up. The fishing vessel they had seen earlier was dipping its nets into the water, grabbing a rich harvest of Miltor.

"No one in Boston invests in fishing anymore," Mudande said. "Too archaic, not interstellar enough. Too wet. The Centaur doesn't care. He was the only one I could find with the right equipment readily available. I'm glad you helped me make friends with him."

Sussman settled back in the boat and watched the nets with their shining loads of squirming fish. "Thank Mastic," he said. "The cat's a true diplomat. More than I am, certainly."

Sussman lay with the back of his head against the wooden gunwale. Llonr thoughts flickered through his mind and he thought of the joy they would feel at having Miltor back. They would do anything for Mudande & Associates at that point. He was starting to get used to the new nerves that had been shoved into his skull. Soon he wouldn't remember how he'd lived without them.

"No argument there." Mudande grinned happily into the sunlight. "Is that the basis of interstellar amity, then? Our pets?"

"Our pets," Sussman replied. "And our employees."

WereWhereWear
Alexander Jablokov

From "WereWhereWear"
by Melanie Mee-Kron Seleznik
Bostonaked: A Journal of the Bodily Arts, April 2080

There is nothing later. Nothing more here. Poised on the quantum chronosequential jump in abstract time, focused on the intersection of the galactic ordinate/abscissa, nexing on the centrality, the primum mobile of fashion—werewherewear.

Were. Its existence is predicated on your desires: "were," as in "werewolf." It changes its shape, its cut, its context. Networks of long-chain anisotropically contractile analomycin—but enough biochemistry! Let the sartoromorphologists worry about it. It Lives On Blood. The Red Limit of fashion statements. C goes no faster. Everyone else sucks your cosmic dust.

Where? Anywhere! Locked into your jugular (this metagarment prefers unoxygenated hemoglobin: a hint for easy maintenance!), W3 keeps you arrayed for all circumstances, from a colorful Basement riot to a soigné affair while stratoplaning at Cloudtop. A nip, a tuck, some modified neurotransmitters, some blood alkaloids, and your late post-merid bullet-resistant Koltsoi-compatible business tunic becomes a waterproof early-twilight fractal lace sark, suitable for muck dancing with your water-rat friends! You will never again be caught inappropriate, prey to confusion, hostility, wit, bombast.

Wear. This is it. Apex. Apogee. Ascension.

[Due to possible legal action, the Editors wish to note that the aforementioned article of clothing is a Targive-modified product. Bostonians wearing, using, or benefiting from Targive products without Targive approval (don't ask how you get it, or how they know) have occasionally vanished, even from top-security enclosures; and, it is rumored, been turned into the next Targive product. Try to judge how dedicated to fashion you are. A byte to the wise, as they say . . . Good Dressing!]

Sail Away
David Alexander Smith

No MATTER HOW perfectly a prosthetic is integrated with your nervous system, your mind senses it as an alien parasite. Diana Sherwood Abt's left hand, a marvel of engineering, was as lifelike as her right and more dextrous at small-muscle manipulations, but no amount of scratching could ease the nonexistent itches in her vanished fingers.

"Computer, what can I do about this?" She brandished her club, craning her neck as she looked out her skywindow on Level 137. To her right were the lumpy slick protrusions which marked the covered remains of some rich person's property, absorbed inside the Old City Ring when construction was begun in 2010.

Out of sight behind them lay the *Beaver II*, her husband Salton's tourist ship. When the tide was high, Diana could just glimpse it, bobbing on the warm thermal undercurrents that rolled in subsurface convection against the city's warm foundations.

"Place your left arm within the sensor field for diagnosis."

Diana complied.

"You are owed twenty-five point sixty-five beans, Miz

Fitzpatrick," the voice continued after a moment's pondering. "Please specify a bank account into which we should credit your funds."

"Twenty-five beans? What for?"

"Refund of your death certificate."

"Refund of my *what*? Who did you call me?"

"Miz Deirdre Fitzpatrick. You were thought to have drowned in the Flood. I congratulate you on your survival. We are pleased to update our records."

"You're nuts. I'm Diana Abt, born Diana Sherwood."

The unseen voice paused. "Yes, you are."

"So I can't be this other person. A person can't be two people at once."

"Why not? Are you not thirty-five years old? Adopted by Iris Sherwood?"

"Yes."

"When you were approximately one week old."

"So she said. Oh, my God." The color drained from Diana's face. "Right after the Siege." She flung herself toward the console and seized it in both hands as if squeezing shoulders. "What name did you say I was?"

"Deirdre Fitzpatrick."

"Who was she? Where was she born? Who were her parents?"

The box chose to answer only the last of these. "Elinor and Toby Fitzpatrick."

Diana's heart was a hole into which her soul fell. "Are they alive?" she whispered.

"Elinor Fitzpatrick died on or about 24 August 2061. Cause of death drowning."

"When the Phneri blew out the Basement," said Diana, her back thumping against the seat.

"The Basement was punctured by order of City Operator Iris Sherwood," the box added as if in justification. "Temperature within Boston was 105 degrees Fahrenheit and rising."

"My adopted mother killed my real mother," murmured Diana in horror.

"Demolition was necessary to provide coolant to the city. Without it, the city—"

"I know what the vent would have happened!" screamed Diana in a fury. "If she hadn't blown it out, I'd be dead! What about my father? What happened to *him*?"

"Toby Fitzpatrick was burned in a methane explosion while installing water-saving devices, 29 July 2061. Declared a Free Citizen of Boston, pensioned. Died 11 March 2088."

Two years ago. My father was alive two years ago. I could have seen him, talked with him. Perhaps we jostled one another in a corridor or shared an anonymous mover ride, our eyes searching the ceiling to avoid contact. Diana put her hand over her mouth.

"Your death certificate refund check has been deposited in your main account as Diana Abt, Miz Fitzpatrick. Shall we update your identity records throughout?"

"Why wasn't this discovered before?" Diana asked, too stunned to put any emotion into her voice. Few are the griefs to compare with finding and losing one's parents in a matter of seconds.

"Recent integration of central archives."

A heavy cough growled behind her. "Madam?"

Diana became aware by the throbbing that she had been pounding her artificial left fist into her right hand. She closed her fingers around the false fist and turned.

Garner Sussman, the housemaster whose big hook nose and dark complexion gave him the grim credibility of an exiled Cherokee warrior, glanced at her hand and she hid it behind her back.

"If you have a moment," Sussman began with a sniff, reading from a datacube cupped discreetly in his brown, short-fingered hand, "we have a potential scheduling conflict between the next Finance Committee meeting of the

Ernest Pole Acquisition Fund—be still my heart—and your trisim sessions. Fortunately, if Maestro Chun Li will just make a few accommodations, I believe we can—"

"Not now, Garner," Diana said impatiently. She was sick and miserable and angry with Sussman for barging in on her, ignorant of her loss. "Any word from his lordship?" She had to get out of Abt's minicube, had to get somewhere to think and grieve.

She passed into her boudoir and stripped to her underwear, not pausing when Sussman appeared. After so many years in the same household, it was hard for her not to think of Sussman as her husband, Salton Abt just a man with whom she shared a continuing if intermittent affair and an irrational fondness for two sullen teenage boys, Ezekiel and Jeremiah. "Or doesn't he bother with me anymore?"

"I expect a call later in the day," Sussman replied, coming to a halt and crossing his hands at the wrists. As always, he made no comment about Diana's undress, but his eyes slipped past her to focus on other things. "With Boston's declining economic prominence, merchant businesses are collapsing right and left, presenting extraordinary bankruptcy-reorganization acquisition opportunities, but I'm sure he'll inquire about you and the boys."

"Me-and-the-boys," Diana said contemptuously. "That's the way he always asks, isn't it?" As if the umbilical still stretched from her to them, and without that connection he would have no interest in his wife. None of this was Sussman's fault, yet he shared in arranging the routines of her life. "Garner," she demanded uncertainly, "look at me. Who am I?"

Slowly, his brick red face turned toward her. "I beg your pardon?"

"Under my clothing." Her plea was forlorn. "Without my name. Am I more than the wife of Salton Abt? Am I someone?"

It was on the tip of Sussman's tongue to tweak her, but

their intimacy was founded on his ability to gauge how much ragging she enjoyed. The cant of her white stringy shoulders told him to guard his tongue. So he tilted his head and lifted an eyebrow, his way of inviting her to answer questions he was too proper to ask.

"I'm still attractive," Diana went on, turning sideways and pressing her hands to her abdomen as Sussman concentrated his gaze on a point above her head. "What's wrong with me?" Diana dropped her hands and Sussman dropped his eyes. "What have I done? I'm no longer in his life. *You* should be his lover, Garner. At least you speak his language. I don't. It doesn't interest me. And it never did. I thought romance and children would be enough."

She went to her bureau, pulled out a sheath capsule, and slapped it against her stomach. Immediately the lavender fluid spread itself over her body until she was wearing a smooth and seamless pantsuit. She drew lines on herself with her fingernail and the material fell away. Defiantly she turned toward him, drew the line higher along her thigh, and peeled off the excess.

As Sussman hesitated, unsure how much commiseration to offer, Diana pushed past him. "I'm going out."

"What about the Te Da cocktail reception at six? You ignored my advice and accepted that dreary invitation, and now you'll—"

In the corridor outside, Boston was abuzz, for the city was preparing to celebrate the crest.

The Cube had long since enclosed itself against any weather up through a hurricane, but living behind embankments is emotionally stressful, no matter how much gallows humor it may generate. Mysteriously, the water levels had confirmed for people's eyes what the Cisos geologists—huge stringlike aliens who liked nothing more than to burrow through granite, making a sound so hideous it set teeth on edge fifty levels up—had been screeching all along.

The pressure was back. Boston was no longer going down the drain.

By now the city was unrecognizable to those who had lived in it before the aliens arrived in 2014. Diana stopped at a kiosk selling lobster munchkins—miniature Targive-modified crustaceans which could not only be eaten, head to tail, but assisted your digestion by crawling down your throat as you chewed.

Who are any of us? Diana thought, walking among the milling thousands who used the big Long Wharf passageway for their daily seven-minute commutes. Those two adolescents elbowing her aside with efficient Bostonian rudeness could have been Ezekiel and Jeremiah, for all Diana could see of their visages under their chrome domes. "Don't be kroomy," one said to the other in a voice slurred with randomized ululations. "Suzzy fnords, everyone knows that." And then they banged their domes together, snapping their fingers.

Diana thought about her two boys, whom she loved but could neither understand nor reach. Everything she said or did was hopelessly wrong, a failing more poignant to her because it hurt so. Insensitivity was her mother's sin and it galled Diana to have inherited it, and thus have lost that bit of moral superiority over the dead Iris.

The older I get, the less I know. Who am I supposed to be? Who were the parents I never knew? I could have found them if I tried. I have Salton's money and Iris's links to Cube info. Why didn't I try?

As she walked, she found herself drawn to Abt's historic boat, moored in what remained of the Fort Point Channel next to South Fusion Station. Salton had bought it in one of his periodic diversifications, a foray into ersatz historical tourism.

Somehow its existence, floating gently on the tide, had been comforting to her. While the city sank, welded to the earth that had betrayed its duty to Boston, this rickety old boat had effortlessly risen. Structure and rigidity, thought to be strengths, were all too often weaknesses.

She passed through an outbound gate, easy enough for a high-key person, and made her way along the Fort Point Channel.

A two-masted brigantine riding at anchor, the *Beaver II* was hulled with oak and teak painted in horizontal lines of black and white. Her figurehead, a flaxen-haired maiden in a gauzy high-waisted dress held at chest level only by proud grapefruit-round breasts, gazed into the harbor, her arms by her sides as if flying through space.

Diana stared at the blond woman, wondering how it felt to be pinioned before the prow of a ship, always leading yet never controlling, sailing you knew not where, never able to see the people who chose the course you followed. "Who's your mother?" she giddily asked the figure.

The ship was deserted. With a shock, Diana realized that the blackness which curtained the sky behind the blaze of orange-and-yellow city lights was night itself. Inside the Cube, time was a matter of convention. Here, sun, moon, and tides rose and fell, indifferent to humanity. OutCubers were abed.

She climbed aboard, feeling in her knees the swell and fall as the *Beaver II* bobbed on the ripples of wake churned by the big cargo boats moving out from IPOB. The old wooden decking under her feet creaked reassuringly, and the ship's ropes hummed with a north-wind vibrato.

"Sail away, sail away," sang Diana. "We will cross the mighty ocean into Boston Bay."

For a moment she was dizzy and she grasped the rigging, the hemp greasing and abrading her right palm as she rocked with the ship.

"You wish to become a slave, Diana Sherwood?" asked an overly precise voice.

"That's *not* my name," she answered without looking

around. Then she recognized the voice and asked in surprise, "Bishop 24?"

The Centaur, a huge insectoid alien with jointed mandibles and many spiny legs, leaned his thorax forward, his catlike yellow eyes seeming to narrow. "Not Bishop 24. Permission to come aboard?"

With a shiver and a swirl of wind, he was instantly beside her. His breath was sweet with the scent of crushed pansy petals. Had he become a vegetarian?

"Who are you, if not the Bishop? Surely there aren't two of you."

"That is no longer my name," answered the Centaur. His head flicked around his left shoulder, then flicked all the way back around his right shoulder, then reoriented on her.

"Why not?"

"I am no longer Bishop of Earth. I am Bishop 25, bishop for the T'ta'too."

"So *that's* what your name meant. We never knew." Another thought struck her. "But if you've done this twenty-three times before, how old *are* you?"

"This was a long and difficult posting," said the Bishop, looking past her. "It is over. The Loophole no longer belongs to Boston but to all of humanity. Humanity has passed its sentience test, and I and my kind are no longer permitted to protect it. The ministry is ended, the see dissolved."

"The sea is dissolved," Diana echoed, changing his meaning. She clutched the light blue gunwale and looked into the darkening harbor. "The oceans shall run dry and the earth split asunder."

"And the dead shall rise up from their graves," continued the Bishop, moving back to the poop deck, "and be judged by what was written in the books, by what they had done, and be grateful. The Book of Revelations."

"Revelations? This has certainly been the time for

them," murmured Diana. "And they have brought the end of the world with a whimper." She snapped back to the present. "No one knows any of this."

"Except you."

"Why now? Why me?"

"The see dissolves as of this night. There is no further injunction against candor." The creature moved toward the ship's stern past the cargo hatch, covered with checkerboard netting, which opened belowdecks. Before him in the twilight rose the lumpy, slick Cube: massive, complex, and strong, lights flickering on its surface. Stars near its edges winked and shimmered with the heat that rose from its vents.

"It's ending, isn't it?" Diana followed his glance. She gestured at the huge building-city that rose above them. "Boston is still powerful, still rich, still arrogant and clever and dominating. But it has become inward-looking, self-contained. It has lost its sense of self."

"You are not speaking of Boston," the Bishop said. He moved his head and the manner of his unspoken question reminded her of Garner Sussman. That thought, almost too painful to countenance, stripped her bare. It seemed natural to confess to him what had happened, so she did.

"I had always known I was adopted," she finished. "Iris made no bones about that. I was the child who was raised by Iris Sherwood, the bot lady. The woman who ordered her Phneri to blow out the city's basement and flood it to cool it. The Butcher of Boston."

The bishop's chrome yellow eyes irised wider, then narrower. "Your mother understood duty."

"*She's* not my mother." Diana sat on the square hatchway cover. "I've lived thirty-five years thinking I was one person, becoming that person, living into a life. But I'm someone completely different. A total stranger to myself. I have no ties to Boston anymore."

"As you wish." The Bishop undulated alongside the

ship's port gunwale. "That is for you to decide. *My* duty here is finished."

He said it with such human satisfaction that Diana looked strangely at him. "Why did you choose this life, Bishop? Do you know anything about your next unfathomable see?"

"Diana Sherwood, I know that the T'ta'too require a sentience test." The Centaur slithered forward, his tone intent and menacing. "That is my duty. It is enough."

"Don't talk to me about duty!" With a fling of her arm, Diana knocked away his outstretched mandible. It was like hitting a prock pipe.

The Bishop coiled back on his torso, his mandibles folding up at his sides. "The sense of duty separates sentients from animals."

"Is your duty to stay in a place only until it no longer hates you?" Diana asked in accusation. "Then to leave? No sentient could enjoy that."

"Enjoyment has nothing to do with it. It is duty." The Bishop glanced about him, his head moving in stroboscopic bursts. "This ship is not authentic."

"It's a replica," she said, disconcerted. "The tea the colonists dumped in 1773 still lies in the mud harbor bottom—the Phneri could probably find it if anyone cared to ask. The masts are fast-grow bamboo cores with a coating of modified shark's cartilage. Authentic Bostonian, isn't it?"

"As authentic Bostonian as your left hand," the Centaur replied.

"You noticed?" For the first time Diana was frightened of the intelligence that obviously lay inside the grotesque multilegged sowbug body. She rotated the hand and flexed its fingers. "It is no part of me."

"Then discard it, if you find the thing so alien." He extended a mandible as if to help her remove it.

Diana retreated. "But I need it," she said, slightly exasperated. "Without it I don't think I could function."

"Ah," said the Bishop with a short, almost perfunctory, nod that made her blush. "Let us go. Sail the ship for me."

"What? Go where?"

"To Hull. Now."

"I can't." Diana retreated, her hands up as if warding off a blow. "I have to get back. Garner will be worried about me."

"The ship can be sailed, can it not?"

"Of course it can. Salton insists that it be kept shipshape." Her husband might be a plutocrat, but he was efficient at it.

"Then let us sail to Hull. My last duties are there."

Diana stared at him. "You must be serious. The Bishop never jokes. Everyone knows that. All right." She shrugged magnificently. "Sure, why not?" A spin across the harbor would take only a few hours and would clear her head.

She found the controls, artfully concealed within the plain wooden tiller, and pressed her thumb against the authorization square with a sudden doubt. Would it work? Who did the city think she was?

"Access approved," the boat replied with enigmatic affirmation. "Cast off."

Diana ran forward and found the bowline looped about its cleat in a self-tightening knot that had not changed in two thousand years of seafaring. Hurriedly she unlooped it, once, twice, three times, and it was free. She coiled and knotted the line and tossed it aboard. Straddling boat and deck, she gave a long strong push with her thigh and the massive ship drifted its nose ever so slightly away from the pier. She always found satisfaction in the idea that a single person could push an entire ship.

When they were under way, she asked, "Why Hull? There's nothing on it. It's nowhere."

"The islands are still legally part of Boston," the Bishop corrected her.

"But the place has been vacant since the Madwoman of

Hull died. Sixty years or more." Garrulous Ethel Endicott Cobb had survived the Bombing of Hull to live in one burned-out shell after another, dodging the city sanitation workers sent to corral her. It was a bedtime story for rebellious children: say your prayers or you'll be kidnapped by the Madwoman of Hull.

"Hull is inhabited," replied the Bishop, who had stationed himself on the foredeck. "As lichens do, humanity will cluster wherever there is rock and sea and the fertilizer of finance." He was moving with herky-jerky precision, using his enormous armspan to haul the big trapezoidal mainsail into place. Wind bellied it and the boat shivered with anticipation.

"Lay off the starboard sheet," Diana ordered, standing by the tiller. Though the ship had a semi-sentient navigation system, she could not rid herself of the belief that the captain should guide her boat on its journey. "Don't choke her."

The Bishop adjusted the rigging. Given more room, the sail bulged out wider, quelling the sharp rippling on its canvas surface.

From the Fort Point Channel they sailed between Logan Airport's submerged sandbars to port and the South Boston Shoals to starboard. As they rounded the Castle Island Fort, sundered from the mainland by the rising water, the breeze freshened and the waves grew tufted whitecaps. "Where to, Bishop?" she called, leaning over the wheel.

The Centaur pointed at a burned and blackened jumble of rocks a few miles southeast. "Telegraph Island. My duties will end on the hill that became an island when the city sank."

"Why did the sinking stop, Bishop? If anyone knows, you do. Why did it start?"

"It is an inevitable consequence of the implantation of a Loophole anchor."

Diana involuntarily shifted the tiller. "A what?"

"A subterranean beacon which establishes a contact zone." The Bishop's head rotated as if on gimbals as he stared at her. "The Custodians implant it as a signal that a new loophole terminus is operational."

"Custodians?"

"The unknown race that builds or discovers Loopholes. Sinking invariably results from the subsurface dislocation and structural collapse engendered by the carrier wave. For your future reference, whenever a region starts to sink, without external cause or catastrophic precursor, you may be certain that an interstellar Loophole has recently been established in your planetary vicinity."

Diana started to laugh with disbelief. "We had twenty-five years to prepare and we wasted them."

The Bishop wagged a mandible at her and she had the impression it was a gesture of laughter. "Of course the sinking culture is generally ignorant of what a Loophole is, and could in any event do nothing about its arrival or the subsequent alien contact. How could you have known?" he said, and Diana felt herself rebuked. "Why blame yourself that you did not know?"

"Did the beacon call you as well?" Diana asked, abruptly departing from this last awkward question. "Is that how you knew to come?"

"The Custodians favor inhabited planets. Usually the resident species is non-sentient and therefore inedible by reason of insanity." He turned and looked past Diana at the City of Boston looming above them.

The carbuncle, the wen, the Christmas cake—the Cube resembled them all. No more cube than sphere, it was in truth a vast irregular hodgepodge of surfaces, steel and prock and stretch rubber strung with gossamer webbing. Gray and brown and black, its planes and curves broken by the rectangular flashes of windows and the soot straws of exhaust pipes, it rose, cantilevered upon itself, like a ragged man-made cliff that sprang from the harbor toward the sky that glowed with the light that leaked from its million shut-tered eyes.

At its peak the city shone with warning lights, bristled with communications antennae. Its roofs and sides were a patchwork of textures. Asphalt shingles and prock wire-mesh were molded around the disjointed contours where older buildings had been fused together like vertebrae. Lower down the builders had used available materials—granite blocks, automobiles crushed into wrinkled wedges—and then coated all exposed surfaces with kittee, a sealant goop that smelled, when the wind and sun were right, like chocolate pudding.

Up close the Cube's foundation was a solid varied rock-face. Kayakers liked to paddle a full circuit around it, peer-ing up into the rusted I-beams, procked arches, pigeon nests and creosoted wood pilings which made up its fractal shoreline.

Boston defied perspective. At a distance its size, so much greater than anything within miles, made it appear that, by a trick of foreshortening, a lump of carved stone had some-how been superimposed over a Mondriaan tangle of straight structural rods. In the night it was intimidating, a hole in the cosmos just beyond one's fingertips. At sunrise it was glorious, rose and pink and gleaming brass where the sunlight hit its metal struts. At midday it was grandiose, forbidding, a challenge to all who came near it.

"It is a fine thing you humans have built here," the Bishop said, his quicksilver gaze seeming to touch the Cube in many places as if reading its vital signs.

Diana had fallen silent, her hand resting only lightly on the tiller as the ship sailed toward the islets of the Hull ar-chipelago. "Yes," she said with reluctant pride. "It is a fine and terrible place. It's the only world I know. It's my family and my home."

"And once mine," said the Bishop, and again Diana heard in his voice the resonance of profound satisfaction.

They sailed for half an hour as the blackened lump of Telegraph Island grew in their sight. An island when the Pilgrims landed, it had in the nineteenth century been melded into the risen, newly-dry flat grid streets of Hull, but when Boston sank, the island had reclaimed its original isolation.

Diana and the Bishop guided the *Beaver II* into a rough concrete dock. She leaped out, caught the bowline the alien tossed her, and made the ship fast.

Around her were the blistered and charred remnants of a gangster fortress the MDC had firebombed and leveled. Grass and dandelions grew in the crevices. Owls hooted in the upper stories. Graffiti had been scratched through the soot to the cement beneath, gray letters etched in a black field. Phneri muttered and splashed quietly along the waterside, fishing and scavenging.

The Bishop unlimbered himself onto land, gazing around as if recognizing friends not seen for years.

"Is it safe?" Diana asked with a trepidation that shamed her.

The Bishop's torso rotated. "I will protect you if it is not."

Diana knew he was being ironic but she was nevertheless terrified, of what she did not know. "I have to be going back," she said hurriedly. "They'll be worried about me."

"You must accompany me."

"Why did you want to come here? What does this place hold for you?"

Without answering, the Bishop moved across the jagged rocks, his big body agile and strong. He climbed and Diana followed him until they both stood near the crown of the hill. All around them lay the rusty twisted steel beams of buildings that had first been homes, then a fortress, and were now rubble. Doorways and windows gaped open. The broken glass beneath their feet had been worn by wind and rain into translucent pebbles, and the tracks and spoor of raccoons and seagulls were everywhere.

"I owe a duty," the Bishop said when Diana had regained her breath. "To a family who lived here when the town was bombed." He gazed about himself as if seeing vanished houses and lost children. "My coming—*our* coming, the arrival of the Loophole and all it brought—destroyed the town of Hull, and with it the St. Croix family. A member of that family saved my life. Then my duty compelled me to destroy his family. Duty always leads to duty. I come here, on this my last night on Earth, to say good-bye."

He bent his torso and ran his claw over the grass and moss which had grown over the cement-block ruins, then straightened and turned toward the Cube across the chill December water, spreading his arms in blessing. After a moment he dropped them and said conversationally, "We will find people here."

Diana looked around. "Where?"

"Strike a light and they will come to us."

She did so. In moments a yellow-white gleam bobbed toward them as if being carried by a man with a limp. As it approached, it threw shadows that revealed a thick grizzled arm holding an antique oil lamp. Its tallow-soaked wick gave steady illumination and a sweet waxy smell. "Are you honest men?" said the gray-bearded man who held the lamp, raising it higher so as to cast their features into better relief.

"What?" said Diana, stupefied.

"An old and sexist joke." He was squat and muscular, with a thick neck and wrists which seemed larger than his brawny forearms. Despite this aggressively peasant build, his eyelines gave the impression of too many hours studying philosophy in waterlogged student lofts. "Who are you? Not you," he growled when the Bishop leaned forward as if to reveal himself. "Her. Who's she?"

"My name is Deirdre Fitzpatrick," Diana found herself

saying. Whether she did this from genuine uncertainty, or the snobbish anonymity which the upper crust seeks to impose on the sloshfooted, or simply an unwillingness to have to explain her past, she never determined, then or later.

"Name's Ettore Nuccio," the man growled. "You two hungry? You look hungry. Nice boat."

"I am not," answered the Bishop. "But my guide is. Will you feed us?"

"Follow me," replied Ettore, presenting his broad sweatshirted back to them and stumping over the rocky headlands.

"Those Phneri at the water could reset these stones into a proper path," Diana muttered half to herself. "And a colony of glowworms would provide enough light to avoiding spraining an ankle."

Ettore led them to a dark, shuttered house which sat at the base of a concrete watchtower. He raised the lamp as he approached the front door. It opened in an embrace of warm light and the glance of many faces, and they went inside.

To Diana's surprise, the living room they entered was wood-paneled and tidy. Ettore extinguished his lamp and hung it on the doorside hook. "Take off your shoes," he instructed, squatting on the landing. A small olive-skinned boy wearing a rag that served as his nightshirt scurried up. "Scat, Petey," said Ettore with gruff affection. "Wait until you're introduced." The imp bit his thumb and vanished with a grin and a wiggle of his small hips.

"This is—lovely," said Diana in astonishment, her eyes drawn to the crackling blaze in the fireplace. The Bishop, whose bulk made the room confining to him, had slid along the wall and was holding himself completely motionless.

"You think we live like savages? Wolf skins and pounding rocks?" Ettore laughed. His teeth were crooked and stained. "The Cube's only a fifteen-minute ride away."

"All your windows are blacked out."

"We kind of like our privacy," he answered, sliding his arm around a thin dark woman with rat's-nest hair and quick fingers. "My wife. Francine, can we manage another plate?"

"Only one?"

Ettore looked at the Bishop and understanding seemed to pass between them. "The big bug isn't hungry."

During the meal that followed, Diana tried to count the children but soon gave up, for they moved like elves through the shadows around the edge of the adults' table, observing their elders with the intensity of entomologists. The food was simple—broiled flounder, haddock, and an alien whitefish transplanted to Earth—but hearty and well cooked, and the oaky white burgundy that Ettore uncorked with solemn care set it off perfectly.

Francine and Ettore made Diana their guest of honor. They showed no conversational loyalty to one another as husband and wife, instead taking turns agreeing or disagreeing with Diana and each other in a rapid pavane that left Diana fighting to hold up her share of the witticisms. After an hour, she realized with a slight start that she was passionately and maladroitly defending the view that only gradual easing of import duties would prevent a depression, a subject about which she had never cared, despite or perhaps because of Salton's endless dinner-table economic lectures. "How do you know so much about the Cube?" she asked to divert attention from a particularly weak argument she had somewhat desperately advanced.

"We're not indifferent to Boston, just outside it," Ettore said with a shrug. "It's a big place. It shouldn't be expected to satisfy everybody."

"But why, if it fascinates you so?"

"We have quirky tastes. Why should Boston stoop to satisfying *us*? Anyhow, with *that*"—he flung his arm northwest—"out there to study, you think we're going to close our eyes to it?"

"Then why the blacked-out windows? Your—cautious—greeting of strangers?"

"We kind of like our freedom," cut in Francine, clearing the plates.

"Let me help with that," Diana said, jumping up. "And you must allow me to pay you for that delicious dinner."

"That'd be great," said Ettore, who then retreated at a glare from his wife. "No, forget it. It's on us."

"I insist. Surely there are things you need?"

Ettore slapped his stomach with both big hands and belched. "Our life's hard work, don't kid yourself," he said with a smile. "We get a few beans from rich guilty benefactors, but we're not rich."

"I can thumbprint you credit."

"No good." He chuckled as her jaw dropped faintly. "Banks. Records. Income tax. Revenuers."

"Then how about tangible wealth?" Diana worked her wedding ring free of her artificial left hand. She held it out, her hand shaking just a little. "It's real gold."

Ettore pinched it like snuff between his big battered thumb and forefinger. After a careful examination, he silently offered it to Francine. She slipped it up and down her finger—she was herself ringless, Diana noted—and, with a minute headshake, handed it back to him.

"Right, Frankie. It's too good." Ettore returned the ring to Diana. "Too much of a gift. You've humbled us. I'm sorry."

"No, no," protested Diana. "I did eat. It was wonderful. And I don't need it anymore."

"Can't. Frankie says when I fuck up, I have to apologize right then and there. That way I don't forget. We're sorry. I'm sorry," he added, reacting to his wife's stern but amused glare.

"I'll find a way to make it up to you. You've been very kind."

"I must leave," interposed the Bishop. He had remained

silent throughout the meal, and neither Francine nor Ettore had shown the slightest inclination to include him in the dialogue. Yet Diana felt that their mutual taciturnity was that of long familiarity, one with the other. She wondered if they had met him before. "My duty calls me to go," the Bishop went on, "as it calls you"—he hesitated and Diana thought he was about to reveal her name, for Centaurs always call a thing by the name it was originally introduced—"Miz."

He could not lie, but chose not to be fully truthful. "All right," said Diana, nodding in gratitude. She started to return her wedding band to her finger but stopped. Where was the bonding in restoring a ring onto an alien prosthetic? Instead she slipped it into her pocket, bent, and put on her shoes, now stiff from their fire-drying.

Francine and Ettore each leaned against a side of the doorframe like caryatids as Diana and the Bishop passed into the chill dewy darkness. Filled with an intolerable depression, she started down the rock-strewn hill.

A realization came to her. "Bishop, you've been helping these people, haven't you? What was it you said? Rock and sea and finance? You've been funding them in untraceable ways. And now you're leaving."

The Centaur looked at her for a long time and Diana thought she saw, reflected in those oversize yellow eyes, a new confidence grow within herself. "And so could you," he finally said, turning away and implacably forging ahead. Below him the ship rested at the pier and in the distance beyond it rose the omnipresent hemisphere of the Boston Cube.

Mildew stains dripped like stalactites down the sides of Ettore and Francine's house. They must have leaks in nor'easter rainstorms. Their roof was haphazardly assembled from corrugated sheets and plywood four-by-eights, evidently designed to look unhabited.

"You know," Diana called to Francine, "with some thatch and a little kittee from Boston, you could seal and

surface your roof, then lay sod over it. You'd have camou-
flage and comfort together."

The frizzy-haired woman twisted her neck, her arms
folded, and glanced over the lintel. "Alas, we have no goop,
nor any means of obtaining it."

"You're kidding. Every three weeks the Spatiens scrape
up Cube goop pitted or eroded by wind or dust. They toss it
out by Lewis Wharf, but all you have to do is heat it gently
and it'll liquefy. The impurities sink and you can skim
worthwhile goop. It's not commercially viable, but—"

"But it'd be plenty for our modest needs, wouldn't it?"
Francine said cheerfully, her eyes alight. "Would you do us
the favor of spending the night? Ettore's got an old whaler
named *Queequeg*. You could show us in the morning."

"I want to, but I don't think I can. I've got kids and a
very hectic schedule tomorrow." Her voice trailed off.

At the foot of the hill, the Bishop had gained the ship
and climbed aboard. He was preparing to cast off. Seeing
her gaze, he stopped and straightened, waiting, watching
her. The gibbous pale moon had risen over the Cube. A few
days earlier it had been full, but in its wane was still bright
enough to stand against the yellow-and-orange glow of
Boston's skyline.

There in the Cube were her life, her children, her husband, and her past. If she returned now, she'd have to
throw herself on Sussman's sardonic, competent mercy and
he would disguise his feelings with barbed asides. It would
all be as if none of this had happened.

Of course, the city will always be there tomorrow, she
thought to herself. We could take a predawn trip and I
could head right back.

After a morning's hard work, she might be tired of these
people and their chosen exile on this blasted rock. Or perhaps—for a fleeting instant she was charmed by the
thought—she'd live out her days there, becoming part of

their family or setting up her own dwelling, the new Madwoman of Hull.

The Cube had sent her forth like a spore. The Cube could afford to birth a new community.

She raised her hand to the Bishop and waved farewell. He answered her movement.

A great city, she thought as she turned back to Francine and the lighted doorway, is not a Loophole, not a wall, not a collection of monuments and buildings. A great city is its people's image of themselves.

They might even call it Boston.

THE BYZANTINES DECORATED their basilicas with vast mosaics. Though each small stone is itself only a square of monochromatic glass, when seen in relation to one another, they make a large image, greater and more subtly shaded than the elements of their composition.

All of us live in a such a mosaic world. It's called reality.

Some fantasy shared worlds seem created from whole cloth, without background or connotation. But the real world is a mosaic full of people and events which, like it or not, we can't control. Logical, random, miraculous, tawdry, horrific: every day brings these events and more, and we take them for granted.

In the summer of 1987, I conceived the idea of a shared-world science fiction anthology set in a real place—Boston.

It could tap into that vast wellspring of experience and memory of Boston. Reality could rub elbows with fancy. In such a place, as in life, today's nobody would be tomorrow's celebrity, today's leader tomorrow's guest lecturer. In an integrated shared world, characters important in one story should be minor in another, just as people's importance to one another varies.

And the place itself could become a personality. What if the world itself becomes the principal character, the anthology's ultimate protagonist?

This anthology would be much more structured than a normal shared world; it would consist of many individual stories that, when read together, gave a picture of a city that was itself a character. Writers would maximize diversity, showing many different perspectives about Boston. We would seek stories that cover a broad spectrum of time, place, style, and character. The novel would link Boston's present to its future and also to its past. Future Boston would be rich and as internally consistent yet diverse as is the current Boston.

A mosaic novel must have unusually talented writers who are more than ordinarily able to work together. For nine years I have been privileged to be a member of the Cambridge Science Fiction Writers Workshop, a continuing Clarion-style gathering that meets monthly. Past and present members of CSFW have won the Nebula Award (multiple times) and the World Fantasy Award, have received nominations for the Nebula and Philip K. Dick Awards, contribute regularly to the leading SF magazines, and have published a dozen novels.

How to build it? Some literary exemplars capture the diversity and multifaceted quality I wanted for *Future Boston.* Milorad Pavic's masterpiece, *Dictionary of the Khazars,* is a thousand-year whodunit which also chronicles a vanished people through three lexicons: one Christian, one Islamic, one Jewish. Many of the best are much longer than a single book: Lawrence Durrell's four-volume *Alexandria Quartet* visits and revisits a single city through the eyes of many lovers. Proust's *Remembrance of Things Past* chronicles hundreds of French characters on the eve of World War I, and Anthony Powell's twelve-volume masterwork, *A Dance to the Music of Time,* covers almost sixty years with exquisite ironic timing.

If we had literary models, we also had real ones. Boston was a hinge between the Old World and the New. I sought similar cities: Amsterdam in the 1650s, when the Dutch opened the Indies; Venice in the 1550s, the only point of contact between the Christian world and the Turkish Empire; nineteenth-century Yokohama during the Meiji Restoration. In these cities cultures clashed, mutated, and melded; wealth was made, the fantastic and exotic were imported, bought, sold, stolen, smuggled, and counterfeited. I wanted to bring to our future Boston that sense of mystery, of danger and wonder lurking in every dark alley. I wanted magic in our brick streets.

Early on we decided that, to take advantage of Boston's rich history, Boston's future would reflect its past—or rather refract it in new ways.

The land on which Boston is built was largely reclaimed from the sea. The Pilgrims settled on the muddy Shawmut headland and immediately set to work building wharves for ocean-going ships. They were visionaries: in 1660, Bostonians built a thousand-foot wharf into Boston Harbor, and a thousand-foot bridge to Cambridge. In the nineteenth century, Back Bay was made land by decapitating Beacon Hill. Tremont Street is named for Tri-Mount, from the three hills which were sacrificed to form rectangular Beacon Street, Newbury Street, and Commonwealth Avenue.

In *Future Boston*, we decided to allow the ocean to recover, bit by bit over the century, all the land that humanity had stolen.

So we sank the place, four inches a year, beginning now.

From its founding, Boston was a port of entry into the New World. To the Indians who greeted them, the Pilgrims were aliens, with impenetrable language, fantastic technology, bizarre customs, virulent diseases, and obscure violent religions. As we sat around my dining room table on Saturday, August 22, 1987, designing the future, we decided we needed an unexpected alien invasion.

It had to be catastrophic, Steve Popkes said. It had to be as unexpected by Earth as the Pilgrims were to the Indians. After debate, we voted on the optimal arrival year and averaged the results—2014. We took the vote at 5:05 P.M., and there it was: alien arrival at 5:05 P.M., August 22, 2014.

Who were they, the voyagers on this interstellar *Mayflower*? Where had they come from? What did they want? As we started to discuss it, Jon Burrowes became extraordinarily emphatic about how it should be, so we all turned to him and said, with evil smiles, "Okay, Jon, *you* write it."

But Jon got his revenge. "The Elephant-Ass Thing" is a story of First Contact in which, after finishing it, the reader knows less about the aliens than if he had read nothing. . . .

Boston has always been a cradle of revolution, whether anti-slavery, feminist, or secessionist: John Hancock, Paul Revere, Sam Adams, and John Brown were Bostonians. Our future Boston again reversed history: Boston seceded from America, leading to Sarah Smith's wonderful line, "On all sides, Boston is surrounded by the United States."

With our canvas thus blocked out, we now had to fill in the details. We created a bible and divided up responsibility for its sections according to individual interests. The design team broke down like this:

Aliens and alien census. Jon Burrowes. Our revenge on Jon's revenge; he now had to chronicle the other aliens.

Culture. Sarah Smith. She created a hundred years of culture, trends, and fashions.

Economics. Steve Caine. Inflation, revenue sources, taxation.

Physics and the Loophole. Geoffrey A. Landis. Who better to design a multiply-connected four-dimensional anomaly and to define its rules of engagement than a Ph.D. on NASA's staff?

Politics. Alexander Jablokov. Anyone who, as a hobby,

studied the political dynamics of the Byzantine Empire and the disintegrating Soviet Union could handle ours.

Technology. Steve Popkes. In short order he laid out a hundred-year cornucopia of inventions and discoveries, chronicled decade by decade.

Through characters. Resa Nelson. Our continuing characters would come and go, appearing in many stories, and for that we needed a combination traffic cop and genealogist. Resa admirably took on the role.

Topography. David Alexander Smith. I bought a half-dozen United States Geophysical Survey maps of the area, laid them like a mosaic on my study floor, and crawled around on hands and knees deciding what would sink when.

Throughout the project, we also received encouragement and editorial guidance from Terri Windling, who was a friend from beginning to end.

To allow structured freedom, we adopted the Heisenberg Uncertainty Principle: nothing existed until it had been described in a story. Observation fixed it. In 2030, Geoff Landis tilted the John Hancock Tower, and everyone had to live with that.

Of course, this gave power. With one throwaway line an author could create distant wars, wreck cities, change the course of mighty rivers, bend steel in her bare hands. So we adopted a second principle: don't specify an offstage event unless you have to.

At first things went fantastically: Jon wrote "The Elephant-Ass Thing," at which we all howled. I surprised myself and the design team with "Dying In Hull," my first short story. Sarah and Resa got excitedly talking one evening and produced "Fennario" and "Three Boston Artists," a unique diptych in time. With his usual brilliance, Alex uncorked "The Place of No Shadows" and "Nomads."

All of these stories were written by the design team and critiqued in our workshop. The resulting feedback was invigorating for us all. Studying the works gave us fuller understandings of each other's creations. In short order followed "Seeing the Edge," "Projects," "Camomile and Crimson," and "The Parade."

We also encouraged the authors to write bits of mortar—the joins between the stories. Out popped "Boston Will Sink, Claims MIT Prof" (the book is real, by the way, published in 1928), "The Uprising," "When the Phneri Fell," "Who Is Venture Capital?" "So You Want to Meet the Bishop," "Physics of the Loophole Effect," and "IPOB Dining Hall Procedures."

After six months, we took stock. We had some fine material—the first flush of stories were sent out to magazine editors, accepted, and published—but they were clustering around a few times and a few themes. Where was the material to describe the secession? What about the last half of the century?

As so often happened during the project, people worked together on the Secession. I wrote a five-page history-book summary. Alex became intrigued and turned it into a twelve-page docudrama complete with human-interest stories, jokes, historical references, and sparkles. (I often imagined myself as the bass player in our Future Boston band, laying out the rhythm line while Alex leapt about the stage, playing with his toes or on his back, his axe screaming the high notes.) Sarah saw in Alex's outline the wet clay of a story. She wrote a draft of "Ye Citizens of Boston," generously awarding equal credit to Alex and myself. This the workshop critiqued. Two drafts later all of Alex's and my scaffolding had been removed, having done its job. "Ye Citizens of Boston" was now wholly Sarah's.

In the meantime Alex had written "Focal Plane," his own uniquely Jablokovian riff on the secession, and "The Adoption," a medley of the anthology's greatest hits. After a struggle I produced, with lovingly brutal critiquing from

CSFW, the capstone story, "Sail Away." In June 1992, we pronounced ourselves done.

We experimented constantly throughout the project. (The unsuccessful experiments, Igor, you will never see.) Others were *too* successful (and showed us how hard it is to tell the story of a city in a single book). Steve Popkes' moving novella "The Egg," a Nebula finalist, grew too large for the anthology and eventually became a short novel, *Slow Lightning*, published in paperback as a Tor Double with Poul Anderson's *The Longest Voyage*. My own novel *In the Cube*, which began as an exploration of the Cube, became a story of families and manipulation (and Diana Sherwood, one of its principal characters, reappears for an anthology cameo in "Sail Away"). Jon Burrowes' wild novel *Vubre the Great* is a cult classic in the making; look for it. And a collaboration between Resa Nelson and myself, "The Last Out," appeared in Jane Yolen's anthology, *2041 A.D.*

It was a labor of love. Eight authors—individuals all, fiercely protective of their freedom to express—combined their prodigious talents and subordinated their equally prodigious egos toward a common goal. *Future Boston* exceeded our expectations. It truly *is* a mosaic novel, more complex than any one person could have written. It has at least a dozen focus characters who interweave through the tales. Ideas and concepts flicker from one story to the next, rebounding in different and surprising ways. Read it again and you will find more than you saw the first time.

We respected each other's talent. We cared about each other's work. We helped each other. We're proud of each other. We're proud of the book.

We hope you have enjoyed it.

ABOUT THE AUTHORS

JON BURROWES is a technical writer whose body lives in Newton (his mind has a winter house on Venus). "The Elephant-Ass Thing" is his first published story.

STEVEN CAINE is a computer programmer who lives in Cambridge.

ALEXANDER JABLOKOV, a full-time writer who lives in Cambridge, is one of the fastest-rising stars in science fiction, with a dozen published stories and three novels: *Carve the Sky* (William Morrow, 1991), *A Deeper Sea* (Morrow, 1992), and *Nimbus* (Morrow, 1993). His stories "Living Will," "The Death Artist," "A Deeper Sea" (the novella version), and "At the Cross-Time Jaunter's Ball," have been included in Gardner Dozois's Year's Best SF collections. A collection of his short stories will be published as a 1994 hardcover from Arkham House under the title, *The Breath of Suspension*.

GEOFFREY A. LANDIS, a physicist at NASA Lewis Research Center in Cleveland, won a Nebula Award for his short story, "Ripples in the Dirac Sea," and a Hugo for "A Walk in the Sun." He has had nearly thirty stories published, mostly in *Asimov's Science Fiction Magazine* and *Analog*.

MATTHEW MATTINGLY, a freelance multimedia artist and painter who lives in West Newton, has illustrated books and periodicals and has exhibited his work in solo and group shows. He has done extensive animation and multimedia work, including the illustrations for the computer-based science fiction hypertext novel *King of Space*.

RESA NELSON, a technical writer, has had several stories published, including "LovePets" (*Pulphouse, Infinite Loop*), "The Dragonslayer's Sword" (*Science Fiction Age*), "The Last Out" (a Future Boston story co-authored with David Alexander Smith and included in Jane Yolen's anthology *2041*), and others.

STEVEN POPKES, a computer systems programmer who lives in Hopkinton, was a Nebula finalist for his short story "The Color Winter." His Future Boston novella "The Egg," was a 1991 *Year's Best SF* selection. Author of two novels, *Caliban Landing* (Congdon & Weed, 1987) and *Slow Lightning* (Tor Double, 1991), he has also published almost a dozen short stories in *Asimov's Science Fiction Magazine* and elsewhere.

DAVID ALEXANDER SMITH, a real estate financial consultant from Cambridge, was a Philip K. Dick Award nominee for his second novel, *Rendezvous* (Ace, 1988), the second book in a three-novel series, of which the first was *Marathon* (Ace, 1982) and the third *Homecoming* (Ace, 1990). His Future Boston novel, *In the Cube*, was published as a 1993 Tor hardcover to excellent reviews. His Future Boston short story "Dying in Hull," a *Year's Best SF* selection, was recently reprinted in *Isaac Asimov's Earth*, edited by Gardner Dozois.

SARAH SMITH, a multimedia designer and programmer who lives in Brookline, has written *King of Space*, an interactive sf novel (Eastgate Systems, 1991) and has published sf stories in *Aboriginal, F&SF* and the anthologies *Shudder Again* and *Christmas Forever*. Her mystery novel *The Vanished Child* (Ballantine, 1992) was a *New York Times* Notable Book of the Year.